POLITICS OF A COLONIAL CAREER

Latin American Silhouettes
Studies in History and Culture

William H. Beezley and
Judith Ewell
Editors

Volumes Published

William H. Beezley and Judith Ewell, eds., *The Human Tradition in Latin America: The Twentieth Century* (1987) Cloth ISBN 0-8420-2283-X. Paper 0-8420-2284-8

Judith Ewell and William H. Beezley, eds., *The Human Tradition in Latin America: The Nineteenth Century* (1989) Cloth ISBN 0-8420-2331-3. Paper 0-8420-2332-1

David G. LaFrance, *The Mexican Revolution in Puebla, 1908–1913: The Maderista Movement and the Failure of Liberal Reform* (1989). ISBN 0-8420-2293-7

Mark A. Burkholder, *Politics of a Colonial Career: José Baquíjano and the Audiencia of Lima* (1990). Cloth ISBN 0-8420-2353-4 Paper 0-8420-2352-6

Mark A. Burkholder

POLITICS
OF A
COLONIAL CAREER

*José Baquíjano
and the Audiencia of Lima*

Second Edition

A Scholarly Resources Imprint
WILMINGTON, DELAWARE

The paper used in this publication meets the minimum requirements of the American National Standard for permanence of paper for printed library materials, Z39.48, 1984.

© 1990 Scholarly Resources Inc.
All rights reserved
Second edition published 1990
Printed and bound in the United States of America
First edition   © 1980 by the University of New Mexico Press

Scholarly Resources Inc.
104 Greenhill Avenue
Wilmington, DE 19805-1897

Library of Congress Cataloging-in-Publication Data

Burkholder, Mark A., 1943–
      Politics of a colonial career: José Baquíjano and the Audiencia
of Lima / Mark A. Burkholder. — 2nd ed.
            p. cm.—(Latin American silhouettes)
      Includes bibliographical references.
      ISBN 0-8420-2353-4.—ISBN 0-8420-2352-6 (pbk.)
      1. Baquíjano y Carrillo, José, d. 1818. 2. Judges—Peru—
Biography. 3. Peru (Viceroyalty). Real Audiencia (Lima). 4. Peru—
History—1548–1820.   I. Title.   II. Series.
KHQ304.B36B87   1989
347.85'03534—dc20
[B]
[348.5073534]
[B]   89–39564
                                                                            CIP

Contents

Illustrations

For My Parents

Preface

When I visited Lima in the summer of 1971, three streets bore the name *Baquíjano*. Further evidence of the prominence of Baquíjano was that a session devoted to him took place at the Quinto Congreso Internacional de Historia de América, held in honor of Peru's sesquicentennial. Moreover, the *Biblioteca Hombres del Perú* several years earlier included him among the eighteen biographies in its first series. José Baquíjano y Carrillo is now recognized as one of Peru's most celebrated representatives of the Enlightenment and a putative "precursor of Independence," but his position in the national pantheon was not secured until the noted historian José de la Riva-Agüero rescued him from obscurity early in the twentieth century.

The present study is neither a full biography of Baquíjano nor another analysis of his thought. The emphasis is upon his efforts as an office seeker, a *pretendiente*, during the quarter-century he pursued appointment to the Audiencia of Lima. Viewed from this perspective, his career serves as a vehicle to illustrate the intensity with which Americans sought high office, means they employed in the quest for preferment, changes in both appointment policy and procedure, and the discrimination and frustration that plagued native sons in particular as their personal goals conflicted with royal policy. By following a single career within a changing imperial setting, this volume provides a perspective that reveals the personal dimension of the political context in Peru and bureaucratic politics in Spain in the late eighteenth century. Thus general features of office seeking are set forth as well as a fresh view of Baquíjano's life.

This approach to Baquíjano's career unavoidably relegates some oft-treated facets to one side while it submits other less well-developed features to the sometimes harsh light of historical analysis. Focusing on his desire for office, moreover, enables one to appreciate anew some of the best known incidents and activities of his life—the proscription of the *Eulogy*, his conflicts in the University of San Marcos, and his participation in the *Mercurio peruano*. The result is an interpretation of his career that differs significantly from previous ones.

In the text that follows I have capitalized *Audiencia* when referring to the Audiencia of Lima. The uncapitalized form is employed for all other tribunals except when used as part of a formal title.

Research incorporated in this book has been conducted during five trips to Spain and one to Peru and Chile. I want to thank the following organizations for the financial support that made this travel possible and allowed me to obtain microfilm relevant to the project: the Institute of International Studies and Overseas Administration of the University of Oregon, the Graduate School of Arts and Sciences of Duke University, The American Philosophical Society (Penrose Fund), and the Office of Research at the University of Missouri-St. Louis.

In addition, I would like to express appreciation to the archivists, librarians, and staffs of the Archivo General de Simancas, Archivo Histórico Nacional (Madrid), Biblioteca de la Real Academia de Historia (Madrid), Archivo del Patrimonio Nacional (Madrid), Archivo Nacional del Perú (Lima), Archivo Histórico del Ministerio de Hacienda (Lima), Archivo Municipal (Lima), Biblioteca Nacional (Santiago, Chile), the Lilly Library, the Yale University Library, Perkins Library at Duke University, the Thomas Jefferson Library at the University of Missouri-St. Louis, and especially to Miss Rosario Parra Cala and her gracious staff at the Archivo General de Indies in Seville. Paul B. Ganster provided friendship during my work in Lima and microfilmed for me a number of documents from the Archivo Nacional, and I wish to thank him as well for his help.

John E. Woodham originally stimulated my interest in Baquíjano while the late John Tate Lanning offered continued support as he directed the doctoral dissertation that has formed an important part of this study. Miguel Maticorena Estrada and Josefina C. Tiryakian also spent hours discussing Baquíjano and late eighteenth-century Peru at this early stage of the present manuscript. John J. TePaske both read the dissertation and made me think far more than twice about the way I should hone the topic. William S. Maltby spent long hours discussing Baquíjano and reading and commenting on a preliminary draft while Steven C. Hause has suffered countless interruptions in his own work to hear out my latest "Pepe" story and offer encouragement and advice. Louis B. Gerteis and James D. Norris as well have endured what they must have thought was an endless saga of Baquíjano's exploits. My long-time friend and collaborator D. S. Chandler has followed my work on Baquíjano from its inception and served as a devil's advocate for over a dozen years. His trenchant critique of an earlier draft literally sent me back to the documents. To these friends and colleagues I give my sincere thanks. None, of course, is responsible for the form or content of the manuscript.

I wish to thank also Theresa Orso, manuscript typist of the College of Arts and Sciences at the University of Missouri-St. Louis, for successfully coping with my illegible hand and the hazards of misplaced accents.

My wife, Sue, has not only watched me alternately damn and rejoice in the progress of this study for over a decade, but shared in the archival research that made it possible. To her I offer both deep appreciation and an assurance that, for me, Baquíjano has now reached the end of the road.

Mark A. Burkholder
St. Louis, Missouri
1980

1

The Environment of Ambition

On February 4, 1812, the Cortes meeting in Cádiz, Spain, selected *limeño* José Baquíjano y Carrillo, third Conde de Vistaflorida, to serve on the newly formed Council of State.[1] When the news reached Lima in late June, the entire populace exploded with joy and spontaneous celebration. Promptly the city council ordered three days of public festivities. Fireworks, banners, music, a magnificent ball, and endless congratulations from aristocrats and plebians alike expressed the city's pride in Baquíjano "the honor of Peru, . . . the worthy son . . . who fills her with glory and pleasure."[2]

Receiving these accolades was a corpulent man of medium height and three score years. Sagging jowls, a high forehead, and heavy-lidded eyes marked a face basking in self-esteem. In a portrait painted in the early nineteenth century, Baquíjano wore the black gown associated with his position as civil judge (*oidor*) on Lima's Audiencia. The clothing was appropriate for he had spent over twenty years seeking appointment to the court. His chest bore the coveted cross of the Royal and Distinguished Order of Charles III, a sign of royal favor that dated from 1791. His left hand grasped an official document bearing the familiar royal stamp. Behind him stood a writing desk and rows of books, probably part of his celebrated library. Prominent among the leather-bound tomes was *Constitutions and Ordinances of the Royal University of Lima*, the new councilor's alma mater and employer for many years.[3]

1

To the crowd thronging Lima's Plaza Mayor as well as to the aristocrats gilding the viceroy's ball in his honor, Baquíjano's appointment to the Council of State climaxed an already enviable career. He had held the senior (*prima*) chair of canon law at the University of San Marcos, been president of Lima's Society of Friends of the Country and written for its celebrated journal, the *Mercurio peruano*, as well as having served for a decade as a judge on Lima's Audiencia. Social prominence he had inherited from his parents. His wealthy Basque father had become the first Conde de Vistaflorida, while his mother was descended from early settlers in Peru and Chile and was related to several of Lima's titled families. Upon the death of his elder brother in 1807, José had inherited the family title and entailed property in Peru and Vizcaya. At the peak of his career, then, his prominence was enhanced upon becoming a *conde* and enjoying wealth enough to display the title with flair.

Inheriting the title and wealth, of course, required only longevity. But Baquíjano's career had demanded continued effort and sustained self-confidence. Despite the wealth and prominence of his family, José had begun life with the disadvantages of being a creole and a second son. Like other younger sons of the aristocracy, he was particularly vulnerable to the influx of peninsulars, who reduced the opportunities of creoles like himself because they married desirable dowered women and took incomes from offices as well. Younger sons were frequently limited by a meager inheritance and often needed employment for comfort if not subsistence. An educated group eligible and anxious for office, younger sons saw each peninsular ecclesiastical or secular appointee as taking a post that one of their number should have received. Accustomed to "respectable" living as youths, they faced the unpleasant prospect of descending to the fringes of respectability, of being the "poor relation." Small wonder creoles unceasingly sought office. Their avidity was often born of desperation.

Although Baquíjano's situation was not desperate as long as his mother supported him, only suitable employment would provide the separate income essential to personal independence. But time joined birth in conspiring against his ambitions. In the 1750s, the decade of his birth, the Spanish Crown inaugurated a sustained effort to expand its authority in America. Temporarily enjoying the financial relief occasioned by peace, after 1750 the Crown was able to stop selling appointments to high administrative and judicial positions in the New World. Returning to more traditional standards, it exerted greater care in assigning men to office in subsequent years than had been possible on many occasions since at least the late seventeenth century. Moreover, it displayed an increasing concern to reduce local influence in government. New offices were established as the century progressed and, as one example, by 1790 powerful intendants resided in most major districts of the Empire. One consequence of the Crown's efforts to secure greater control was a contraction of Americans' opportunities for high-ranking government employment.

Additionally, in the second half of the eighteenth century, Peru's fabled wealth and commercial opportunities paled in comparison to those of New Spain. Changing trade patterns and the loss of Upper Peru to the new Viceroyalty of the Río de la Plata contributed to Peru's economic malaise. Although a son of one of Lima's wealthiest families, José could not anticipate a life without employment. Furthermore, a competitive spirit and craving for public recognition of his abilities impelled him to pursue a career that would reward merit and intellectual prowess and be worthy of his social background in addition to providing a secure and comfortable income.

By the 1770s, when José first sought an audiencia appointment, creole supplicants were receiving chilly receptions in Madrid's antechambers. Frustration followed for Baquíjano and other first-generation creoles with similar backgrounds and ambitions. Reared in an atmosphere of opportunity, they vented their disappointment by criticizing the new appointment policy and calling for a return to the appointment of native sons. Simultaneously most continued to believe that expanding their registers of merit with additional service would eventually yield the coveted appointment. Persistently they juggled family merit and personal services into endless pleading petitions.

Baquíjano's efforts to gain appointment to Lima's Audiencia spanned nearly a quarter century. Expelled from Spain after an initial failure to secure preferment, the limeño spent over fifteen years tortuously building a record that justified reward. At last, in 1797, he received his title of office as a criminal judge in Lima's high court, the first native son named to the tribunal in two decades. Routine advancement to the civil chamber followed in 1806. When Napoleon forced Ferdinand VII to abdicate in 1808, Baquíjano, now the third Conde de Vistaflorida, was one of America's most eminent creole magistrates and one of its few native sons, a logical choice for the Council of State.

Baquíjano's life illuminates the ambitions and frustrations of the creole elite in Peru. His success in joining the Lima court came only after he surmounted difficulties that would have overwhelmed a man of lesser ability, determination, and financial resources. The enormous obstacles he faced in spite of his social and economic advantages highlight the difficulties faced by Americans whose backgrounds were more modest. Moreover, as the son of a peninsular, his success brought little solace to the vast majority of creoles—both of whose parents were American.

To appreciate fully the social advantages and environment that stimulated Baquíjano's ambition, it is necessary to examine his family and the opportunities of his youth as well as the record of native-son appointments to Lima's Audiencia. Only after this background is provided can one adequately understand Baquíjano's unrelenting pursuit of an Audiencia appointment.

Lima, the City of Kings founded by Francisco Pizarro in 1535, lies in the Valley of Rimac, one of some forty river oases along Peru's west coast. Established for its proximity to prime agricultural land and the harbor of Callao, Lima quickly became the center of Spanish culture, administration, and trade. By 1560 a nearly complete microcosm of Spanish society was present.[4]

Unlike Cuzco, the former Inca capital, Lima was a Spanish rather than Indian city and new immigrants from the peninsula steadily augmented its growing creole population. By 1614 almost twelve thousand persons of Spanish origin resided in the city. The whites represented just under half of the total population, but their preeminence went unchallenged in the racially mixed capital. The population expanded during the seventeenth century and was over thirty-seven thousand in 1700. From the mid- to late eighteenth century, Lima's population remained at about fifty thousand persons, a number far larger than that of Philadelphia, Anglo-America's leading metropolis. The whites of Lima accounted for some two-fifths of this total.[5]

With population growth came building and expansion. A plan

of the city for 1613 reveals a full range of governmental, ecclesiastical, and cultural edifices. On the block Pizarro had
originally granted himself stood the viceregal palace. Also adjoin-
ing the Plaza Major were the cathedral and *cabildo* (city government) building. Convents, monasteries, hospitals, schools, the
University of San Marcos, the Inquisition's offices, and countless
artisans' and retail shops further filled the city. Lima's core was
compact and a short walk from the Plaza Mayor sufficed to reach
most attractions. Pizarro had granted the original settlers *solares*,
lots a quarter of a block in size, radiating from the Plaza Mayor,
and families with wealth and prestige continued to congregate
close to this center.[6]

Although agricultural production provided wealth throughout
the viceregal period, silver underwrote Peru's economy. Pizarro
and his fellow captors of the Inca Atahualpa in 1533 first tasted
the region's munificence. But the silver flood really began in the
1580s when the amalgamation process that employed mercury for
separating silver from its ore was applied to the rich lodes of
Potosí in Upper Peru. Silver production, and the trade necessary to
furnish the miners with food, equipment, and other supplies, produced fortunes quickly.

Lima benefited particuarly from mining and trade. The monopolistic trading system the Spanish crown established for its New
World possessions made Lima the entrepôt for all but the Carib-
bean portion of Spanish South America. Silver from interior mines
passed through the city on route to Spain and the Peruvian silver
fleet returned from Panama with European goods to distribute
throughout the region. Merchants engaged in this trade joined together formally in a guild (*consulado*) in 1613 to exploit better
their monopolistic advantages. In general terms, Peru's overall
silver production declined from its late sixteenth-century peak
throughout the seventeenth century and well into the eighteenth.[7]
Declining exports and increased American self-sufficiency affected the fleet system, and sailings after the mid-seventeenth century were irregular. An alternate investment that emerged as
increasingly important was coastal trade.

Although the lucrative trade in Asian goods via Mexico was prohibited in 1631, ships plied north to Guayaquil carrying grain,
wine, and oil; they returned laden with cacao, tobacco, lumber,
and other products. The Chilean trade grew more important be-

ginning in the late seventeenth century. An earthquake in 1687 disrupted grain production around Lima and the importation of Chilean grain soon soared, an opportune expansion for Lima's merchants. An explosion of French contraband trade via Cape Horn, however, challenged the merchants during the War of the Spanish Succession (1700–1713). Subsequently came the final collapse of the traditional Panama trade in the late 1730s and then, beginning in 1748, the onset of regular sailings of register ships from Spain to the Pacific Coast. Faced with these threats, Lima's merchants and shipowners fought hard to retain hegemony over coastal trade.[8]

Despite the breakdown of the traditional trading system, it appears that following the 1687 earthquake Lima's merchants emerged as the strongest economic group in Peru. The *hacendados*, their closest competitors, suffered a relative eclipse as the area's agriculture suffered from disrupted irrigation as well as the scarcity and high cost of labor. This reversal meant a loss for Peru's conquistador-descended nobility and a corresponding gain for the peninsular-dominated group of merchants.[9] Merchant strength at mid-eighteenth century, however, was more collective than individual. Many merchants had fortunes of fifty to one hundred thousand pesos, but few had over five hundred thousand pesos. *Juan and Ulloa* reported that probably no more than ten or fifteen commercial houses had merchandise and cash exceeding half a million pesos in value.[10] These magnates formed a prominent part of Lima's elite.

Eighteenth-century observers placed the number of Lima's noble houses at between two and three hundred. The Dutch observer Tadeo Häenke divided their ancestors into three groups: conquistadors and first settlers, peninsular officeholders of noble birth, and successful merchants.[11] Most conspicuous were the titled nobles, listed as twenty-seven in 1721, no less than forty-five a quarter-century later, and forty-nine in 1790.[12] Although some titles originated with peninsulars, most *condes* and *marqueses* in eighteenth-century Peru were Americans. Americans were not only often the original recipients, but creole successors regularly inherited titles first granted to peninsulars.

Titled nobles became numerous in Lima in the late seventeenth century. The number of titles granted in the 1680s alone was nearly equal to all previous concessions in Peru. By 1750 over eighty-five had been conferred to persons in Peru.[13] While some titles lapsed and others returned to Spain, the number active in 1750 bespeaks a concentration of prestige unequalled elsewhere in America.[14]

The designation of *conde* or *marqués* alone identified the titled subdivision of Lima's elite. Possession of a title was not synonymous with great wealth, although titled nobles were among Lima's richest residents. Titled nobles had arisen from each of the groups Häenke identified. Additionally, the divisions themselves betrayed the observer's unconscious male bias, a bias that permeated contemporary commentators' views but accorded ill with reality.

Wives and daughters provided the bond uniting Lima's aristocracy and gave it more homogeneity than the tripartite division implied. Men served all royal offices, but strictly speaking these posts formed the only area they monopolized. Women could and did participate in commerce, although it goes without saying that they held no merchant guild (consulado) positions. More importantly, though, they owned land and urban property and through convents controlled still more. Unwed peninsular bureaucrats reaching Lima were eligible spouses for daughters descended from families that claimed descent from conquistadors or sixteenth-century settlers. If the bureaucrat were already married, his children would often later establish families in the city. Moreover, high mortality rates of women—especially during childbirth—occasioned a sizable turnover among spouses, and successive marriages between high-ranking bureaucrats and daughters of first a wealthy peninsular merchant, whose own wife was generally locally born, and later a long-established landowning family were not unknown. Intermarriage among bureaucrats, businessmen, and first families suggests fluidity within the elite more than strict subdivision. Furthermore, the three groups' economic activities differed more in scale than kind.

By the mid-eighteenth century, marriage had bound these families into a sufficiently homogenous social group that efforts to divide them revolve around a sterile search for unbroken male successions or an enumeration of successful peninsulars—most of whom had married into the web. While the peninsulars themselves faced resentment from descendants of earlier immigrants, their own offspring entered the aristocracy without dispute. Descended from businessmen or bureaucrats on the paternal side, the children's maternal lines often represented earlier blends of men in these fields as well as conquistadors or first settlers.

Marriage with colonial women afforded successful peninsulars entry into the previously established elite from the sixteenth century on. As each generation reproduced itself, new opportunities arose. Overall, daughters probably enjoyed better opportunities than sons to improve their material condition for the simple reason that more single peninsular men immigrated than women; thus, colonial white women were in demand.

Juan Bautista Baquíjano de Beascoa was one of many "noble" but financially unpretentious Basques who sought fortunes in America in the early eighteenth century and ultimately married a *criolla* of long-established family. Juan Bautista was born in 1701 into an *hidalgo* family of long residence near the Vizcaya town of Durango.[15] As a young man he sought success from within Lima's business community and, like many aspiring Basque merchants, joined compatriots from his home region. In particular he associated with Martín de Zelayeta, a knight of Santiago who was one of Lima's most prosperous merchants.[16]

Juan Bautista's success in business was phenomenal. At his death in 1759 he was one of Lima's wealthiest residents, his fortune probably not exceeded by that of a dozen persons. Commerce and agriculture formed the bases for his riches. His ship, *Nuestra Señora de las Mercedes*, regularly plied between Peru and Chile to stock warehouses that in 1759 held 500 *quintales* (50,000 pounds) of Chilean copper, 1,000 quintales of fodder, 1,700 boards of Chilean lumber, and 5,200 pounds of Paraguayan *yerba maté*. Two rural properties (*chacras*) between Lima and Callao were complete with fifty male Negro slaves, eighteen oxen, and over 250 mules, the latter part of an immense and profitable transport industry that flourished in the region. Moreover, the stamped silver and financial instruments in the merchant's possession were worth over 500,000 *pesos*. At the time of his death, another 50,000 pesos were on their way to Cádiz, presumably to pay for merchandise.[17]

Juan Bautista clearly perceived that well-placed debtors, friends, and relatives could benefit him. The inventory of his property revealed over eighty financial obligations due him. Most of these were for sums below 1,500 pesos. There were over a dozen, however, that exceeded 5,000 pesos; by far the largest, a debt of just over 50,000 pesos, was owed by Gen. Francisco Vásquez. How many of these obligations were in exchange for merchandise and how many were loans in cash is unknown. In several instances, however, the debtors were persons of prominence. Among those encumbered were the supernumerary oidors of Lima, Domingo de Orrantia, son of an eminent peninsular merchant, and Manuel Zurbarán y Allende. Although the sums involved were small—800 and 300 pesos respectively—they represented levers of influence to be employed as necessary. Zurbarán's debt was three years old when his creditor died; given its modest size and the failure to repay it, it is probably fair to consider the amount a retainer. Another official, the *contador* Francisco de las Heras, had died in debt to Juan Bautista. In addition, the successful Basque was a creditor for the Conde de San Xavier, the Conde de Torre Velarde, and the Marqués de Casa Boza.[18]

Among Juan Bautista's close acquaintances was the Chilean attorney Domingo Martínez de Aldunate. Martínez de Aldunate became a supernumerary oidor of the Audiencia of Chile in 1748 and, soon after assuming his post, sold his Lima house to Juan Bautista for 24,000 pesos. Juan Bautista, holding the Chilean's power of attorney, sold a slave in his behalf two years later.[19] Not surprisingly, the two men had friends in common. In 1744 Manuel de Salamanca, governor of Chile, gave his power of attorney to Martínez and listed Juan Bautista as an alternate.[20] With this kind of relationship, one suspects that Juan Bautista felt the Chilean end of his business ventures was secure. Another friend was Cristóbal Mesía y Munive, a Chilean attorney named a supernumerary oidor of the Lima Audiencia in 1755. In 1759 Juan Bautista listed Mesía as an alternate executor for his estate.[21]

Among his relatives, too, Juan Bautista could call upon important persons. As the only member of his family to leave Vizcaya for Peru, he lacked relatives in Lima until he contracted a marriage that more than remedied the deficiency in 1746. María Ignacia Carrillo de Córdoba y Garcés, born in Lima in 1726, wed the middle-aged Basque merchant in a marriage that, in many ways, typified the unions between successful peninsular males and young women from families long established in America. María's paternal line had reached Peru in the late 1570s when Hernán Carrillo de Córdoba, an experienced Andalusian soldier and city

councilor of Córdoba, transferred his military abilities to New
World conflicts and soon joined the Chilean frontier struggle between Spanish settlers and the indigenous population. Nine years
of risk to his "person, arms, and horse" in Chile, services for
Viceroy Francisco de Toledo (1569–81), and later successes
against corsairs while a military assistant to his brother-in-law,
Viceroy Conde de Villar Don Pedro (1585–90), brought Hernán
royal approbation in 1601.[22] Through her maternal line as well,
María was related to the earliest settlers beginning with Pedro Lisperguer, who reached Peru in the 1550s and also soon went to
Chile where, unlike Hernán Carrillo de Córdoba, he established
his family.[23]

Descendants of these early settlers held *encomiendas* and served
military and municipal offices. María's uncles furthered the family's social standing by marrying titled wives, the marquesas of
Santa María de Pacoyán and Santa Lucía de Conchán, and serving as alcaldes of the Lima city council.[24] Her father, Agustín Carrillo de Córdoba, continued the tradition of public service and was
a prominent official in Lima for many years.

Agustín began his career as a military officer in Chile. While
there, he married Rosa Garcés de Marcilla in 1699, daughter of a
successful peninsular father and a creole mother. Like many other
Americans, Agustín traveled to Spain to offer his services during
the War of the Spanish Succession. In common fashion he combined aid to the king with personal advancement. For 5,000 doubloons delivered to the hard-pressed royal exchequer, he obtained
an appointment as regent of Lima's Tribunal of Accounts.[25]

Agustín held the prestigious and important regency for over
thirty years. The post provided a salary equal to that oidores
earned and a base for furthering family interest. Certainly
Agustín's position could not have harmed his brother Luis's commercial activities as a member of the Lima consulado. The
regent's services, whatever immediate benefits they provided for
his family, received high praise from Viceroy Marqués de Villa
García (1736–45). The viceroy informed Philip V that Agustín
was dedicated, mature, intelligent, and honest (and consequently
in financial need) in fulfilling his obligations both as regent and as
judge on the unpopular commission for the tax on foodstuffs
(*sisa*).[26]

María Ignacia's siblings also enjoyed prominence. Her brother

Melchor, a cleric skilled in Indian languages, joined the eminent Lima cathedral chapter in 1751. Luis, another brother in cloth, served as a chaplain in the viceregal palace. An older sister, Ninfa, married the Panamanian-born *fiscal* of the Audiencia of Charcas, José Casimiro Gómez García.[27] In 1751 Gómez García moved to Lima as oidor and thus provided the family with entry to the Audiencia. Through the oidor, whose sister married Manuel Gorrichátegui, an important family tie was established. The oidor's brothers-in-law, Agustín Gorrichátegui, the future bishop of Cuzco, and his brother Manuel, a member of cathedral chapters in Spain, would be important in José Baquíjano's career.

From her maternal side, María Ignacia brought ties to the important Boza family. First cousin Antonio de Boza was a contemporary of her brothers, Luis and Melchor. Although born in Chile, Boza made his career in Lima. A *colegial* of both San Martín and San Felipe, he entered the practice of law in 1737. Subsequently he became noted for both his university service and actions as *asesor* for Viceroy Conde de Superunda (1745–61). Another cousin was Domingo Martínez de Aldunate, the future Chilean oidor, who was Juan Bautista's business associate.[28] Through his marriage to María Ignacia, Juan Bautista had joined a family involved in education, the Church, city offices, the business world, and the high bureaucracy. The family's ties in 1746 extended from Lima to Panama, Charcas, and Chile.

Juan Bautista's marriage tightened his personal links to Lima's aristocracy; two years later Ferdinand VI provided the merchant the opportunity to crown his financial and social success with a title of Castile. In 1748 the King authorized the sale of three titles free from taxes (*lanzas* and *media anata*); the proceeds were to reimburse the former bishop of Concepción, Chile, for his expenses in rebuilding that city's cathedral following an earthquake in 1737. In the early 1750s, Viceroy Conde de Superunda granted Juan Bautista one of these titles with the name Conde de Vistaflorida. As the royal confirmation read, this honor recognized his "quality and merit, and [his] having delivered the amount of twenty thousand pesos" to the former bishop. The new conde was the eighty-ninth resident of Peru to receive a title.[29]

Gaining a title was the Conde de Vistaflorida's last major accomplishment. Not all his wealth could save him from eighteenth-century medical practices. On June 12, 1759 he died, the victim, some said, of his physician's gross incompetence. Clearly the Conde had expected more years, for he had not yet established an entail for his eldest son, an oversight he charged his wife to remedy.[30]

Following her husband's death, María Ignacia took over the household. As a wealthy young widow whose extended family also resided in Lima, María Ignacia's position was demanding but not impossible. Left with riches and a title, her concern was preservation rather than elevation of social status; accordingly, she planned traditional futures for her seven children. The eldest son, Juan Agustín, would become the family's social and financial head. José, the second son, would enter a profession. The five daughters would contract marriages to preserve, if not strengthen, the family's social and economic position. As for herself, she would maintain her husband's involvement in commerce and agriculture and oversee her offspring's maturation.

To assist in maintaining the family's financial base, the Condesa enlisted her brother Luis, a cleric who had developed commercial interests. The choice was fortunate; together María Ignacia and Luis proved formidable in business. Despite executing the disbursements decreed in Juan Bautista's will and despite the depressed state of Peru's economy, the Condesa left a fortune when she died in 1791 which exceeded that left her by her husband.[31]

The Condesa joined several other women in taking a prominent part in Lima's mercantile activities. Her enterprises extended beyond the capital and its port to the interior of Peru "and even [to] remote and foreign countries."[32] One regular investment was continuing her husband's participation in the grain trade between Lima and Chile. In addition to trade and maintaining land, warehouses, slaves, mules, and equipment near Callao, the Condesa invested in both rural and urban property. Her last major purchase was an estate valued at 85,000 pesos. Land, however, was less important than financial instruments in a fortune that totaled nearly a million pesos at her death. The Condesa had extended credit or cash for individual sums exceeding 30,000 pesos. Both titled and untitled persons were in her debt, and woe unto debtors remiss in their obligations.[33] In 1790 the Condesa headed a list of worried Lima creditors whose attorney wrote Charles IV requesting that an important debtor not be granted a moratorium. Allegedly the scoundrel had threatened to seek one solely to avoid paying his obligations, despite having assets that could be liquidated.[34]

Juan Baustista's death did not alter the Baquíjano family's need for well-placed friends and relatives. And, since he alone of his family had come to Peru, his death changed none of the relationships. Family ties, however, required renewal in each generation. Marriages provided social cement as families sought to retain or raise their station. Colonists had long recognized the mutual benefit produced by uniting new wealth with old prestige as exemplified in the marriages between Juan Bautista and María Ignacia and, earlier, between her maternal grandparents, Antonio Garcés de Marcilla and Ana de Lisperguer.

Despite the brief duration of her marriage, the Condesa had seven children available for matrimony. Few families could bear the expense of every child marrying, but for any family with social pretensions several strategic alliances were in order. The Condesa's success in overseeing suitable marriages explains the family's continuing prominence and involvement in bureaucratic, military, and commercial affairs.

Juana Rosa married the Peruvian noble Andrés Francisco Maldonado y Salazar, a militia captain in Lima who later became captain in the Regiment of Nobles and a city *alcalde*. Her spouse's rank in society was indicated by his father's first wife, a sister of José Clemente de Traslaviña, a limeño oidor of the Audiencia of Chile from 1740 to 1776.[35] Another daughter, Francisca Paula, also wed an officer, José Antonio de Salazar y Breña. Salazar, although a limeño, became one of the few pensioned *caballeros* of the Order of Charles III in 1774, and by the mid-1790s held a militia colonelcy in Lima.[36] A son of this marriage, Manuel, became the fourth Conde de Vistaflorida in 1817.

A third Baquíjano daughter, Josefa, married José Remírez de Laredo, the second Conde de San Xavier y Casa Laredo. Josefa's marriage linked the Baquíjanos to another prominent, wealthy family, that of Francisco Buenaventura Remírez de Laredo, the Peruvian son of a peninsular treasury official in Trujillo. He had initiated a successful business career in Chile, and he married Francisca Javiera Calvo de Encalada y Recabarren, daughter of the Chilean magnate the Marqués de Villapalma, in 1736. For her dowry, Francisca brought an appointment as *corregidor* for the

Peruvian province of Huamalíes. Even before he returned to Peru, Remírez de Laredo's fortune was mounting and, perhaps aided by capital produced from exploiting the *corregimiento*, he continued to prosper. He purchased another appointment as corregidor in 1750 and, not long afterward, procured the title Conde de San Xavier y Casa Laredo for 20,000 pesos.[37]

The second Conde de San Xavier y Casa Laredo's siblings added further prominence to the family. His sister, Francisca, married Antonio de Ulloa, the famed traveler to South America and later governor of Huancavelica and Louisiana. Brother Gaspar combined a military and legal career and, after several audiencia appointments, reached the Council of the Indies. Gaspar boasted membership in the Order of Santiago and, after 1786, bore the family's title.[38]

As for José Remírez de Laredo himself, he brought his family more despair than honor. While a naval officer in Spain he established a reputation for causing trouble. Hopeful that personal supervision would restrain his excesses, his parents prevailed upon Antonio de Ulloa to secure José's return to Lima. But the good intentions bred from fourteen years' separation foundered when the young naval lieutenant returned to gambling. Then, with his father ready to disinherit him, José suddenly reformed. According to his mother, the marriage to María Josefa had calmed the son's "usual libertinage." Despite later charges by hostile critics that marriage into the Baquíjano family had only increased his difficult behavior, tranquillity prevailed within the Remírez de Laredo household. José's circumspect behavior during his father's final years softened the old man's attitude, and he bestowed both the title and the entailed property on the officer.[39]

Family peace proved only temporary; the strain of adjudicating the estate produced violent quarrels between the new Conde and his mother. She wrote bitterly that he never called her "mother" but only "the executrix." As the dispute progressed, the Conde had a friend print a libelous piece against his mother's attorney. Amidst the furor this action created, the Conde fled Lima on a departing naval vessel. Tragedy ended the case when the ship sank and he lost his life; death alone had spared him arrest and imprisonment upon reaching Spain.[40]

Marriage with the Remírez de Laredo family had produced a score of relationships, including a tie between José Baquíjano and the third Conde de San Xavier, another limeño anxious for high office. The brash lieutenant's death, however, afforded still another opportunity for a strategic marriage.

In the late eighteenth century, viceroys still followed their predecessors' custom and brought relations and clients with them when they assumed office. Following Viceroy Francisco Gil de Taboada y Lemos (1790–96) came his nephews Vicente and Francisco Gil de Taboada. Vicente soon became Intendant of Trujillo, a post he filled until 1820. Quickly appointed to the highly desirable post of captain of the viceregal guard of halberdiers, Francisco continued a military career and eventually became a brigadier. Before his uncle's term ended, Francisco married the widow Josefa Baquíjano.[41] Again the Baquíjano family had created marital ties with a prominent family.

A fourth sister, Mariana, also revealed the family penchant for marrying well-placed peninsulars. In 1776 she wed the Salamancan Gerónimo Manuel de Ruedas y Morales. Her dowry, agreed upon two days after Ruedas took his seat as oidor on the Lima Audiencia, was 68,563 pesos, a sum that exceeded the judge's total expected salary for the next thirteen years.[42]

Ruedas, previously incumbent of both *fiscalías* for the Lima court and subsequently the first regent for the Audiencia of Charcas, exemplified the value of university service for gaining an audiencia appointment. Trained in civil and canon law at the University of Salamanca, he proceeded to the University of Bologna's Colegio Mayor of San Clemente Martyr. There he held a professorship for eleven years, his stay ended by appointment to Lima's criminal fiscalía in 1767. Viceroy Manuel Amat capitalized on Ruedas' background by naming him to the committee that produced the 1771 reform plan for the University of San Marcos.[43]

The remaining Baquíjano daughter, Catalina, married Domingo Ramírez de Arellano in 1773. Domingo was the eldest son of a family long entrusted with important local offices in the Spanish town of Viguera. In his teens he accompanied an uncle to Peru and immediately entered the urban cavalry militia, joining the Regiment of the Nobility of Lima; when admitted to the Order of Calatrava in 1776, he was a captain of dragoons. Although he continued to hold militia commissions until his death in 1811, Domingo's primary interest was business. By the 1780s he was carrying cacao from Guayaquil to Lima in his ships, the *Santa*

Ana and *Las Mercedes*, and engaged in trade with Spain. Upon the death of Luis Carrillo, he became the Condesa de Vistaflorida's principal business adviser and, following her death, the effective executor of her estate. Additionally he managed the second Conde de Vistaflorida's properties in Peru. His prominence in Lima's merchant circles received public recognition when the consulado elected him prior in 1793. Catalina's marriage thus helped to preserve the Baquíjano family's importance in commerce.[44]

The five Baquíjano daughters had contracted marriages that strengthened the family's eminence in Lima. Together they had created or expanded familial links to the city council, the merchant guild, the militia, the Audiencia, and even the viceroy. The importance of the extended family in Lima society and local affairs could not be denied.

While the Baquíjano daughters remained firmly entrenched in Peru, their older brother, Juan Agustín, followed a different course. The eldest son of the family, Juan Agustín was born in Lima on April 13, 1748 and succeeded his father as the second Conde de Vistaflorida at the age of eleven. Undoubtedly at his mother's insistence the young Conde, unlike most noble Peruvians, went to Spain for formal education. Unlike his younger brother José, of whom he repeatedly despaired in later years, Juan Agustín displayed only modest interest in the world of learning, preferring to focus on practical affairs. After scarcely two years in Madrid's Seminary of Nobles, he returned to Peru where he soon became captain of a militia cavalry company in the province of Cañete where his mother owned property. This post later enabled him to gain membership in the Order of Santiago in 1784. Aside from a term as an *alcalde ordinario* for the Lima city council in 1775, Juan Agustín remained apart from political office. He also refrained from marrying, although his wealth and title certainly would have made him eligible for a stunning match with a daughter from another of Lima's most prominent families. Peru, in fact, exerted little but financial attraction for the second Conde and by 1780 he abandoned it permanently in favor of Spain.[45]

The Conde's decision to emigrate to Spain did not by itself distinguish him from other wealthy Americans. Many creoles paid the price to see the peninsula, loiter around the court, and beg favors for themselves, their relatives, and friends. American aspirants for membership in a military order, for example, could regularly locate a cluster of fellow countrymen to swear to their unblemished past and good family.[45] But Juan Agustín Baquíjano differed from most creoles in Spain in not wanting to return to the New World. Rather, he soon established himself as a resident in Madrid, providing his American relatives with a convenient voice at court.[47]

In his new home the Conde continued his parents' involvement in financial activities. He invested in the new Bank of San Carlos, Spain's first national bank, bought stock in the merchant guild of Cádiz, purchased government bonds, and made private loans. By 1796 he had amassed a fortune he placed at nearly five million *reales*. This wealth included not only land in Peru and Vizcaya, but, more importantly, various notes and government bonds.[48]

Juan Agustín maintained business connections in Lima where he worked closely with his uncle, Luis Carrillo, until the latter's death, and then with his brother-in-law Domingo Ramírez de Arellano, whom he placed in charge of his Peruvian affairs. At various times the Conde also dealt with businessmen in Mexico, Buenos Aires, and Santo Domingo. In Madrid he loaned money to many people close to the court. His investments served him well when a royal decree of 1789 ordered all nonresidents to leave Madrid. The Conde protested successfully that members of the court owed him money and this tangible consideration demanded his continued presence. It is unclear how important Juan Agustín was in the court's financial circles, but it is worth nothing that Jorge Escobedo, Councilor of the Indies and former Visitor General to Peru, owed him the substantial sum of 90,000 reales when he died in 1805.[49]

Taken together the Baquíjano family had flourished. At mid-eighteenth century the Basque merchant Juan Bautista de Baquíjano was favorably placed in Lima society. His commercial success and marriage to María Ignacia Carrillo de Córdoba anchored him in the city's financial and social elite. As the couple's daughters grew up, they made favorable matches that demonstrated the family's standing. The elder son, Juan Agustín, furthered his own fortune while creating new financial ties in Madrid. Thus the Baquíjano family enjoyed prominence in Peru and recognition at court. The combination provided a social background that nourished José Baquíjano's ambitions.

José Xavier Leandro Baquíjano y Carrillo de Córdoba was born in Lima on March 13, 1751 and baptized ten weeks later. The visitor general of Peru's Inquisition officiated, while limeño oidor Domingo de Orrantia and a future oidor, the Chilean Christóbal Mesía y Munive, Conde de Sierrabella, witnessed the sacrament. Orrantia and Mesía symbolized the environment of native-son and other creole success that enveloped José literally from his earliest days. The child's godfather was his father's close friend, the wealthy Basque businessman, Martín de Zelayeta. An immigrant remembered over a century later for his charitable contributions, at his death Zelayeta left José and his siblings legacies of 4,000 pesos each.[50]

José began life in the comfortable surroundings of a wealthy, aristocratic household. The family home stood three blocks from the southwest corner of the Plaza Mayor on Calle Gurumendi, later Calle Baquíjano. As was typical of merchant homes in Mexico City and Buenos Aires in the late eighteenth century, part of the house served as a retail outlet for the Spanish and French textiles his father imported. The domestic furnishings corresponded to Juan Bautista's wealth and pretension. Fourteen slaves were present. The living room displayed some thirty paintings, the most prominent featuring religious themes. An immense table made in Africa and sixteen gilded chairs filled the room. In the merchant's study stood an elaborate desk, ten chairs, and more paintings. Dining occasioned lavish display. When José was a boy silver service for sixteen was available, and this allowed a large plate, six smaller plates, four forks, and four spoons per person.[51] Within this opulent setting, young José met relatives and close family friends. Throughout his life he belonged to Lima's upper class, a group that expected deference, respect, and favor. The relationships he enjoyed from his youth stimulated a belief that his background entitled him to the high position held by the witnesses at his baptism, Orrantia and the Conde de Sierrabella.

Although the posthumous inventory of the first Conde de Vistaflorida's possessions listed no books, both he and his wife recognized the importance of education and started José studying Latin and the liberal arts as a young boy. His formal education began in April, 1762, when he entered Lima's Seminary of Santo Toribio.[52]

The choice of Santo Toribio for José's schooling reveals that family ties outweighted prestige. Although the Seminary boasted an illustrious past and reknowned alumni, it ranked behind the Jesuit College of San Martín as the school favored by Lima's aristocratic families. Among San Martín's alumni were Audiencia ministers as well as high-ranking clerics. Twenty-eight of the Lima cathedral chapter's members between 1730 and 1760 had attended San Martín as opposed to only two from Santo Toribio.[53] Considering the first Conde's concern with prestige and personal social advancement, had he lived José probably would have attended the Jesuit college as had his uncles, Melchor Carrillo de Córdoba, a member of the cathedral chapter from 1750 to 1760, and José Casimiro Gómez García, an audiencia minister in Charcas and Lima. For a youth intent on either a high-ranking clerical or secular career, San Martín offered more promise than Santo Toribio.

Since the Conde died when José was only eight, the Condesa supervised the boy's education. Santo Toribio attracted her for its new rector rather than its reputation.[54] The Panamanian Agustín de Gorrichátegui y Gómez, himself an alumnus of San Martín, was the brother-in-law of her older sister, Ninfa. Named rector of Santo Toribio in 1760, Gorrichátegui brought to his post an avid interest in the modern philosophical ideas that were gaining circulation through publications such as those by the noted Spanish eclectic, the Benedictine Father Benito de Feijóo y Montenegro. Dr. Toribio Rodríguez de Mendoza, the guiding spirit of the celebrated Convictory of San Carlos, Lima's post-Jesuit school, later praised Gorrichátegui's pioneering efforts in introducing modern ideas to Peruvian students. Following the rector's promotion to Bishop of Cuzco in 1770, Dr. Ignacio de Castro publically proclaimed Gorrichátegui's attention to modern physics. The young intellectual noted that for the new bishop nature conformed "not to our ideas, but our ideas to the effects observed in nature." He avoided a philosophical system and relied upon modern mathematics rather than "vague peripatetic notions" that have never produced real explanations.[55]

The devotion to modern thought Baquíjano later displayed so conspicuously in his writings was born under Gorrichátegui's guidance and encouragement. Justinian's *Institutes*, rather than the ideas of Descartes or Newton, however, constituted the course at Santo Toribio. This José mastered quickly, his examinations winning unanimous approval. His new learning received public display in a formal academic act in December 1764. The skillful way he presented and defended his thesis impressed the audience and the Archbishop of Lima, to whom José thoughtfully had dedicated the act, later recalled the young student's success in glowing terms.[56]

The Archbishop's further reference to José's "outstanding progress" in Santo Toribio justly describes his rapid accumulation of degrees. The University of San Marcos conferred the baccalaureate in canon law on February 18, 1765 and scarcely two months later he successfully stood examination for the licentiate and doctorate in that faculty. When he received these advanced degrees on April 29, 1765, the precocious youth was but fourteen years of age, even younger than his famous compatriot and near contemporary Pablo de Olavide had been when receiving the doctor's hood.[57]

Baquíjano vividly exemplified the facility with which boys of prodigious memory could amass academic credentials. But there was another side to his early triumphs. Through encouragement and financial support his mother had effectively eased him into a path leading to a professional career. The Church, government, higher education, private practice of law, or a combination of these offered respectable employment for a second son of noble birth. Although degrees in canon law obviously aided a career in the cloth, they formed an acceptable background for the other areas.

Baquíjano first sought a vocation in teaching, a field that would occupy him intermittently for nearly thirty years. He began to tutor students in jurisprudence at Santo Toribio shortly before receiving his advanced degrees and subsequently continued as a faculty member. Contemporaries corroborated his later boast that he taught well.[58]

Nearly all teachers in the colonial world received modest if not wretched salaries. Consequently tutors, teachers, and professors sought an additional stipend. For a man with legal training, the logical sequel was to become an *abogado*, an attorney licensed to practice before an audiencia. This step opened the way to numerous government positions as well as private practice. Degrees in canon or civil law alone did not enable qualifying as an abogado because knowledge of Spanish law was mandatory. Since no colonial university offered such practical training in the 1760s, however, a student needed to study privately or to apprentice himself to a practicing attorney to obtain this extra command. Apparently Baquíjano followed the latter course before passing the Audiencia's examination on December 5, 1769.[59]

Becoming a licensed attorney did not move José to forsake a possible ecclesiastical career. Yet the certification further prepared him for his future pursuit of judicial office. Qualifying as an abogado was common among aspirants to the judiciary in the eighteenth century and after 1750 nearly all audiencia ministers had previously been so licensed.[60] Baquíjano at age eighteen was retaining flexibility in choosing a career. While no direct evidence suggests that he was seriously contemplating a judicial career at this time, each professional step fit into a recognized pattern for men eager for an audiencia position.

Baquíjano's formal professional training ended in 1769. During the following year, however, an opportunity to broaden his education arose. Agustín de Gorrichátegui was named Bishop of the Diocese of Cuzco in 1770 and offered his relative a post as personal secretary. When the new prelate left for the ancient Inca capital in August, Baquíjano resigned his teaching responsibilities at Santo Toribio and also turned his eyes to Indian Peru.[61] His travel and residence in Cuzco provided a personal knowledge of the *sierra* that few of his fellow writers in the *Mercurio peruano* years later could match.

Baquíjano's tenure as Gorrichátegui's secretary marked a turning point in his aspirations. Immersed in the intricacies of the bishop's responsibilities, José soon found little attraction in a life devoted to the Church. The idea of a secular career captured his attention and, after attending the Lima Provincial Council in 1772, he remained in his natal city.[62]

José's decision to remain in Lima represented the triumph of local ties over career possibilities elsewhere. Furthermore it highlighted his awareness that the viceregal capital was the fount of local patronage and offered the best opportunities for building a secular career worthy of royal reward. Lima was his base. His relatives' influence was focused in the capital and, as a known scion of a titled family, his possibilities for favor and success there increased accordingly.

Abandoning an ecclesiastical career further delimited José's vocational choices. The decision coincided closely with the emergence of a definite goal—obtaining appointment to the Audiencia of Lima. The tribunal not only offered an attractive salary but also represented the pinnacle of prestige among the courts in South America. Its location, moreover, was optimal for a man whose home was the City of Kings. With his objective certain, professional steps previously taken without a clear perception of their ultimate use gave way to actions designed to enhance his attractiveness for high judicial office. By the end of 1772 José knew that he wanted appointment to Lima's Audiencia. The following twenty-five years chronicled his efforts to fulfill this ambitious goal.

At first glance, Baquíjano's decision to seek appointment to his home tribunal might seem fatuous. Lima's court in 1772 had only fourteen positions and each incumbent enjoyed indefinite tenure. Moreover, as a general rule the Spanish Crown considered limeños undesirable appointees to their home Audiencia. Recent work, however, has demonstrated that creoles' fortunes varied in gaining appointment to their home and other New World tribunals from 1687 to 1821 and forced abandonment of the simplistic contention that Americans suffered "virtual exclusion" from high office.[63] Yet the unique success of Peruvians in gaining audiencia positions requires more extended treatment in order to appreciate adequately why Baquíjano believed his goal reasonable and within grasp.

From the time the Crown named the first Americans to audiencia positions in the late sixteenth century until 1750, eve of Baquíjano's birth, Peruvians excelled in receiving the coveted appointments. Not only did they secure well over half of all American appointments (121 of 223), but also, and more importantly, many obtained posts on their home court in Lima. For the years from 1687 to 1750, the percentage of native sons among Peruvian appointees was over fifty. This record deserves emphasis both for its uniqueness and for its importance in creating an environment favorable for Baquíjano's ambitions.

In 1538 Emperor Charles V ordered that creoles descended from explorers, conquistadors, and first settlers be given civil positions. These posts, moreover, were to be "where their ancestors served" the Crown.[64] Americans regularly contended that this phrase meant the favored appointee was to be a native son, a man born in the district in which he received office.

For many years most historians either ignored the distinction between "native sons" and "other creoles" or considered it moot on the grounds that an American named to a high-ranking post went to "a colony other than that of which the Creole official was native." Separating the two groups is crucial, however, for geography normally circumscribed the general creole desire to hold office. The family was colonial society's most important component and, since few creoles cared to abandon voluntarily the security and reliability it afforded, most sought to serve in the region of their birth.

The distinction between "native sons" and "other creoles" is especially important when one considers audiencia appointees, for the high courts enjoyed considerable power and prestige both for their judicial responsibilities and their importance as advisory bodies to the chief executive of their districts. Since ministers served for life or at the pleasure of the king, they provided a continuity in government absent from the offices of viceroy, captain-general, or governor. Moreover, unlike a creole corregidor named to an alien province for a limited term, an American designated to a distant audiencia could never be certain of returning home. Much as an appointee born in Spain, he entered his post as an "outsider." Consequently creoles who pursued audiencia appointments regularly sought to remain native sons. When this was impossible, they preferred an initial appointment to a tribunal from which normal advancement would be to their home court rather than an office in a higher ranking court outside this promotion channel.

Although no law in the *Recopilación*—the codification published in 1681—specifically prohibited creoles from serving audiencia posts, marriage and property restrictions implied the exclusion of most native sons.[65] The Crown considered native-son appointments exceptional and as requiring a specific dispensation of nativity. It never yielded to native-son entreaties that locally-born men should hold all audiencia positions, nor would it even grant, as it did for several courts in Spain, that native sons should serve designated seats on their home tribunals.[66]

Americans, on the other hand, began arguing for native-son appointments from at least the first half of the seventeenth century. In 1642 the limeño Nicolás Polanco de Santillana, knight of Santiago and fiscal of the Audiencia of Charcas, presented a memorial asking the Crown to give special consideration to professors of the University of San Marcos, who were alumni and native sons, when it filled Audiencia and ecclesiastical positions in Lima. Twenty-five years later the American attorney Pedro de Bolívar y de la Redonda, himself an alumnus of San Marcos, invoked extensive legal traditions as he argued that native sons should hold all positions.[67] If implemented, the result would have given each region's leading families *de facto* local rule.

Local families appreciated the potential benefits native-son ministers could offer. Men with power were expected to benefit their relative and friends. Indeed, Americans often lamented that high-ranking peninsular officials furnished numerous relatives and clients with local offices. A serving native son would provide at least some prominent families with direct representation in colonial government's highest ranks. Of course such representation could prevent evenhanded administration of justice and consultation favorable to royal interests. Precisely for these reasons, the Crown opposed naming native sons and sought to impede other appointees from establishing any local ties.

Peruvians, like men in the empire's other mainland regions, particularly desired appointment to their home tribunal. Success meant having gained the highest position to which a Peruvian trained in the law (*letrado*) could reasonably aspire. Oidores, *alcaldes del crimen*, and civil or criminal fiscales commanded social prestige and power. Their offices carried a salary of 1,350,000 *maravedís* (nearly four times the amount received by the most highly paid professor at San Marcos), the possibility of remunerative commissions, and countless opportunities for illegal gain. For an aspiring family, a son on the court represented capital social gain. An established aristocratic family in Lima would view a son on the court with equal pleasure, for he would help to perpetuate the house's eminence as well as to provide an additional income, an income whose importance grew as Peru's mining yield declined.

Lima's ample educational facilities gave Peruvians an advantage over most colonists. A seminary, colleges, and the University of San Marcos furnished students with the requisite academic background for a career in an audiencia. In addition, numerous barristers provided the practical legal knowledge students needed to become practicing attorneys. Limeños benefited especially from their ready access to a complete legal education. They avoided the expense of living away from home that, for example, befell Chileans until the mid-eighteenth century. Moreover, from the mid-seventeenth century onward, students who received an education in Lima were unavoidably exposed to success stories of earlier alumni and professors who went on to serve on audiencias in Lima and elsewhere. Polanco's representation in 1642 revealed clearly the University's concern to place its sons in prominent positions.

The preeminence of Peruvians in gaining appointments until 1750 is seen in Figures 1 and 2.[68] In obtaining positions both in Lima and elsewhere, they eclipsed creoles from every other region. Mexico, the district next in representation, provided only six appointees in the years from 1602 to 1687 and but twenty-six during the subsequent period to 1750.

The opportunities for Peruvians to advance their self-interests peaked between 1687 and 1750 when the Crown systematically sold audiencia appointments. Caught in desperate financial straits, the Crown bartered dispensations from any restrictive legislation or policy the prospective buyer sought. Thus, for example, it allowed men not yet twenty-five years, the age of major-

FIGURE 1

Peruvians and Appointments to American Audiencias

	Pre-1601	1602–87	1687–1750	Totals
Peruvians	2	46	73	121
Other Americans	1	36	65	102
TOTALS	3	82	138	223

FIGURE 2

Place of Birth for Appointees to the Audiencia of Lima

	1543–1601	1602–87	1687–1750	Totals
Peru	0	8	38	46
Other Parts of America	0	5	4	9
Spain	59	99	26	184
TOTALS	59	112	68	239

ity, to serve at home, hold property, and marry a local woman.
Peruvians demonstrated a particular avidity to purchase appointments, and the importance the transactions held in facilitating
their presence on Lima's court is indicated in Figure 3.[69]

Revealed in the totals in Figure 3 is the singularity of Peru as a
source for Audiencia ministers, but to establish a perspective from
which to appreciate Baquíjano's aspirations, it is necessary to examine the background of other successful native sons. If all were
the offspring of audiencia ministers, a merchant's son would be
foolish to seek such preferment. On the other hand, if education at
a university in Spain were a prerequisite, the pool of potential
aspirants would be limited. Examining the thirty-eight native sons
named to Lima from 1687 to 1750 helps to identify the kind of
men who could reasonably expect appointment (see Appendix A).

Almost without exception, the native sons enjoyed either af-
fluence or ample credit. Exploiting the Crown's penury, twenty-
eight purchased appointments for sums that often surpassed
20,000 pesos. Yet although money was frequently the candidates'
most prominent credential, the Crown required some professional
training as well. Eligibility demanded at least a baccalaureate in
civil or canon law, and most native sons exceeded this modest requisite and claimed other qualifications as well.

The native sons' educational and professional accomplishments
are revealed in Figure 4. Nearly all held advanced legal degrees
conferred by the University of San Marcos after previous attendance at a Lima college, usually that of San Martín. Additionally,
at least a slight majority had qualified to practice law before the
Audiencia.

Strikingly, despite Lima's rank as South America's preeminent
tribunal, very few native sons had previously served on another

FIGURE 3

Appointees to the Audiencia of Lima, 1687–1750

(purchasers in parentheses)

	1687–1711	*1712–30*	*1731–50*	*Totals*
Peruvians	19 (16)	3	16 (12)	38 (28)
Other Americans	2	0	2 (2)	4 (2)
Spaniards	10 (1)	15	1	26 (1)
TOTALS	31 (17)	18	19 (14)	68 (31)

court. This anomaly reflected the bypassing of normal advancement to Lima produced by the sale of appointments. Only a handful of native sons, in fact, claimed previous public service, one a purchased appointment as president of the Audiencia of Charcas,[70] three as advisers (*asesores generales*) to the viceroy of Peru,[71] two as protectors of the Indians in Lima and Charcas,[72] two others as legal advisers to local institutions,[73] and one as a treasury official.[74] In only one case did this experience rather than monetary payment account for the later Audiencia appointment.[75]

The paucity of noteworthy prior government or university service was due principally to the Crown's willingness to sell appointments to young, inexperienced men. Half of the native sons were under thirty-three years when named, the youngest being merely nineteen. Moreover, after formal education in Peru, many youths then went to Spain; there they sometimes spent years seeking preferment, time they might otherwise have employed in actual service to local or royal government.

In education, age, travel to Spain, lack of previous experience,

FIGURE 4

The Thirty-Eight Native Sons Named to the
Audiencia of Lima, 1687–1750
Education and Professional Activities

EDUCATION		*PROFESSIONAL ACTIVITIES*	
University:		Attorney:	
San Marcos (alone)	34	Lima	20
San Marcos and Salamanca	2	Royal Councils	1
Other	1	No information	17
Unknown	1		
Colegio:		University Service	
San Martín (alone)	27	Professor	8
San Felipe (alone)	2	*Opositor*	4
San Martín and San Felipe	4	Substitute	3
Unknown	5		

Highest Degree			Previous Audiencia Appointment	
	1687–1711	1721–50		
Doctorate	9	18	None	28
Licentiate	8	1	Charcas	7
Bachelor	1		Chile	2
Unknown	1		Santa Fe de Bogotá	1

and the necessity to pay for their appointments, Peru's native sons showed many common traits. Additionally, many had parents who displayed similarities. Twenty-four native sons had fathers from Spain.[76] Nearly all of these appointees' mothers, on the other hand, were from Peru, seventeen from Lima.[77] In other words, nearly two-thirds of the native-son appointees from 1687 to 1750 were first-generation creoles on their paternal side. Furthermore, the fathers of a majority came from the three Basque Provinces (11), Navarre (4), and Santander (2).[78] Nearly every peninsular father had either a military commission or position in local administration. Only two, however, had been audiencia ministers, and their sons were first appointed to a tribunal other than Lima before 1687.[79] At least eight fathers were active merchants. Seven of the eight fathers who were definitely merchants also held military or administrative appointments.[80] Three of these eight merchant fathers came from the Basque Provinces, three from Navarre, and one from Santander. These men, too, were particularly prominent among fathers belonging to military orders. Six of the seven fathers so honored were from the Basque Provinces or Navarre and five were merchants.[81] The only titled father among the twenty-four peninsulars was the famed merchant prince from Santander, the Marqués de Torre Tagle.

Combining these characteristics, one finds that a "typical" native-son appointee from 1687 to 1750 was the offspring of a peninsular father from northern Spain and a limeña mother. His father held a military commission or a position in local government, and the family had enough wealth to provide him with a complete legal education in Lima, a trip to Spain, maintenance at court, and, probably, at least part of an appointment's cost. Besides the advantages his family had provided, this "typical" appointee, a young man, had few if any specific accomplishments to relate. One can readily perceive that Baquíjano's family background, youth, education, and lack of government service in 1772 corresponded closely to that displayed by the "typical" native-son appointee.

An examination of appointments from 1687 to 1750 emphasizes the singular success of Peruvians in serving audiencia posts at home and elsewhere in America, while a consideration of the native-son appointees helps to define the kind of men who succeeded and, thus, the kind of men who most realistically could believe that they, too, might become ministers. These approaches alone, however, do not provide a full setting for appreciating Baquíjano's ambition. Equally critical is the continued presence of native sons on Lima's Audiencia during his formative years.

Pre-1750 appointees were a majority of the court's fourteen permanent seats throughout Baquíjano's youth. At his birth, fourteen of eighteen men who held appointments were native sons.[82] Although their number gradually declined, seven still held seats in 1772. These men were visible evidence of the career successes of native sons between 1751 and 1772 which underlaid Baquíjano's perception of his own possibilities. During these years, the court never had more than three peninsulars; creoles born in Panama or Chile, but educated in Lima, filled its complement.

Although authorized fourteen ministers, Lima's Audiencia also had four extra judges holding appointments in 1750. These supernumeraries, as they were called, awaited vacancies left by the regular ministers in order to assume full responsibilities and salary. Their presence gave the court a surplus of ministers that continued into the 1760s and precluded numerous appointments between mid-century and 1772. Thus they buffered the court against the Crown's general effort to tighten control over the American audiencias. Certainly the four new ministers could not have dampened José's ambition. Cristóbal Mesía y Munive was a Chilean educated in Lima. Panamanian José Casimiro Gómez García was Baquíjano's uncle and Gerónimo Ruedas Morales, one of the two peninsulars, later became his brother-in-law.

Viewed from the perspectives of family, individual ability and educational achievement, Lima's tradition of local men gaining audiencia appointments at home and elsewhere, and native-son prominence on the home tribunal during his youth, Baquíjano's environment was one that could only nurture ambition in the young man. Within this setting, his desire to join Lima's court seemed eminently reasonable. Little did he appreciate in 1772 that his environment was unique in the American colonies and that since the time of his birth the Crown had frequently displayed antagonism to native-son service elsewhere in the empire.

2

To Court and Disgrace

The Lima environment had excited Baquíjano's ambition, but, at a time when the Crown was steadily limiting native sons on the American courts, his eventual appointment to the Audiencia came only after a lengthy personal campaign. During the quarter century between 1772 and his appointment in 1797, hope and frustration alternately marked his life. Repeatedly his efforts either to obtain an appointment or simply to accumulate personal achievements worthy of one foundered unexpectedly. Underlying his difficulties was a dramatic shift in the Crown's appointment policy. Free from wartime expenditures, the Crown terminated the sale of audiencia appointments in 1750, returned to more traditional standards of evaluation, and began to demand solid professional credentials from its appointees. Moreover, during the remainder of the colonial period, it seldom named native sons; peninsulars in particular benefited from the new direction, receiving three-quarters of the initial appointments in the years from 1751 to 1808. The very uniqueness of Baquíjano's success within the new context gives added point to examining his career.

Baquíjano's career followed an irregular course until 1797. A first trip to Spain terminated in disgrace in 1776, and subsequent efforts to forge a notable record through government and university service aborted in an unforeseen uproar that followed the publication of a speech he delivered at the University of San Marcos in 1781. Unseemly contests for the rectorship and the first chair of civil law at San Marcos further marred the 1780s, but early in the following decade, Baquíjano's fortunes rose sharply. He gained the first chair of canon law at San Marcos and became president of Lima's Amantes del País and a major contributor to its journal, the *Mercurio peruano*. Expanding upon these successes, he convinced the Lima city council to name him its representative at court, returned to Spain and, after petitioning persistently for several years, gained at last the coveted appointment to Lima's Audiencia.

As we have seen, the unique success of Peruvians in obtaining audiencia appointments provided the environment in which Baquíjano's ambitions matured. As a youth he had known some, if not all, of Lima's ministers and his family's prominence insured that the social relationships were between equals. Academic achievements, unanimously acclaimed intellectual prowess, and high social rank predisposed José to believe that he deserved an appointment. Still, he recognized that the king's advisers expected candidates to have a record of public service. Consequently, once having chosen his goal in 1772, he sought offices that would furnish him the needed credentials to demonstrate that he had gained the confidence of local officials.

At this point the Condesa de Vistaflorida, who acquiesced if not rejoiced in her son's new choice of career, probably aided him. An important member of Lima's merchant community, she undoubtedly exerted influence necessary to secure José's appointment as a legal adviser (*asesor*) for the merchant guild in early January 1773.[1]

Baquíjano's only known activity as asesor was helping to write a treatise on Peru's commerce. This document analyzed the region's commerce historically, emphasizing causes for its decline and suggesting means to revitalize it. Written shortly before Charles III created the Viceroyalty of the Río de la Plata, an action that had severe repercussions on Peru's economy, the treatise would doubtless make fascinating reading, particularly when compared to Baquíjano's comments on Peru's economy in the early 1790s.[2] Unfortunately it remains undiscovered, and one has only Baquíjano's word that implementing the proposals would have benefited Peru and the royal treasury.[3]

Even less material documents José's activities in the second position received in 1773. On March 17 the Marqués de Villafuerte informed Lima's city council that illness and other absences hindered the two authorized legal advisors (*asesores del número*) from serving their offices with necessary dispatch. Consequently, he proposed that the council appoint José as a supernumerary asesor to serve during the regular advisers' absences and infirmities. The city fathers concurred and swore the young attorney into office immediately.[4]

Although José was one of only three supernumerary asesores the city council named between 1756 and 1781, the wording of his appointment varied little from that of twenty-nine honorary asesores named during these years.[5] Indeed one suspects that these appointments, regardless of title, were designed more for the patronage they represented than any labor to be received. Limeños who aspired to audiencia positions commonly listed such an office in their vitas (*relaciones de méritos*).

Baquíjano's subsequent actions illustrated forcefully the extent to which he, as other ambitious youths, sought local asesor posts as expressions of public confidence rather than vocations. One week after it had appointed him, the city council wrote a recommendation in his behalf.[6] The letter reveals when Baquíjano initiated proceedings to have a personnel file formed, a routine prelude to the solicitation of a royal appointment. Moreover, it discloses that by late March 1773 José had committed himself to journeying to court.

Parents in the Spanish colonies had long borne considerable expense to send one or more sons to Spain. Although a few youths formally enrolled in Spanish universities or, like José's older brother, Juan Agustín, entered the College of Nobles in Madrid, far more sought immediate rewards. Baquíjano followed a long-established tradition among upper-class limeños when he decided to join the court in its regular pilgrimages to successive palaces. Testimony of unblemished ancestry that Peruvians provided in order to enter a noble order reveals the constant presence of their compatriots at court. More significant in light of José's ambition, most Peruvians named to Lima's Audiencia were in Spain when appointed.

The court was the fount of patronage; moreover, for Americans, whose closest relatives were located far from its antechambers, personal solicitation was particularly helpful. Yet travel to Spain offered more than a place in an employment line. For men with genuine intellectual curiosity, Spain provided opportunities for stimulation that far surpassed those available in the colonies.

The aid of relatives and friends was often crucial for a youth who sought to enter Spain's court circles. Personal ties permeated early modern society, and a well-advised officeseeker attempted to maximize them. Thus, when Baquíjano reached Cádiz in early 1774, he immediately contacted the dean of the city's cathedral, Manuel de Gorrichátegui. Brother of José's former mentor and a distant relative, Gorrichátegui took leave from his post to escort José to Madrid. En route the pair must have stopped for at least one night in Seville, an enchanting city that afforded rest and refreshment and an opportunity to visit with Pablo de Olavide, the most illustrious Peruvian in Spain.[7]

Olavide, a known enthusiast for avant-garde French authors, combined intellectual pursuits with service in high office. While still in his teens he had taught in Lima's University of San Marcos and obtained an appointment as a supernumerary oidor to the Audiencia. When Baquíjano reached Seville, Olavide was the Intendant of Andalusia. As a first generation creole of similar background, Olavide must have brightened José's vision of personal triumph. Later Peruvians perceived that the two men shared common abilities and interests and praised them in the same breath.

Unfortunately one can only speculate about any conversation Baquíjano and Olavide might have had. After polite greetings and relating the latest news from Lima, José undoubtedly would have confided his ambition to serve on Lima's court and solicited any possible assistance. Olavide, in turn, might have regaled his young compatriot with court gossip amid practical suggestions about whom to see regarding his goal. One wonders, however, whether he would have told how his own appointment to the Lima Audiencia had come *"por vía de beneficio,"* at a cost of 20,000 pesos.[8]

Following their stay in Seville, Baquíjano and his escort would have traveled north toward Madrid. Once settled in the capital, the cleric introduced José to persons who might aid him in his pursuit of office.[9] Although the information these unnamed advisers passed to the young Peruvian is unknown, it is probable that it included a description of the appointment procedure then in operation.

The way in which the Crown made audiencia appointments had long been hallowed by bureaucratic tradition, and during the mid-1770s it operated smoothly. Once the Secretary of State for the Indies had ordered the Cámara, the chamber of the Council of the Indies responsible for nominations, to provide a written recommendation (*consulta*) of candidates for a vacancy, an official announcement of the opening was posted. This notified *pretendientes* and their agents that applications were due within twenty days.[10] Immediately aspirants began submitting formal requests for consideration (*memoriales*) and relaciones de méritos. When the deadline passed, officials drew up lists that enumerated the candidates and frequently presented what the *camaristas* would consider the most notable qualifications of each.[11]

Although the memorials varied in length from several sentences to several pages, most were brief and referred the reader to an appended vita for detail. With few exceptions, each applicant either avowed that he was a bachelor or included a notarized statement from his wife that attested to her willingness to accompany him to the ends of the empire. As some candidates discovered to their chagrin, failure to reveal their marital state was sufficient cause to prevent their applications from reaching the Cámara.[12]

During most of Baquíjano's first trip to Spain, four camaristas determined the fate of each candidate. Felipe de Arco Riva Herrera, the sole *capa y espada* minister among their number, was the most senior member (*decano*) of the Council. His tenure began in the mid-1740s when he received an appointment as the dowry of his wife, a lady-in-waiting for the queen. In the fall of 1770 he advanced to the Cámara.[13] Marcos Ximeno had joined the Council of the Indies in 1764 after a career in the Spanish audiencias and moved to the Cámara three years later.[14] The two remaining camaristas, although also peninsulars, brought American experience to their tasks. Domingo de Trespalacios y Escandón had spent over twenty years in the New World, most of it on the Audiencia of Mexico. Like Ximeno he was named to the Council in 1764 and advanced to the Cámara in 1767.[15] The fourth active member of the Cámara was José de Gálvez, the former visitor general to New Spain, who began to serve in 1772.[16] Together these men made the recommendations that, while Baquíjano was at court, almost without exception resulted in the appointment of one of their nominees. Indeed since 1750 few men had received an initial audiencia appointment without having been proposed on its consulta by one or more camaristas.

At the time Baquíjano reached Spain, the Cámara normally provided the king with a consulta for each vacant audiencia position. Although for most of the Cámara's existence the consulta had listed only three names ranked in order of preference, since 1751 all votes were revealed.[17] Since each camarista voted for three men, it was possible for the total number of candidates presented on the consulta to be triple the number of camaristas. Voting itself was by voice with the most junior camarista casting the first vote for each of the three places.[18] This meant that until he became Secretary for the Indies in February 1776, Gálvez initiated the voting throughout Baquíjano's solicitations. In the written recommendation delivered to Charles III, however, the votes were listed for each of the three places beginning with the nominees of Arco and proceeding by seniority.[19] After the king's decision, official notification was delivered to the successful pretendiente or his agent. All that then remained was to pay the appropriate tax (media anata) and fees for the paper work involved, obtain the title of office, and assume possession of the post. The entire process from the announcement of a vacancy to the issuance of a title of office easily took about six months.

Baquíjano's arrival in Madrid added one more letrado to the pretendientes seeking audiencia positions. Available evidence suggests that for the period in which he sought an appointment—from late 1773 to early 1776—a total of about 250 men competed with varying frequency for the openings. The number of aspirants for each post increased dramatically between 1773 and 1776; while less than fifty candidates normally sought an open position at the time of his arrival, by 1776 over eighty were common and more than one hundred not unknown.[20] The greater interest by the latter date probably reflected the increased optimism provoked by an unprecedented expansion of the number of posts available.

Although it appears that less than a quarter of the pretendientes were creoles, enough Americans traveled to Spain in pursuit of appointment that one suspects they frequently met in the corridors of government office buildings, jostled in anterooms, and offered each other consolation if not encouragement. Baquíjano undoubtedly ran into fellow limeño Manuel Antonio de la Bodega y Mollinedo, a youth of approximately his own age who had attended the University of San Marcos before journeying to Spain for study at the University of Alcalá and solicitation of an office. Another future minister, Francisco Xavier de Moreno y Escandón, also trod the corridors in a lengthy search for an appointment. Born in the district of Santa Fe de Bogotá in 1751, he too had attended universities in Spain after study at the university in Bogotá. The Mexican attorneys Francisco Xavier de Gorospe y Padilla, Tomás González Calderón, José de Saravia y Castro, and José Joaquín de Arias de Villafañe, *caraqueño* Sebastián de Talavera y Medina, and *charqueños* Juan de Dios Calvo Antequera and Francisco López y Lisperguer further added to the swarm of pretendientes that descended with the announcement of vacant positions.[21] And these men exemplify only those Americans, perhaps half of the total, who sought an audiencia appointment from the vantage point of Madrid.

Other Americans regularly relied upon agents to further their pretensions. Francisco López, for example, encharged his affairs to fellow Chilean Juan de Salas. His compatriot, Alonso de Guzmán, employed the popular agent Tomás Pérez Arroyo. Doctors Antonio Alvarez de Ron and Pedro Vázquez de Noboa, both professors at the University of San Marcos, also employed agents.[22] Their failure to gain a position illustrates the frequent inadequacy of this approach for persons who had not previously obtained a royal appointment to a lesser letrado post.[23]

In his eagerness to obtain an appointment, Baquíjano initiated his solicitation even before reaching the peninsula. As any pretendiente not personally in Madrid, he relied upon an agent to submit the memorial for him. On December 1, 1773, Manuel Aganza penned a brief note that stated Baquíjano's desire to be considered for a position of criminal fiscal of the Audiencia of Lima, which had been left vacant by the promotion of Antonio Porlier to a fiscalía of the Council of the Indies and the routine advancement of Gerónimo de Ruedas to the post of civil fiscal.[24]

Baquíjano's fate in this first effort foreshadowed the results of his initial trip to Spain. Whether through lassitude or failure to receive his client's authorization in time, Aganza presented the memorial after the deadline for applications. Consequently, Baquíjano's papers did not circulate with those of the initial group of pretendientes. Even an earlier remission, however, probably would not have altered the conclusion. Although only twenty-six applied—scarcely a quarter of the number that would be pressing for American appointments three years later—the competition was stiff. The fiscal of the Audiencia of Guatemala and the protectors of the Indians for the courts in Lima, Charcas, and Bogotá had all submitted their credentials; fourteen of the applicants would receive audiencia appointments before Baquíjano was successful. The ranking on the consulta left no doubt about how distant Baquíjano was from an appointment on the eve of his arrival at court. The fiscal of the Audiencia of Charcas, an experienced minister who ultimately received the post under consideration, was the Cámara's unanimous first choice. After him were ranked the protectors of the Indians for Charcas and Bogotá.[25]

The advancement of an audiencia minister to the Lima court illustrated their respect for the *ascenso*, or promotion based on progression through a hierarchy of posts. Lima capped the line of promotion for the South American courts, and few men joined it between 1751 and 1808 who had not previously served in a lower ranked tribunal. Indeed in the early 1760s, the Cámara was specifically ordered to propose only ministers on American courts when it recommended candidates for the Audiencia of Mexico. Although no parallel order has been found for Lima appointments, in practice the ascenso was normally observed.[26]

Baquíjano had engaged an agent to manage his solicitations since late 1773, but he assumed personal direction of his campaign in 1775. Relentlessly he petitioned the king and the Cámara when vacancies appeared in the audiencias of Chile, Charcas, and Lima.[27] An application he submitted in July 1775 for the post of criminal judge on the Audiencia of Lima typified the requests. After mentioning his doctorate in law, birth in Lima, and residence in Madrid, José stated simply that he had pursued his studies with the intent to continue his forebears' tradition of royal service and thus now sought an Audiencia appointment. Verification of his merits and services was filed with the secretariat for the Council of the Indies. As was routine, he noted his unmarried state before concluding with a request that he be named to fill the vacant position.[28] Neither this petition nor personal entreaties, however, secured him a single vote for this or any other post in Lima. The man named alcalde del crimen was an oidor on the

Audiencia of Chile who received unanimous support from the
Cámara for first place on the consulta.[29] Again the ascenso had
been respected.

At the end of November 1775, after nearly two years of solicitation, Baquíjano at last knew his efforts had not been totally in
vain—his name appeared on a consulta. Felipe de Arco, the one
non-letrado camarista to vote, selected José as his candidate for
third place on the recommendation for the position of protector of
the Indians in Charcas. Next to the record of Arco's vote was
placed the notation, "He came to Spain with good recommendations."[30] Although the appointee was the unanimous first-choice
candidate, Fernando Márquez de la Plata, José's spirits were certainly buoyed by word of his modest success. He did not know it at
the time, of course, but this single third-place vote for the protectorship would be the closest he would come to an appointment for
over twenty years.

With the memory of his recent achievement fresh in his mind,
José must have read with delight the announcement that on March
11, 1776, Charles III had ordered the expansion of each American
audiencia.[31] The number of vacancies to be filled was without
precedent, and scores of pretendientes hastened to apply.
Baquíjano, who at last had turned twenty-five years of age on
March 13 and was thus unquestionably eligible for appointment,
joined the other hopefuls in promptly requesting consideration.

Among the first new posts to be filled was the criminal fiscalía
in Chile. Although other pretendientes' memorials began arriving
at the end of March, José's remission of April 16 was within the
time limit.[32] Since the list of pretendientes was formed alpha-
betically by first name, "Josef" secured him place number fifty
among the one hundred and one applicants.[33] Unlike his earlier
solicitations for positions in Lima, this competition was restricted
to persons who held no audiencia appointment because Chile was
a court of entry. Examining the other pretendientes will illumi-
nate some characteristics of officeseekers at this time and help to
place Baquíjano within their number.[34]

It is probable that twenty-one of the other one hundred pretendientes were creoles and, with only two of them definitely from
Chile, potential native sons were in short supply. Moreover, both
Chileans, along with eight other creoles, relied upon agents to submit their petitions, while only nine of the seventy-nine peninsulars

did so. Clearly peninsulars took advantage of their location to oversee their solicitations personally.

Over ninety percent of the applicants held a post-baccalaureate degree. Although Baquíjano was one of but thirty-six men with a doctorate, the successful candidate held a licentiate degree, the degree possessed by a majority of the *pretendientes*. Since two of the three men who held the baccalaureate alone received audiencia appointments the following year, it appears that a higher degree provided no benefit to candidates in the 1770s.

One *pretendiente* described himself *"de estado soltero y libre,"* a description that fit more than sixty percent of his competitors.[35] The fact that Baquíjano was a bachelor, however, provided only a slight advantage over the married applicants, all of whose wives had agreed to accompany them should they be named.[36] And this advantage probably reflected the greater ability of bachelors to remain at court for a prolonged period without employment while seeking office rather than any conscious policy by the Crown to favor bachelors.

What, then, affected the resolution of the *consulta?* The appointment of Ambrosio Cerdán y Pontero provides a glimpse of the answer. Cerdán was a *licenciado* from Barcelona whose father had served for many years on the audiencia there and whose grandfather had been on the Council of Castile. He was unfettered by the self-imposed geographic constraints that reduced Baquíjano's interests to Lima and its feeder courts of Charcas and Chile, hence Cerdán applied for appointment to courts in New Spain as well. Such broadcast solicitation provided him with more exposure and consequent familiarity to the *camaristas* and his name began appearing on *consultas* in 1773. Although his family background was uncommon among appointees to American courts, the young bachelor's residence in Madrid for several years to solicit an office was routine.[37]

The need to devote a prolonged period to seeking an audiencia appointment deserves emphasis. Persistence was an asset and many *pretendientes* passed years in Madrid responding to announcements of vacancies in the New World and hoping to reach a *consulta.* From Baquíjano's first attempt to secure an appointment in late 1773 until the close of 1777, when the great wave of namings produced by the expansion of 1776 had ended, every entry position except the *fiscalías del crimen* that were given to pro-

tectors of the Indians was filled by consulta. Only two appointees
to Manila were not on the consulta for the office they received.[38]
In other words, during Baquíjano's first campaign in the 1770s, it
was almost impossible to obtain appointment without support
from the Cámara, support that usually needed to be a majority if
not unanimity of votes for first place on the consulta.

From the time Baquíjano began his solicitation until he submitted his memorial for the fiscalía del crimen of Chile, twenty entry positions of oidor or fiscal became available. Eighteen of these
went to men receiving their first audiencia appointment. The
Cámara's votes are available for eighteen of the twenty positions,
and a brief examination of the eventual success of the forty men
who received votes confirms the consulta's importance at this
time.[39] Excluding Francisco Ignacio González Maldonado, who
received an advancement from Manila to fiscal of Guadalajara in
1774, the other thirty-nine men had held no previous audiencia
position.[40] By the close of 1780, however, thirty-two of them had
received appointments to American courts.[41] Although six of the
remaining men never obtained an audiencia post, the seventh,
Francisco Carbonel del Rosal, was eventually named an oidor in
the Canary Islands.[42] Two things are revealed in these figures: to
obtain an appointment in the mid-1770s it was essential to be
listed on a consulta; once on a consulta, continued solicitation provided the pretendiente with a high probability of eventual success.

Masked in these statistics is a true measure of the disadvantages
creoles faced as they sought office. Those Americans who wanted
to serve on their home courts suffered an additional handicap. The
harsh fact was that José's first campaign occurred during the last
stage of the Crown's quarter-century effort to reduce local influence in the American courts. Only two creoles received initial
appointments while he was soliciting, and but one was a native
son.[43] Since Francisco Antonio de Moreno y Escandón had served
for a decade as protector of the Indians in Bogotá, his advancement to the new criminal fiscalía was routine. Charles III terminated Moreno's native-son status in 1780 when he transferred
him to Lima, despite the Cámara's recommendation of other candidates.[44]

The Lima environment had seriously misled Baquíjano. The
presence of numerous native sons during his youth had made obtaining an appointment appear deceptively simple. Not only was

the Crown's overall appointment policy since mid-century unfavorable for his ambitions, but also its vigilance over the
qualifications of applicants had increased significantly since the
swell of limeño appointments in the 1730s and 1740s. José had
deluded himself, moreover, when he thought that he would be
considered seriously as a candidate while still in his early twenties
and shy of the statutory minimum age of twenty-five years.

After three years in unsuccessful pursuit of a royal appointment,
Baquíjano left Spain. The timing of his precipitate exit, however,
was determined by events not directly related to his ongoing attempts to secure an office. Within months after he accompanied
José to Madrid, Manuel de Gorrichátegui became disillusioned
with his young charge. In late November 1774 the cleric wrote a
confidential letter to Julián de Arriaga, the Secretary of State for
the Indies, that not only dealt the final blow to Baquíjano's dreams
for appointment in the 1770s, but continued to haunt him for over
twenty years.[45]

Manuel asserted that Baquíjano was highly talented and well-
educated. Already he possessed an astonishing knowledge of law,
history, philosophy, and other subjects. However, the cleric wrote,
"true knowledge consists of fear of God." Through association
with evil men José had imbibed perverse doctrines; devoid of "true
knowledge," he no longer deserved compassion. He "only thinks,"
Manuel lamented, "of abandoning himself to pleasures and living
without any law but that of libertinage and corruption." Through
extravagant display the young limeño had spent nearly thirty
thousand pesos in less than eight months. In consideration of
Baquíjano's skeptical attitude toward religious beliefs and his
dedication to iniquity, his escort stated that he could no longer
recommend him for a government position. Indeed it was to clear
his troubled conscience that he was informing the Secretary of
State about José's intemperate behavior, repenting that he had
placed him in a position to expect a high office. The Secretary, he
suggested, would benefit both the youth and his family if he were
to order the profligate to Peru, away from the corrupting life he
had discovered in Spain.

Beyond a doubt José had relished the opportunities at court to
spend money freely and had plunged into what became a lifelong
passion for gambling. Within a few months he had consumed
more than his patrimony by living in a manner that, as his mother

later acknowledged, no doubt ruefully, was appropriate for his family and station.[46] Yet some of his money went for more than transient enjoyment. Wandering throughout Madrid's bookstalls, he gathered volumes for what became a "rich and select" personal library.[47] Oblivious to his more somber companion's charges, he participated in literary gatherings and learned a foreign language, probably French.[48]

For well over a year Baquíjano pursued his pleasures and appointment with no awareness that his trip would terminate in disgrace. Unknown to him, Arriaga had commissioned an aide to examine secretly the charges raised in Gorrichátegui's letter. The investigation was still in progress when the Secretary died and consequently it was his successor, José de Gálvez (1776–87) who received the report in early 1776. The contents confirmed the cleric's allegations that José had been gambling heavily and overspending his income. Moreover, the aide supported the suggestion that the best way to end the difficulty would be to send the wastrel back to Peru.[49]

Gálvez, of course, was already familiar with Baquíjano's credentials as a result of his efforts to gain an office. Never impressed enough to support the Peruvian for even third place on a consulta, the Secretary now concurred with his aide's evaluation. Five days after Baquíjano's memorial for the fiscalía del crimen of Chile, the Secretary informed him that Charles III had ordered him to leave the court. Within one month he was to be in Cádiz, ready to board the first ship sailing for Callao.[50]

Forty days later the sorrowful youth informed Gálvez that he had reached the southern port. On December 23 he wrote the House of Trade's president for permission to board the *Alquiles*, then preparing the sail for Callao. License in hand, Baquíjano at last left Spain on December 29, 1776.[51]

Sailing toward home, Baquíjano undoubtedly reflected on the magnitude of his disaster. Everything consequential had gone wrong. He had failed to obtain an appointment to Lima's Audiencia or even to a minor tribunal; his patrimony was spent, squandered by gambling; and the king had expelled him from the peninsula. As the ship plied toward America, José undoubtedly hoped never again to hear of his youthful immoderation. In his disgrace he must have considered his goal of serving on Lima's court almost beyond reach. Yet his abilities remained and, from recent experience, he now knew that the Crown valued, indeed frequently demanded, prior government and university service as qualifications for its ministers. With the Spanish sojourn ended, it was imperative to rebuild his career.

3

Resurgence of Hope
and Frustration

When the *Alquiles* left Cádiz, Baquíjano shared the passenger accommodations with *malagueño* Melchor Jacot Ortiz Rojano, the newly appointed first regent of the Audiencia of Lima. Given Jacot's penchant for gambling, perhaps his selection eased Baquíjano's mind that his own overindulgence had not irretrievably precluded a judicial career.[1] At the same time, however, the peninsular's presence reemphasized the Crown's policy of placing outsiders rather than native sons on the tribunal. Jacot not only exemplified the king's explicit rejection of native sons, but personified the altered political environment that Baquíjano would find in Lima.

A variety of royal decisions in 1776 affected both Peru's economy and its political leadership. The viceroyalty suffered major dismemberment when the Crown detached the provinces of the Río de la Plata and created another viceroyalty with its capital in Buenos Aires. Attaching the mining district of Charcas to the new viceroyalty undermined traditional trading patterns and greatly reduced the flow of silver into Lower Peru. Although relieved of the financial burden of subsidizing defense expenditures for the Río de la Plata, Peru found its already weak economy further impaired. Nonetheless, Charles III had resolved that the region's contribution for imperial expenses should rise. In early 1776 he named José Antonio de Areche Visitor General for Peru and charged him to improve tax collection and the administration of justice. In addition, as part of an empire-wide expansion of the audiencias, the king augmented Lima's tribunal by two oidores, an alcalde del crimen, and a regent. This wide-ranging set of changes brought two powerful new officials to Lima. Jacot and Areche carried instructions whose implementation afforded ample opportunity for conflict both between themselves and with the viceroy.

The final change immediately visible in Peru in 1776 was the replacement of Viceroy Manuel de Amat by Manuel de Guirior, the former viceroy of New Granada. Amat had ruled Peru firmly for fifteen years. During his tenure he aroused such distaste among the Lima elite that only with difficulty could he secure persons to post bond for his *residencia*. Guirior showed himself more affable and quickly established cordial relations with Lima's leading families. By the time Jacot and Areche reached the city, the viceroy was becoming a bulwark for local interests. Baquíjano found himself drawn into the three-way struggle that developed, and ultimately his improving prospects vanished as a result of political conflict beyond his control.

Baquíjano arrived in the new political setting in mid-1777 shame-faced and without employment. Once resettled, however, he soon began to assume positions that would bolster his credentials for later solicitation. His availability and eagerness to serve helped him to secure temporary appointments as a professor at the University of San Marcos and as protector of the Indians on the Audiencia of Lima by the end of 1778. A viceregal appointment to a university chair in 1780 further strengthened his record. By the following year Baquíjano was prepared to resume active pursuit of a permanent appointment to Lima's high court. In only four years he had moved from disgrace to cautious optimism.

For over fifteen years Baquíjano centered his professional activities at the University of San Marcos. Successively he held the chairs of *Institutes, vísperas* of civil law, and finally prima of sacred canons as he moved up the academic hierarchy. Teaching law at a university was a traditional employment for letrados and one that could bring substantial rewards. In the second half of the seventeenth century, professors who held a chair in law at the

Spanish universities of Salamanca, Alcalá, or Valladolid were assured a subsequent high-ranking appointment.[2] In mid-eighteenth-century Spain, men still sought a university chair not so much to teach, as to use it as a "temporal and transitory trampoline from which to spring to commissions, prebends, and positions of political importance more lucrative than the chair."[3] The reliance that pretendientes for audiencia appointments placed upon statements of academic activities and accomplishments as late as the 1770s indicates the weight they gave to such service. Merely entering the competition for a chair was regularly reported in letrados' relaciones de méritos.

Professors at American universities, usually creoles educated in the Indies and without ties to Spain's six powerful *colegios mayores*, historically had not gained audiencia positions as easily as their Old World counterparts. Nonetheless, Baquíjano did not have to turn to his peninsular brother-in-law for inspiration. Peruvian examples existed of men who, like Gerónimo Ruedas y Morales, had held a chair before advancing to a court. In the late seventeenth century, before sales disrupted traditional appointment practices, law professors at the University of San Marcos were included as a matter of course on lists of candidates assembled for the use of the Cámara of the Indies when it considered vacancies on the entry audiencias of South America.[4] At the time of Baquíjano's birth, Pedro de Castilla, former senior professor of civil law at San Marcos, was serving in Lima's civil chamber. And, of course, Pablo de Olavide had stepped from his chair at San Marcos into an Audiencia appointment.[5]

During Baquíjano's youth, the number of former professors and competitors for academic chairs who served on Lima's Audiencia was low, a reflection of the Crown's willingness to sacrifice customary criteria for cash in the 1740s. Moreover, since many purchasers to the court were Peruvians, they had faced the bottleneck created by the lack of chairs at San Marcos and thus the impossibility that most could engage in university service. After sales ended in 1750, however, such activity became commonplace again for aspirants to the judiciary; most of Lima's ministers who began their audiencia careers in America from 1750 to 1778 had actively sought, if not actually served in, a university chair.[6]

The desire to become a professor in late eighteenth-century Peru, however, was not automatically translated into reality: the number of applicants regularly exceeded the number of vacancies. Vacancies were particularly limited at the University of San Marcos, which had only seven chairs of law open to persons not attached to the Convictory of San Carlos.

Then as now, nonetheless, it was possible for the number of persons who taught at a university to exceed the number of chairs. When a professor took a leave of absence, a substitute filled his position, a circumstance which made the opportunities to teach more frequent than might first appear. It was precisely the availability of such an opening that enabled Baquíjano to initiate a university career. Within months after his return from Spain, the University needed a supernumerary professor (*regente*) to fill the chair of *Institutes*. In February 1778, rector Joaquín Bouso de Varela named him to serve until the incumbent returned.[7] José thus began fifteen years of teaching with an interim appointment to the least prestigious chair of law. Despite the nature of the naming, he had taken an important step on a major road to an eventual Audiencia appointment.

Baquíjano's appointment was a professional starting point, but it did not place him in an intellectually vital ambience. Indeed the very existence of a separate chair of *Institutes* testified to the failure of efforts to draw the University out of the intellectual lassitude characteristic of Spanish and American universities in the mid-eighteenth century.

Despite occasional earlier advocates of modern knowledge and a curriculum more responsive to contemporary needs and devoted to contemporary ideas, a thoroughgoing attempt to infuse San Marcos and other Hispanic universities with a curriculum that stressed experience, experimentation, useful knowledge, and the critical use of reason began only after the expulsion of the Jesuits in 1767. The Company had departed from Lima leaving a valuable library, some scientific instruments, and wealth that the Crown planned to apply to education. Accordingly, in 1768 it ordered Viceroy Amat to provide a proposal to resurrect San Marcos. An innovative plan resulted in 1771 that would have transformed the University had it been implemented.[8]

The 1771 plan outlined bold changes in administration, faculty, and curriculum. It replaced the annually elected and unpaid rector with one who would serve a three-year term at an annual salary of eighteen hundred pesos. Even more dramatic was the

proposed abolition of rank and salary distinctions among professors within each faculty. Henceforth, except in medicine, each
professor would receive one thousand pesos and rotate annually
among the faculty's chairs. Specified texts were listed so that professors would be forced to teach using more modern authors.
Moreover, the plan called for the construction of a library within
the University and a laboratory facility that would enable modern
physics to be taught. To initiate the reform, the viceroy would appoint a rector and seventeen professors.[9]

As a first step Amat appointed a new rector, Bouso de Varela, to
execute the plan. The viceroy's hopes foundered, however, when
the money needed to effect the innovations did not appear. Jesuit
properties sold slowly and the net proceeds were not only less than
anticipated but frequently received in installments. Extending the
rector's term did not resolve the financial impasse. Consequently
Bouso de Varela could not realize the proposed changes and a
standstill prevailed until Guirior's tenure as viceroy.[10]

Guirior recognized that he could not implement the 1771 proposal. Besides, it was to have been modified when the new plans
for the universities of Salamanca and Alcalá de Henares appeared.
Since the plan of studies for Salamanca was available, he thought
the time was opportune to revise the proposal for San Marcos in
light of its provisions. Consequently he acceded to clerical
pressure for a new rector, an action that insured the abandonment
of the 1771 plan, and called for a new, more limited reform proposal. His struggles with Areche from 1778 to 1780, however,
drew his attention away from San Marcos and he did little else except to fill several chairs by decree and to urge his successor to
promote mathematics and experimental science.[11]

One of the chairs that Guirior filled by decree was the vísperas
or second chair of civil law. Baquíjano's success in the chair of *Institutes* influenced the viceroy to grant him this advancement in
July 1780. As a carryover from the 1771 plan of reform, the new
appointment included the specific charge that Baquíjano incor-
porate Spanish law into his explanation of Roman law.[12] As José
later pointed out repeatedly, he was the first professor in Peru to
teach Spanish law *(derecho patrio)*.[13] Guirior himself considered
instituting the instruction of Spanish law as among his most important contributions to the University.[14] Certainly it was an

action fully in tune with the times; the 1771 Plan of Studies at the University of Salamanca also had called for such instruction.[15]

Baquíjano's appointment as vísperas professor of civil law left him with only two possible professional advancements in the University: the prima or first chairs of civil and canon law. These chairs were open but rarely; often they became vacant only through the death or retirement of the incumbents. Thus Baquíjano could not plan on advancing quickly as a professor. There was, however, another possibility for improving his vita. This was to obtain the rectorship, an office that bestowed great prestige on its occupant and was an asset to one's relación de méritos. At least nine of San Marcos' rectors had later become audienca ministers, a detail Baquíjano surely knew.[16]

Within a few months after receiving the vísperas chair, Baquíjano decided that he would seek to become the next rector of San Marcos, the highest administrative official in the university. The timing of any overt steps toward the office was delicate, however, for the current rector, the cleric José Ignacio de Alvarado, was to be replaced by a secular member of the university community (*claustro*) who would be elected on June 30, 1781.[17] From Baquíjano's perspective the date of the election was unfortunate. If he did not seek election then, it would probably be at least six years before another opportunity arose, an unpleasant delay for an ambitious young man. Yet there was no point in seeking the rectorship unless he anticipated winning the election. That was the crux of the matter. Baquíjano was not confident of victory in 1781, but he anticipated that his chances would increase in the near future. Consequently, the best strategem was to support an extension of Alvarado's term.

Shortly before the election was to have been held, the cloister named a commission that included Baquíjano to ask Viceroy Jáuregui to extend Alvarado's term for one additional year.[18] It is unknown who inspired the idea, but it certainly meshed with Baquíjano's plans. The viceroy more than agreed; he granted Alvarado three additional years.[19] Although this was more than Baquíjano wanted or the cloister had requested, at least it insured that no election would be held before José was ready.

The extension meant that Baquíjano would be able to use the eulogy that rector Alvarado had commissioned him to deliver at the University's formal reception of Viceroy Jáuregui in August as a means of drawing the cloister's attention to his oratorical skills and intellectual abilities. His presentation, he thought, would serve him well when he contended for the rectorship.

Another reason as well undoubtedly convinced Baquíjano that the moment was not ripe for an assault on the rectorship. Since late 1778 he had held interim employment on the Audiencia, first as protector of the Indians and then also as fiscal del crimen. Together these posts consumed a substantial amount of his time, too much to allow him to pursue adequately a contested campaign for the rectorship. And it was not worth giving up the certain merit to be accrued from the Audiencia service by resigning to seek the post of rector.[20]

Baquíjano's appointment as protector of the Indians and his subsequent appointment as vísperas professor of law clearly exemplified the close relationship that existed between university and government service. His original academic appointment to the chair of *Institutes* had demonstrated the rector's confidence in his knowledge of law. His abilities thus publically confirmed, José had an advantage when a government opening occurred. Once named interim protector of the Indians and fiscal del crimen, his subsequent appointment to the vísperas chair was justified on the basis of his government service. Although the University's *Constitutions* prescribed that quadrennially the victor of a formal trial lecture would receive the chair, Viceroy Guirior simply named Baquíjano to serve it. He justified circumventing the *Constitutions* both because José's talent and application in the chair of *Institutes* were well known and because his services as an interim minister of the Audiencia demanded too much time to allow preparation for a vigorous trial lecture.[21]

A series of fortuitous circumstances enabled Baquíjano to join the Audiencia in a junior and interim capacity while retaining his university position. In 1776 Charles III had united the responsibilities of the protector of the Indians to those of the criminal fiscal and abolished the separate protectorship. A variety of reasons, however, prevented two permanent fiscales from serving steadily in Lima before 1781 and, as a result, interim appointees briefly perpetuated a separate protectorship and helped to fill the fiscalías.

Baquíjano's chance came when Viceroy Guirior named the

Marqués de Sotoflorido to be his legal adviser. To accept the new responsibility, Sotoflorido had to resign as interim protector of the Indians. Guirior and Jacot then selected Baquíjano to succeed him on December 3, 1778.[22] Several possibilities help to explain this choice. The position was temporary and thus unattractive to persons who already held permanent, full-time employment. Baquíjano's academic chair testified to his knowledge of law and allowed him adequate time to fill the vacancy. Moreover, Jacot knew José well as a result of their voyage from Cádiz and was impressed with the young professor's abilities. Since the regent was active in selecting the replacement for Sotoflorido, this relationship undoubtedly benefited Baquíjano. Finally, it is possible that José's brother-in-law, Gerónimo de Ruedas Morales, then still serving on the Audiencia, exerted influence in his behalf.

An appointment to serve as interim fiscal del crimen, a post that occupied Baquíjano until late 1781, followed that of protector.[23] Because he held the protectorship, Baquíjano was automatically a logical candidate for the additional responsibility. Customarily a protector served temporarily as criminal fiscal when an unexpected vacancy occurred and, indeed, the title of office for a royally-named protector carried a provision that required such service.[24]

José's appointment arose from the complete absence of permanent fiscales in February 1778. As an interim measure, Guirior named Ruedas to serve in the capacity of fiscal and protector.[25] Ruedas had served as fiscal for nearly seven years before becoming an oidor and thus was eminently qualified for the appointment. But since he had already received promotion as regent for Charcas, this temporary measure was unsatisfactory.

Even the king's appointment of two new fiscales in 1778 had little effect. José de Castilla was also named fiscal of the general *visita*, an action that limited his Audiencia service. The second fiscal named, Joaquín de Galdeano, took possession of his office in late 1778, but conflict with Visitor General Areche quickly brought his suspension from the tribunal.[26]

Guirior then assigned oidor the Marqués de Corpa to serve the fiscalías. Yet even this did not eliminate the problem. As a long-serving criminal judge before his promotion in the fall of 1777, the oidor had heard numerous criminal cases and could not legally handle them later as fiscal. To remedy this difficulty, on February

20, 1779, Guirior turned to the newly named interim protector and appointed Baquíjano to serve as fiscal in the cases that Corpa was legally impeded from hearing.[27]

Together the protectorship and the fiscalía provided Baquíjano with nearly three years of experience on Lima's Audiencia. Despite the interim nature of the appointments, he was allowed to wear the magisterial robe of a judge and thus partake of the tribunal's prestige. Nonetheless, he drew no salary or other remuneration for his service, a fact he carefully brought to the king's attention later. He also claimed years afterward that no judge or tribunal had disagreed with the opinions he had rendered as a minister.[28] While the boast was clearly exaggerated, the Audiencia did inform the king in 1793 that the interim minister had filled his appointments with "integrity, zeal, and exactitude."[29]

Baquíjano's services as protector of the Indians involved him in mining, commerce, education, and Indian uprisings, as well as more mundane criminal cases. He had to learn the conditions in Peru's mines to prevent Indians from being sent to those where their lives or health would be endangered. He actively promoted ending the notorious *repartimiento* of merchandise by which corregidores forced Indians to purchase unwanted merchandise at exorbitant prices.[30]

Once Baquíjano urged hastening the judicial process in response to an Indian noble's allegation that he was being mistreated and that a local militia officer's alliance with a corregidor, an *escribano*, and other powerful local individuals was delaying implementation of viceregal orders in his favor.[31] On another occasion he demonstrated that two men accused of rustling cattle were not Indians as they claimed, but *chinos* or "of distinct caste" and thus not entitled to his services. Indignantly he denounced such fraudulent claims and the useless time and labor they required, efforts that deprived *bona fide* Indians of his services. Asking to be released from the case, he successfully proposed that the criminal chamber order the culprits to retain a private attorney and to pay the court costs already accumulated.[32]

The protectorship also drew Baquíjano into civil cases. When a new college and university were proposed for Arequipa, Baquíjano opined that revenues earned by the former Jesuit college in the city from pious works created to benefit the Indians could be applied to the proposed institutions. The only stipulations he advocated were the Indian chieftains, nobles, and their descendants should receive both fellowships established expressly for them and one-fourth of the other fellowships available.[33]

Baquíjano took his responsibilities seriously and combed Spanish legal codes for statutes favorable to the Indians he defended. In the last analysis, however, he emphasized the long-accepted view that Indians were perpetual minors by nature and thus deserved leniency. When Bernardo Tambohuacso, chieftain of Pisac, was accused of conspiring with Lorenzo Farfán de los Godos and several other *mestizos* of Cuzco to prevent the establishment of a customs house, Baquíjano scorned the chieftain's statement that he had Indians available for an uprising. The assertion was merely a vain boast or the product of a demented mind. Tambohuacso was a "pusillanimous, dull-witted chieftain" whom the mestizos had induced to listen to talk about a rising. The court should note that the *Recopilación* called for gentle means of correction before employing rigorous ones. In the face of the Túpac Amaru rising that erupted in highland Peru in 1780, however, the criminal judges remained stern. Pushing aside Baquíjano's arguments and a legal question of ecclesiastical immunity that arose from the chieftain's seizure at the door of a church, the court concurred with its fiscal and ordered Tambohuacso's execution.[34]

A case that involved a convicted thief who had jumped bail and allegedly commited a series of robberies brought forth Baquíjano's attitude toward Indians with great clarity. The fiscal contended that José Soria, alias Piñita, was a "famous and incorrigible thief" and thus should be executed. Baquíjano, however, deemphasized the importance of the crimes, pointing out, among other things, that since the accused had employed master keys to open the doors, he had not technically "broken into" the houses. More importantly, he sought to discredit the Indian's statement. In prose worth quoting at length, Baquíjano maintained that in his deposition Soria

> proceeds with an inconstancy that reveals not just a little the pusillanimity of his mind and the consternation and fear in which he found himself. Had any Spaniard or other *casta* made the declaration in the same terms, one would have been able to believe some of it, but coming from an Indian, one

should view it very suspiciously. By his ignorance and natural fear an Indian will blame himself falsely or at least ex-
aggerate his role. Indians merit such little faith in their
depositions that the testimony of six does not equal that by a
single Spaniard or mestizo. The politician of the kingdom
who with much prudence and experience considers the Indians' character is one of this opinion. The propensity that
they have for lying is so great that at times they hide the truth
without heeding their own danger.

There is another reason that supports distrusting this declaration. The fellow criminals who implicated him in the robbery of Don Joaquín Narváez exposed the drunkenness in
which he was found when involved in the robbery. The proof
given demonstrates that Soria is a habitual drunkard. Drunkenness is a dominant vice among Indians and it would not be
strange if he were inebriated when his declaration was taken,
particularly when it is commonplace that even those persons
who in other circumstances repudiate and abominate strong
drink use it to lessen the uncomfortableness of the jail.[35]

In short, how could the court credit a statement made by an ig-
norant, fearful, lying, inebriated Indian—a man who, to Baquíjano, exemplified all of the common failings of the race?

Baquíjano's perception of what he considered inherent
weakness in the Indians he was to defend placed him firmly in the
mainstream of colonial attitudes. While lamenting the Indians'
"vile state," the suffering widows and orphans, and the general
misery that characterized their lives, he offered no new approach
for ameliorating their state.[36] His concern was to fulfill his responsibilities as protector in a praiseworthy manner, and this meant
within the constraints of the traditional conception of the Indian
as a perpetual minor.

Baquíjano's service in the protectorship and interim fiscalía
marked a notable advancement in his career. For the first time he
had tasted high office, and the experience further strengthened his
resolve. Nearly three years of labor gave a solid foundation to his
claims of public service and thus increased the possibility of securing an Audiencia appointment. Moreover, the responsibilities justified his appointment without election to the vísperas chair of
law. Unquestionably the positions increased his visibility within

Lima. With greater reknown, however, came expanded possibilities for being drawn into public political disputes.

From the perspective of Baquíjano's ambition, the appointments were particularly important as a possible stepping stone to a regular Audiencia post. The mandated appointments of all remaining protectors in the Indies to newly created criminal fiscalías in 1776 reinforced the potential benefit of his interim service.[37]

Baquíjano definitely thought that his government and university service justified a renewed pursuit of an Audiencia appointment. Soon after becoming interim protector and criminal fiscal and even before receiving the vísperas chair, he submitted evidence of the new achievements and paid to have his vita brought up to date.[38] Eager to bolster further his record, he decided to seek the rectorship of the University of San Marcos in the near future.

Emphasis upon Baquíjano's relentless ambition to gain an Audiencia appointment and his preparations in 1780 to renew his pretensions provides a new vantage point from which to consider the best known episode in his life—his eulogy of Viceroy Agustín de Jáuregui in 1781 and the subsequent proscription of the printed text.[39] Far from thinking that the *Eulogy* might blight his career, Baquíjano believed it would advance his ambitions within the University of San Marcos and, in turn, his likelihood for an Audiencia position. One suspects that no person was more shocked than he at the condemnation of the printed address and the resulting reversal of his fortunes.

The man responsible for the *Eulogy*'s proscription was Visitor General José Antonio de Areche, who informed José de Gálvez of the verbal presentation and later denounced the published version in detail. Considering that Areche's displeasure alone initiated the actions that led to the formal condemnation of the *Eulogy*, one must examine the background to comprehend his response.

Pleased and amply rewarded for his own celebrated *visita* to New Spain (1765–71), Gálvez inaugurated his tenure as Secretary for the Indies by naming visitors-general for New Granada and Peru. He carefully selected men from whom he confidently expected thorough investigations and successful implementation of changes that would improve administration and increase the flow of taxes into the royal coffers. To Peru he sent Areche, the fiscal of

the Audiencia of Mexico and his supporter during the New Spain
visita. Areche reached Lima in mid-June 1777 armed with broad
powers and detailed instructions, and prepared to fulfill his
charge. He remained as visitor until mid-1782 when Jorge Escobedo replaced him by virtue of a royal order of September 13,
1781.[40]

General visitas regularly provoked conflict between visitor-
general and viceroy. In 1777, moreover, Jacot, the Audiencia of
Lima's first regent, added a further dimension to the setting. The
result was a three-way conflict among Areche, Viceroy Guirior,
and Jacot that continued until both Guirior and Areche left
Lima.[41]

Both time and temperament played a part in the conflict. Guirior, first on the scene, benefited from substantial local antipathy
to his predecessor and quickly established cordial relationships
with leading families of Lima and with the Audiencia, on which
sat several prominent limeños and other ministers with strong
local ties. Upon assuming office, the viceroy demonstrated concern with fiscal and economic matters, suggesting *inter alia* the
importation of two German silver mining experts to teach improved mining techniques and the movement of treasury officials
(*oficiales reales*) from one office to another to discourage fraud.
During the eleven months before Jacot arrived in June 1777, Guirior developed a strong base of local support.[42]

The regent's appearance introduced a new element into the political environment. Fresh from the Chancellery of Valladolid,
Jacot was appalled at conditions in Lima's Audiencia. Discovering
innumerable unresolved cases in the court's archive, he quickly
concluded that the ministers were indolent, worked too few hours,
and observed an excessive number of holidays. The day after his
arrival he demanded that the tribunal meet for mass at seven-
thirty each morning, begin work at eight o'clock, and continue for
three hours without a break.[43]

Not content with altering time-honored routine, Jacot also promoted personnel changes. In late August 1777, he informed
Gálvez that five oidores, including three who were locally born
and another who was married to a limeña, worked only to benefit
their friends and relatives.[44] The correspondence of his first
months in office bore repeated charges that the Audiencia was not
fulfilling its responsibilities and that changes were badly needed.

The judges, naturally, resented the attacks on their way of life and their relations with the regent quickly grew strained.[45]

Jacot included Guirior in his attacks on the court, claiming that the judges cooperated with the viceroy in exerting their energies to thwart rather than provide justice. The viceroy's entertainment of the oidores was detrimental to impartial justice. In addition, he exceeded viceregal prerogatives by claiming cases for himself that belonged to the Audiencia or even to local magistrates. Because of his own unwillingness to compromise in judicial matters and his "rectitude, zeal, disinterest, and love of the royal service," Jacot claimed, the ministers, and the viceroy and his friends, the Marqués de Sotoflorido and Dr. Antonio Boza, were conspiring against him.[46]

Guirior in turn informed Gálvez that the regent was determined to overextend his rightful authority. After repeated squabbles, the viceroy submitted a lengthy list of alterations he believed necessary in the regent's *Instruction* to permit cooperation. Gálvez's office promptly dismissed the suggestions, and mutual recrimination between regent and viceroy continued as long as Guirior retained his position.[47]

Areche's arrival in Lima within a week after that of Jacot increased the opportunities for friction. The regent initiated the conflict when he refused to attend the visitor's public reception. His fealty to the letter of the law augured ill for cordiality between the men, and time did not improve their relationship. As late as May 1782, within days of the visitor's replacement, Jacot was still complaining that Areche was trying to diminish his authority.[48]

Although Areche and Guirior cooperated during the visita's early months, the nature of the visitor's commission inevitably created conflicts. Areche's instructions ordered him to oversee the investigation of all of the viceroyalty's tribunals of justice and the exchequer and he conscientiously and personally supervised as much work as possible.[49] Consequently, he quarreled with the viceroy repeatedly, particularly over the imprecisely delineated powers each held concerning the royal exchequer. During the last two years of Guirior's tenure, Areche bitterly contested the viceroy's actions over such matters as improvement of the Huancavelica mercury mine, tax payment by Lima merchants on grain imported from Chile, and the establishment of a lawyers' association in Lima.[50] Jacot succinctly summarized the state of affairs in

June 1780: "The Kingdom [is] quiet, and the Viceroy and Visitor [continue] in their hatred and separation. Nothing is new."[51]

Guirior's opposition to Areche's actions, especially in financial matters, reflected his belief that the visitor was intruding in areas rightly his own. Moreover, the viceroy understood and sympathized with the interests of powerful groups in Lima. Merchants and large landholders alike supported him and thus opposed Areche.[52] The general populace, too, soon forced the visitor to revise an initially favorable evaluation of its attitude, and in early 1778 he joined Jacot as a subject for *pasquinades*.[53]

The conflict between Areche and Guirior dramatically illustrated the visitor's influence with Gálvez and the extent of his power. Repeated condemnations of Guirior's obstruction of the visita stirred king and secretary to action. On January 10, 1780, Charles III wrote that he found it "convenient" to relieve Guirior of his command.[54] The viceroy's failure to cooperate with Areche and desire to have the visita terminated, Gálvez later recorded, had prompted the king to dismiss the viceroy before Peru was completely ruined.[55] Not content with removal, Gálvez ordered a secret investigation of charges brought against Guirior: lack of respect for the laws in his public conversations, declared opposition to the Secretary for the Indies, obstruction of the visita, and involvement in "a public celebration in Lima" scandalously entitled his "coronation."[56] The origins of these damning allegations were in letters that Areche had written to Gálvez. The regent's complaints, too, undoubtedly reinforced their impact.

Guirior learned of his dismissal only upon his successor's arrival. On the evening of July 19, 1780, news reached him that the *Monserrat* had docked in Callao. Agustín de Jáuregui's secretary appeared shortly and presented Guirior with the royal *cédula* announcing his removal and the captain general's appointment. As dismay spread throughout Lima, Guirior went to Callao the following day, and delivered command of the viceroyalty to Jáuregui.[57] Areche, no doubt, allowed himself a wry smile of satisfaction. His chief opponent eliminated, he must have felt confident of his ability to overwhelm lesser detractors and to accomplish his tasks.

Areche's position in mid-1780 seemed stronger than at any prior time. The summary manner of Guirior's deposition publically confirmed the king's continued support of the visitor. The Audiencia had also felt the consequences of the visita. When Areche's investigation corroborated Jacot's charges of intimate connections between numerous ministers and influential Lima families, the king acted decisively. He retired three oidores, transferred another to Mexico, and ordered an alcalde del crimen to Bogotá. The blow was without parallel in eighteenth-century Peru. Although it did not completely eliminate local influence on the court, it provided unmistakable evidence that the Crown supported the visitor's recommendations and intended to tighten its control at the expense of local interests.[58]

Had Areche and Viceroy Jáuregui established an amicable relationship, Baquíjano's *Eulogy* would probably have quietly disappeared from view, sparing historians the task of analyzing it and robbing Peru of a "precursor of Independence." But *amicable* describes relations between Areche and Jáuregui no more aptly than it would characterize those between the visitor and Guirior.

The root of the conflict that soon surfaced was Areche's desire to act unhampered by existing institutions and without criticism. He opposed the office of viceroy *per se*. He believed that trained civilians headed by a superintendent should oversee mining, commerce, agriculture, patronage, and all other domestic and financial matters. The viceroy should be reduced to handling military affairs and, acting as a captain general, have authority only to secure external defenses and internal tranquility.[59] Although the king specifically vested Areche with the customary viceregal control over the royal exchequer when he named Jáuregui, even this did not satisfy the visitor.[60] His opposition to the office of viceroy easily extended to its incumbent and within a year of Jáuregui's arrival the visitor had repeatedly denounced him to Gálvez.[61]

Areche's complaints centered on three areas: Jáuregui sought to expand his authority; he catered to the same vested interests that Guirior had; and he did not suppress malcontents in Lima who maligned the visita. As early in the tenure of the new viceroy as April 1781, the visitor suggested to Gálvez that Jáuregui might need replacing.[62] Clearly Areche was prepared to see the worst in anything Jáuregui did months before Baquíjano eulogized him at the university reception.

The visitor's dissatisfaction and contempt for the viceroy paralleled his view of the inhabitants of Lima in general and the University of San Marcos in particular. Areche perceived the capital as ruled by particular interests and cabals working against him and, therefore, against the will of the king. Not content with keeping the capital in a state of open disrespect and disorder, its citizens had spread lies about the visitor that had reached the interior of the viceroyalty. The resulting disarray could be corrected only when Lima was brought to heel.[63]

The University of San Marcos also felt the visitor's anger. He had opposed the election of Dr. José Ignacio Alvarado to the rectorship in 1778 for the doctor wanted to lead San Marcos away from reform and, in the visitor's opinion, was a reprehensible gambler and troublemaker. In addition Areche believed that, despite its customary policy of contributing generously, the University had not given a voluntary contribution for the present war with England just to spite him.[64]

When Areche listened to Baquíjano deliver a belated welcoming oration for Jáuregui in August 1781, he was predisposed to censure any speech given in Lima, let alone at the University or in praise of the viceroy. When Baquíjano executed his charge and eulogized Areche's opponent, he unavoidably stimulated the visitor's bile. Considering the visitor's antagonism toward Jáuregui and dislike for Lima and the University, his hostile reaction to the *Eulogy* was almost predictable.

The University of San Marcos traditionally honored each new viceroy with a sumptuous reception. For Viceroy Jáuregui its employees spent twenty-five days hanging ornaments, cleaning the silver and other decorative fixtures, and placing colored lamps in the doorway and patio. The University circulated elaborate rules for the poetic contest and purchased costly prizes for the winners. The reception was spectacular. Amid ample food and drink the guests enjoyed music and poetry in a festive setting of decorations and fireworks. The University even distrbuted doubloons to each guest.[65]

At the appointed hour Baquíjano arose to deliver the major address. As the guests settled back in their seats, he began an hour-long oration that focused on the familiar Spanish theme of justice as personified by the viceroy.[66] For nearly thirty minutes the eulogist floridly described Jáuregui's bravery, indomitable spirit, and devotion to Spain while serving in military positions. He then turned to Jáuregui's accomplishments as Captain General of

Chile. He called particular attention to his subject's successful Indian policy, a policy marked by humanity and justice and one that coincided with Baquíjano's own conception of good government. In the closing minutes, Baquíjano lauded the viceroy's attitudes. Jáuregui knew that actions should not be taken against the will of the people, that good policy ceased being so if the people opposed it. He appreciated the responsibility of his office, the burdens of the people, and the needs of particular groups, for example, the merchants. His very appointment as viceroy confirmed royal recognition of his meritorious services.

There is no reason to believe, as some writers have, that Baquíjano "left his auditors gasping with amazement."[67] More probably, the listeners sighed with relief as the oration finally ended. Only Areche was sufficiently aroused to commit his reaction to paper, and his testimony cannot be interpreted as accurately reflecting a common response. Most listeners probably reacted as the viceroy did. Perceiving nothing untoward in the speech they let it pass from mind. Baquíjano himself pocketed the handsome four hundred peso honorarium and retired to his study to embellish the text with footnotes before delivering it to the printer.[68]

Areche himself did not immediately condemn Baquíjano's presentation, indeed did not even mention his name in correspondence to Gálvez until early November 1781—more than two months after the reception. The visitor's letters during the interim merely amplified earlier charges against Jáuregui and the visita's detractors in Lima. Jáuregui had too much power, was lazy and apathetic, and indolently had not repressed attacks on the visita. His appointment had been a mistake, a strange neglect of requirements for competence in office.[69]

The visitor's complaints did not secure Jáuregui's immediate removal, but Gálvez promptly acted on his condemnations of malcontents in Lima. A royal order of April 24, 1782, informed Jáuregui and Jorge Escobedo, named to succeed Areche in September 1781, that they were to take the measures necessary to discover the persons spreading false and pernicious ideas against the government. Quickly they were to make one a public example to prevent similar scandalous disorder in the capital.[70]

When Areche finally mentioned Baquíjano in his correspondence, it was within the context of his ongoing diatribe against Jáuregui and the *maldicientes* of Lima. In his initial reference he criticized the orator for attributing to Jáuregui power he did not have to correct abuses in the collection of government revenues from merchants. His paranoia surfacing, the visitor related that he suspected the University had given him a choice seat at the reception to make certain that he could hear clearly such comments. When the speech was printed, he would send Gálvez a copy so that he could see for himself what it contained.[71]

True to his word, on November 22 Areche informed the Secretary that he was sending two copies of the *Eulogy*.[72] They never arrived, however, and thus the initial official reaction to the tract was based solely upon Areche's unverified and highly colored testimony, a testimony far more condemnatory than the final government verdict.[73]

To Areche the *Eulogy* was a godsend—printed confirmation of his many allegations against Jáuregui and Lima's *maldicientes*.[74] And this time, to his horror, the spokesman was an interim minister of the Audiencia, a professor at the University, and a man the city respected. That Baquíjano served a public office made his presentation all the more execrable.

The visitor's censorious letter sought to convince Gálvez and Charles III that immediate action was imperative to curb Lima's malcontents. Within his argument were three supporting tenets: Lima was full of troublesome citizens who shared the opinions he perceived in the *Eulogy* and who were the cause of Peru's difficulties; Viceroy Jáuregui was both unwilling and incapable of containing these vituperative spirits and their spiteful propaganda; and Areche himself had labored blamelessly in the royal service and was able to verify his virtuous behavior.

Before the University reception, Areche had never mentioned Baquíjano in his correspondence. Now, suddenly, the professor loomed as a representative of the rampant license that the visitor perceived in the capital, a malevolent reader of prohibited books, a spokesman for educated dissent, and, even worse, an irreverent, dangerous leader of public opinion. Considering the visitor's frequent complaints about members of the Audiencia and close advisers of Guirior, one would expect to have found him denouncing Baquíjano in letters of 1779 and 1780 if the professor really had been an important leader of anti-Areche sentiment.

In late 1781, however, Areche quickly made up for the lack of prior references. He claimed that Baquíjano was spiteful about being expelled from Spain without a position and had introduced into Lima the commonly believed rumor that Gálvez was anti-American. Lima bore heavy responsibility for the troubles still plaguing Peru in the aftermath of Túpac Amaru's rising. Her citizens' unbridled tongues resulted in libelous and dangerous lies spreading throughout the countryside. Contrary to the orator's contention, most limeños did not love the king, pay him his due, nor promptly act to support his authority.

Former Viceroy Guirior bore ultimate responsibility, according to Areche, for allowing the atmosphere that enabled such dangerous spirits to develop. However, Jáuregui shared the blame for he had not cleansed the city. Rather he accepted advice from the same counselors as had his predecessor. The success of their efforts was manifest in his response to the *Eulogy*. Jáuregui had heard the false, though flattering, doctrines Baquíjano had proclaimed in the reception and allowed the speech to be published without deletions. Even worse, he followed the precepts it contained, demanding authority that was not his while simultaneously failing to employ his rightful powers to quell Lima's tale-mongers. To Areche, the viceroy was incompetent; until replaced by a firm hand, Lima would remain obnoxiously vocal and persistently harass the visitor's every effort to purify Peru's government.

Areche believed Baquíjano had suggested changes for Jáuregui to institute, criticized existing conditions in a manner that attacked the prerogatives of the king, insulted Gálvez (particularly in two footnotes), and directly assaulted the actions of the visita. Consequently he defended at length His Majesty, the royal ministers, and most heatedly himself and his assistants. His defense sought to demonstrate that Baquíjano, representing the visita's enemies in Lima, had groundlessly attacked his just and meritorious measures. The *Eulogy*, he declared, would serve not only as a stimulus for discontent in Peru, but also as a propaganda weapon for Spain's European rivals who would display this collection of lies as the true picture of Spanish government in the Americas. The king and his Council of the Indies should examine the tract to determine the proper steps for preventing another such outrageous occurrence.

Briefly summarized, Areche considered the *Eulogy* a "seditious, denigrating paper." It was an intrinsically dangerous document that symbolized all that he hated in Lima. It represented both a

spiteful populace purposely trying to thwart royal efforts at
reform and a weak viceroy who allowed this vocal dissent to go
unarrested. The fact that Baquíjano delivered it in the first place
and then actually published it without removing the objectionable
comments confirmed the opinions Areche had formed about the
viceroy and Lima citizens months earlier.

Areche's report contained devastating charges; their gravity
easily explains the royal order to proscribe the *Eulogy*. But, unfortunately for Areche's case, no one in Lima corroborated his interpretation and Gálvez himself accepted the arguments only until
his office subjected the *Eulogy* to a critical examination.[75] Indeed,
the fiscal of the Council of the Indies considered Areche's attitude
toward Baquíjano simply another example of his prejudicial antipathy toward Americans in general. The visitor, he stated,
seemed to believe "that there neither is nor has been in those
kingdoms of America either an ecclesiastical or secular person
who is not stained by the greatest excesses or crimes."[76] In the
short run, however, Gálvez's support of Areche determined the
royal response and undermined Baquíjano's hopes for an Audiencia appointment in the near future.

When Jáuregui's reply to the royal order of April 24, 1782, that
demanded action against the Lima malcontents reached Gálvez's
office, it stimulated an immediate clarification based upon
Areche's condemnatory letter. The Secretary for the Indies signed
a confidential order on August 1, 1783 that began: "The King is
informed that among the most pernicious and subversive papers
spread in that kingdom was one entitled *Panegírico* [sic] that Don
José Baquíjano pronounced in eulogy of Your Excellency in the
University of San Marcos of that Capital of Lima the day of Your
Excellency's reception in it." The order expressed the king's un-
ceasing amazement that Jáuregui had not only heard the speech,
but actually allowed it printed, an attitude "so contrary to your
obligations as viceroy to remedy abuses of this nature." It concluded by instructing the viceroy to work with Escobedo to collect
immediately all copies of the tract and to send them to Gálvez's office where the necessary actions would be taken.[77]

Jáuregui, who, as Areche had emphasized, saw nothing "pernicious and subversive" in the *Eulogy*, bowed before the royal ad-
monishment and ordered the *Eulogy* collected. In April 1784, he
sent to Spain a box containing the three hundred twelve copies

found of the six hundred printed. The remaining copies were allegedly spread throughout the viceroyalty. Before the Secretary acknowledged receipt, Jáuregui had been replaced as viceroy and died.[78]

Not until mid-July 1785 did the *Eulogy* finally reach Madrid and the Peruvian desk of career bureaucrat Antonio Porcel. The timing of Porcel's examination did not help Baquíjano. Within a week of the *Eulogy*'s arrival, his office had responded negatively to a commotion over the rectorship for the University of San Marcos. Baquíjano's involvement as a principal in the conflict combined with the attention provoked by the *Eulogy* served him ill in both cases. The temporal conjunction marked Baquíjano in Porcel's opinion as a troublemaker, and this view further colored his recommendations. Yet Porcel examined the *Eulogy* thoroughly and consequently his evaluation, with which Gálvez concurred, must stand as the official government statement on the tract.[79]

Porcel considered Baquíjano's discussion of Jáuregui's personal and military merit in the first part of the *Eulogy* beyond reproach and, consequently, not of interest to Gálvez. Thus he focused his analysis on the second part in which the author had examined Jáuregui's orders and actions. Here Porcel found that Baquíjano had not directly attacked government actions, but had criticized them obliquely. While supposedly praising the justice of a royal measure, he "incidentally mentioned the effects brought by failure to observe it." Then, instead of briefly noting this neglect, he used defamatory arguments employed by Spanish and foreign authors when condeming the Spanish Conquest and possession of the Americas. These infamous authors included Bartolomé de Las Casas, Niccolo Machiavelli, Montesquieu, Simon Linguet, the Abbé Raynal and Robert Boyle. "Their pernicious doctrines," Porcel alleged, "he quoted with great praise."

The official further observed that Baquíjano had "satirized severely" the customs of the court and lampooned former Viceroy Guirior as "the governor whose name America has sculpted in the annals of virtue." Finally, he concluded, "keeping in mind the time of its publication and the ungovernable character of its author, the leader of one of the parties that has motivated the clamorous appeals on the election of the rector of the University of Lima, the *Mesa* believes that this paper is seditious and merits being seized with great care."

To prevent similar occurrences, Porcel made four proposals modified only slightly in the subsequent royal order that Gálvez sent to Viceroy Teodoro de Croix and Escobedo on August 10, 1785.[80] The two officials were to oversee the collection and secret burning of the remaining copies of the *Eulogy*, to investigate the practice used in granting permission for printing books and the "very irregular" authority Jáuregui had said the University of San Marcos enjoyed to print its students' works without the government's prior permission, and to collect from Baquíjano and any other subjects that had them the *Encyclopedia*, works of Machiavelli, Montesquieu, Linguet, Raynal, and other books the Inquisition or the government prohibited. Finally, they were to reprimand Baquíjano severely for his use of prohibited books and for the objectionable liberties he had taken in writing the *Eulogy*, to observe his conduct, and to employ whatever corrective measures they deemed necessary.

Porcel's comments centered upon Baquíjano's use of prohibited books. These references, of course, appeared solely in the footnotes added following the reception. The official mentioned none of Areche's numerous, serious complaints, nor did his report contain any reference to Baquíjano's allegedly having headed opposition to the visitor's actions, having attacked the appointment of the administrator of customs and enforcement of customs regulations, or having accused Gálvez of being anti-American. Although unable to substantiate Areche's charges, Porcel perceived at once that Baquíjano's footnotes contained references to prohibited books. The copy of the *Eulogy* that he examined is now in the library of the General Archives of the Indies and contains the markings and marginalia. He particularly noted the reference to Father Las Casas and the subsequent discussion of cruelties Spaniards had inflicted on the Indians during the Conquest. Had Baquíjano not added the footnotes, the Crown probably would not have condemned the *Eulogy*. As it was, the presence of prohibited references was *prima facie* evidence of wrongdoing. Combined with his simultaneous unsuccessful suit over the rectorship, Baquíjano's fate was sealed.

Viceroy Croix summoned Baquíjano upon receiving the condemnatory royal order. As instructed, he reprimanded the professor and ordered the surrender of the prohibited books cited in the order. Baquíjano immediately submitted those books that he owned and, obviously stunned by this blow to his career, quickly sought to clarify the *Eulogy* and to obtain royal pardon for his errors.[81]

In a written memorial Baquíjano affirmed his obedience to the king and offered sincere repentence for any indignation he had caused. He had added the objectionable notes out of a desire to make a name for himself, citing them for statements fully supportable "in all faultless books of politics." Far from adopting the "harmful maxims" the prohibited books contained, however, he had read them only for his own instruction. His personal life was exemplary and his fulfillment of the protectorship of the Indians had been marked by zealous observance of the laws. Neither in the notes nor in the body of the *Eulogy* had he intended "to deprecate in the slightest degree the deeds of the ministers to whom the King had entrusted the command and government" of the colonial possessions. Only the dignity of representing the University and speaking before the collected body of learned men of Peru had stimulated him to employ "the proper rhetorical devices" in describing a perfect governor in the way that "religion, the moral policy of all civilized nations, and, most of all, our wise laws desire him." If Croix wished, he would gladly provide complete information verifying his conduct, respect for the magistrates, subordination, and moderate thought.[82] In short, Baquíjano acknowledged erring in the *Eulogy*, particularly in adding references to prohibited books. At the same time, he excused himself on the grounds of insufficient reflection and the desire to make himself conspicuous. Croix accepted the memorial and wrote Gálvez that the professor had repented.[83]

The last royal order dealing with the *Eulogy* was that written to commend Croix for his execution of the 1785 order. As late as 1798, however, the Cámara of the Indies referred to the official condemnation of the *Eulogy* when it denied Baquíjano the advancement he sought in the Lima Audiencia.[84]

There is no doubt that the furor over the *Eulogy* hindered Baquíjano's government career. What needs emphasis, however, is that the consequence was totally unanticipated, the result of the complex political situation in Lima, and the last thing that Baquíjano wanted. Frustrated in his attempt to gain a position on the Audiencia in the 1770s and ignominiously returned to Peru, in 1781 he was successfully rebuilding his career. Unopposed by

Areche, Guirior and Jacot had named him an interim minister of the Audiencia and Guirior had appointed him to the second chair of law in the University. His selection to deliver the major address at Jáuregui's reception was another honor and further displayed confidence in his abilities. Thus, when he gave the eulogy, Baquíjano's future seemed bright.

Baquíjano's praise of Jáuregui was sincere. He knew the viceroy personally, recognized his success as captain general in Chile, and appreciated his outlook. But, ever mindful of opportunity, he closed the speech by challenging Jáuregui to revive and implement the laudable educational reforms that Charles III wanted. It was with his career in the University of San Marcos in mind that Baquíjano added footnotes to the speech before passing it to the printer. These notes displayed his erudition and familiarity with contemporary knowledge. By citing prohibited sources, even though acceptable authors voiced the same ideas, he hoped to gain the attention of the cloister and become a university leader. The attraction of adding service as rector of San Marcos to his growing list of attainments was irresistible.

4
Advancing a Career

Unaware that Gálvez was about to issue a decree that would destroy his prospects for a rapid appointment to Lima's Audiencia, Baquíjano gathered support to oust the rector of San Marcos. His objectives were simple: to get the current rector removed and himself elected. This meant securing a majority of votes from the cloister composed of persons who held doctorates in one of the University's faculties or a Master of Arts degree. To initiate his plan he circulated a petition among friends and allies in the cloister that called for the election of a new rector notwithstanding that the incumbent, Alvarado, had nearly a year left of his three-year extension. With forty-five signatures attached, Baquíjano presented the petition to Viceroy Jáuregui, who then referred it to the cloister for consideration.[1]

At this early stage Baquíjano was master of the situation. In a meeting held on July 11, 1783, he informed the gathered cloister of the proposal. Acrimonious discussion followed, but José had packed the session with supporters. When the question was called, the body supported the petition by ninety-two to sixty votes and Jáuregui immediately ordered an election for August 5.[2]

The margin of victory confirmed Baquíjano's belief that his electoral prospects were high. He had seized the initiative and, since the incumbent was ineligible for reelection, had a head start against any opposition. Any thought of an easy victory vanished, however, when the upstaged Alvarado lent his support to a strong contender who soon appeared.

69

Alvarado had been stung by Baquíjano's action. After having benefited from his patronage, the young professor had led a revolt against his authority. Baquíjano's belated call for a return to the constitutional provision regarding the rectorial term after having originally accepted the extension granted by Jáuregui was unforgivable. Consequently, although unseated from office, Alvarado remained active in university politics.[3]

The man who acceded to the former rector's blandishments and agreed to oppose Baquíjano was Doctor José Miguel de Villalta y Santiago Concha, the scion of one of Lima's most distinguished families. Villalta's father and maternal grandfather each had served on the Audiencia for decades, and in 1783 two oidores— Antonio de Querejazu and Melchor de Santiago Concha—were among his relatives. One uncle, Francisco, was a prominent ecclesiastic in the city and a cousin would become an alcalde for the Lima cabildo before the decade closed. Particularly through his maternal side, Villalta was linked by blood or marriage to many of the city's most important houses.[4]

Unlike Baquíjano, Villalta was neither a professor nor an aspiring bureaucrat. Although he had entered the prestigious colegio mayor of San Felipe in 1761, he later abandoned academic pursuits to oversee several rural estates. Unlike his brother, Manuel, who gained reknown for military service during the Túpac Amaru revolt, the unassuming José Miguel owes his historical reputation exclusively to defeating Baquíjano for the rectorship.[5]

The former rector's desire for revenge on the one hand and Baquíjano's brash ambition on the other ensured a nasty campaign. Although both candidates came from eminent families, Villalta enjoyed greater access to the keys of authority. Due to the archbishop's temporary absence, Francisco de Santiago Concha was the ranking cleric in Lima, a position he allegedly employed to sway voters toward his nephew. The oidores Querejazu and Santiago Concha and their sons also allegedly solicited votes for Villalta while the Marqués de Sotoflorido and the prima professor of civil law, Antonio Alvarez de Ron, helped Alvarado's old supporters.[6]

Opponents to Baquíjano objected to his style and youth. Not only had José sought Jáurequi's support for the removal of Alvarado after he originally had been elected by the cloister, but, as one influential foe noted, he had decided that he alone should be the rector.[7] This inflexible ambition antagonized a number of senior members of the cloister.

Indeed Baquíjano found himself in a dilemma. To obtain the rectorship at his age would be far more impressive than to gain it years later. Yet the combination of haste and youth affronted older cloister members who considered seniority alone an important asset. Villalta himself was nearly twenty years older than Baquíjano and thus putatively more mature and qualified; most of his important allies carried enough years to be Baquíjano's father or even his grandfather.[8] Such was the importance of seniority among voters that at least one of José's relatives denied him support for that reason.[9] For electors concerned about seniority Baquíjano's unquestioned intelligence and literary talents substituted inadequately for his lack of years.

The presence of ecclesiastical voters added a further dimension to the electoral conflict. Although the office of rector alternated between clerics and laymen, both groups held the franchise and participated in each election. Alvarado was a canon of the cathedral's ecclesiastical chapter and thus his removal threw down the gauntlet to that venerable body. His colleagues Santiago Concha and Pablo de Laurnaga, the rector of Baquíjano's *alma mater*, the Seminary of Santo Toribio, joined him in providing Villalta with clerical patronage that Baquíjano could not match. Their influence produced subsequent charges that they had intimidated other clerics as part of general meddling in the election.[10]

Contemporaries agreed that family pressure, bribery, and illegal use of influence marked the unseemly campaign. Quickly the contest involved family honor and, to the dismay of royal authorities, the contentions extended beyond the cloister and enveloped Lima's most prominent families as well as its "lowest people." Popular conversation focused on the spectacle and on election day crowds gathered as coach after coach deposited the voting doctors and masters in front of the University.[11] The balloting continued for over three hours; finally at about 9:00 P.M., after the absentee ballots had been included, the candidates agreed that the election had been fair.[12]

Baquíjano's assent was premature. The impressive margin of victory in securing the election had left a residue of ill-placed confidence. When the votes were counted, Villalta emerged with a plurality of ninety-four. Baquíjano received ninety-one votes and the remaining eleven were either for minor candidates or in-validated.[13]

The shock of defeat prompted immediate reflection upon the election's validity. Despite his agreement to abide by the results, now Baquíjano refused to accept them. Before the victor could take the oath of office, Gaspar Remírez de Laredo, a former alcalde of the city and Baquíjano's relative by marriage, protested that the election should be annulled. Baquíjano's opponents, Remírez charged, had employed bribery, threats, manipulation of ballots, and the power of the archbishop to win.[14] Thus began the protests and recriminations that ultimately carried word of the charges and the subsequent legal process to both the Secretariat and Council of the Indies.

Although he enjoyed Jáuregui's favor, Baquíjano failed to get Villalta removed from the rectorship. When the viceroy and Audiencia ordered a new election, Villalta successfully appealed to prevent it. Baquíjano, in turn, responded with the accusation that the rector sought to serve his term by stalling. Since over twenty-five votes were contested and he had lost by only three, he should receive the post.[15] Baquíjano repeatedly affirmed that Villalta was not the legal rector, and he missed no opportunity to hinder the University's operations.[16] Personal gain not university improvement was his objective.

The angry professor's protest failed. When Teodoro de Croix replaced Jáuregui as viceroy on April 4, 1784, Villalta was still rector. Annoyed that the continued antagonism hindered the University's operation, Croix resolved to settle the problem. He ordered a cleric elected when Villalta's first year in office ended and, as consolation, named Villalta vice-rector and senior counselor, a post a retiring rector automatically held for one year. In addition, the viceroy prohibited both Baquíjano and Villalta from attending the election.[17] Together the actions restored some harmony in the cloister.

Antonio Porlier, a former minister on Lima's Audiencia, who had been promoted to a fiscalía of the Council of the Indies, recommended complete approval of Croix's actions. Noting that Baquíjano had renounced any right to protest the results, the fiscal declared that the election had been valid and, despite the unusual prohibition of Villalta's reelection, the call for a new election did not discredit him. He further charged that Baquíjano had fomented the controversy and proposed that he be reprimanded and ordered to pay the legal costs of the case.[18] In mid-August 1786 a chamber of the Council of the Indies that included Baquíjano's powerful enemy Areche forwarded the case to the full council, which, in turn, concurred with the fiscal's proposals in late October.[19]

Baquíjano's loss far exceeded the payment assessed for court costs. Gone was the chance to obtain the rectorship at an impressively young age. More importantly, the episode further blackened his name with Secretary Gálvez and offered corroboration for the character analysis that Areche had previously provided when condemning the *Eulogy*.

Visitor General Escobedo's reflections to Gálvez on the election confirmed Baquíjano's role in the deposition of Alvarado and his heated efforts to secure the rectorship. While the visitor emphasized that both contestants and their supporters had engaged in disreputable practices, he made it clear that Baquíjano bore primary responsibility for both the inception and prolongation of the uproar.[20]

Escobedo perceived correctly that Baquíjano "did not accept the loss well."[21] Irate that he had lost, particularly to a man whom he considered without qualifications for the position, José protested his defeat before the viceroy and the Audiencia. Moreover, he harassed Villalta throughout his year in office with total disregard to the impact on the University. In January 1784, for example, he protested that since Villalta was not the legitimate rector, two recent cloister meetings should be struck from the record. In one, the cloister had given "the so-called rector" authority to reduce the price of university degrees to raise money. Consequently Villalta had sold six in order to divide the proceeds among the faculty at the Christmas holiday. This, Baquíjano averred, was illegal.[22] The protest prompted Jáuregui to order the University to suspend filling any chairs until the cloister clarified the questions raised.[23] In mid-May, the cloister again considered a memorial by Baquíjano. This time he charged that Villalta should not begin preparations for Viceroy Croix's reception; rather, the next rector should undertake them.[24]

Baquíjano continued to harry his opponent even after he had left the rectorial chair. A master at manipulating regulations, he outdid himself for pettiness at the University elections of 1785.

The cloister reelected Rector Francisco de Tagle y Bracho and three of the four counselors by unanimous acclamation. The fourth counselor and vice-rector, however, was Villalta. Beyond anyone's memory, the cloister had unanimously endorsed the rector's choice for this position. Baquíjano protested selecting Villalta by acclamation, however, and demanded a secret ballot, a constitutional, but unheard of, request. When the cloister agreed, Baquíjano then insisted that its absent members were entitled to vote. The demand irritated many in the assembly since it could not be executed the same day and finally the meeting adjourned without electing a vice-rector. Victorious in the first round, Baquíjano pressed his case before Viceroy Croix who, after extensive consultation with various legal advisers, finally appointed a vice-rector in an effort to prevent a secret ballot and the reappearance of the two parties formed by the Baquíjano-Villalta rectorship election. Villalta appealed to the Council of the Indies, but, since the case remained pending before the Audiencia of Lima, he received no satisfaction.[25] Baquíjano had won a small, spiteful victory, but one that offered no benefit to his career.[26]

Defeat in the rectorship election left Baquíjano only two opportunities for advancement in the University—the first chairs of law and sacred canons. These capped their respective faculties and incumbents of the former in particular had subsequently gained audiencia positions. As proprietary chairs, however, they fell vacant only through their occupants' resignation or death. With only two vacancies during the 1780s, they afforded aspirants even fewer opportunities for advancement than did the rectorship. The chair in canon law became available in July 1782, so early in his university career that Baquíjano, with uncharacteristic modesty, refrained from applying.[27] He displayed no such compunction, however, when the professor of civil law died in 1785.

It was not until 1788 that the University held trial lectures (*oposiciones*) to fill the chair. Eleven candidates finally appeared, but the competition quickly narrowed to Baquíjano and the Chilean cleric Dr. Domingo Larrión.[28] Their contention soon released passions comparable to those displayed during the rectorship election in 1783.

Memories of the rectorship controversy, in fact, affected the selection for the prima chair. Dr. Larrión received considerable backing from the ecclesiastical chapter. A canon since 1777, by the election he had belonged to the chapter for twenty years and now the corporate solidarity that had earlier benefited Alvarado and Villalta was extended to him.[29] Archbishop Juan Domingo González de la Reguera, whom Baquíjano had antagonized when he accused him of meddling in the rectorship election, provided support as well.[30] González de la Reguera's antipathy toward José was so great that he persecuted at least one cleric and cloister member because of his friendship with Baquíjano.[31] Such hostility, which the aggrieved cleric reported to Secretary of State Porlier less than two months before the chair was filled, augured ill for José's candidacy.

In a manner reminiscent of the earlier rectorial contest, Baquíjano's family joined in the fray. His sisters and in-laws lobbied, cajoled, and according to Larrión, "employed other very irregular means" in their efforts to secure José's election.[32] The candidate himself circulated a discourse that argued that clerics were prohibited by statute from holding the prima chair of civil law. This "academic manifesto" and an appended satirical verse that ridiculed Larrión were spread throughout Lima and the surrounding region.[33]

Baquíjano's actions and his family's efforts only confirmed opponents in their contempt for the "ungovernable and turbulent spirit" he displayed.[34] His irrepressible ambition caused comment as well among persons disinclined to force every issue.[35] Once more an abrasive and conceited style worked against him.

Even more than in 1783, seniority played a part in the contest. Larrión was sixty-five years of age in 1788. After receiving his early education in his native Santiago, Chile, he had moved to Lima for further study. In 1759 he began to teach at the University of San Marcos. When he sought the prima chair of law he had served in three chairs, been an attorney in numerous legal cases, and was in mid-career in the cathedral's ecclesiastical chapter.[36]

Among his adherents, Larrión's extensive university service was an important asset noticeably absent in his far younger opponent. Baquíjano, after all, could claim but two years as the regent of the chair of *Institutes* and nine years in the vísperas chair of civil law. Larrión's agent later claimed that when it elected his client, the cloister had considered not only the trial lecture, Larrión's age, thirty-six years of university service, earlier trial lectures, and additional activities in Lima, but also Baquíjano's "youth and lack of services in the School."[37] Even some of José's distant relatives had thought that Larrión had "indisputable justice, merit, and seniority."[38]

On July 13, 1788 the voters cast their ballots to resolve the extraordinarily hard-fought contest. Eleven electors expressed their disdain for the proceedings by refusing to vote and a number more cast ballots that were later invalidated. Baquíjano, nonetheless, remained confident that his superior ability would triumph. At 2:00 P.M., before the votes were counted, he joined Larrión before the rector and agreed that "the voting had been made to his complete satisfaction and that he had no objection to make." This misplaced certitude vanished instantly, however, when the results were announced. Of six hundred eighty-five votes, Larrión received three hundred seventeen and Baquíjano three hundred six.[39] By the narrowest of margins, José once more felt the sting of defeat.

Disbelief blended into disappointment that in turn yielded to anger and protest. Flanked by two of his sisters the loser sought an audience with the viceroy to protest his defeat on the grounds that clerics were barred from holding the civil chair.[40] Croix adroitly parried the appeal by assuring Baquíjano that he could pursue the point judicially, but Larrión was to occupy the post immediately.[41] Frustrated by this response, José temporarily withdrew his complaint and the winner was duly installed late on the day of his election.

Temporary retreat did not signify reconciliation to defeat. On the contrary, with his usual obstinance Baquíjano petitioned Croix on July 14 to order Larrión to deliver the text of his trial lecture so that it could be printed and forwarded with his own to the Council of the Indies. The councilors could then judge his qualifications against those of the victor, a man José reasserted was disqualified by his ecclesiastical state as well as having "less aptitude and ability for filling the position."[42]

Anxious to prevent another fracas such as had followed Villalta's election, Croix turned to the Audiencia for an opinion.[43] By a majority vote the *real acuerdo* denied the request for Larrión's text. In addition it responded irritatedly to Baquíjano's disparagement of his rival's ability and ordered the offensive words expunged from the record. The viceroy concluded his participation in the case by forwarding testimony of the election and Baquíjano's protest to the Council for a final ruling.[44]

What began as a complaint to the viceroy by a disgruntled loser willing to pursue any avenue to advance his career slowly evolved into an important case concerning the general question of clerical professors and chairs of civil law. Agents for the two litigants presented repeated memorials full of the usual blend of self-adulation and righteous indignation.[45] While repeated examples of clerics who had held chairs of civil law weakened Baquíjano's argument on the one hand, his reputation as a captious trouble-maker on the other hand insured that the Council's fiscal would view his briefs charily.

After examining the charges and counter charges, the fiscal opined in October 1790 that Baquíjano's claim that superior merit entitled him to the chair was but "an effect of blindness" or exaggerated self-esteem. The Council should order him to remain silent and the victor to retain the chair. The younger professor had clearly calumniated Larrión when he claimed that his opponent's clerical state and lack of ability disabled him from serving. For his actions and temperament, Baquíjano should pay the costs of the case. Furthermore, the viceroy should personally reprimand him for his derogatory remarks about Larrión and other related actions, warning him to behave "in the future with more reflection and maturity" or face severe consequences.[46] The Council concurred with the fiscal's evaluation and issued the corresponding cédula in April 1791.[47]

The adverse decision added another link to Baquíjano's chain of failure before peninsular authorities. Whether the Secretary for the Indies was Gálvez or Porlier, whether the fiscal for New Spain or Peru rendered an opinion, whether the Council acted through one chamber or more, the result was unchanging. Officials in Madrid perceived José as an incessant problem. And lest they forget his prior transgressions, opponents repeatedly referred to the condemnation of the *Eulogy* and the adverse judgment in the rectorship case. The cédula that confirmed Larrión's victory described the loser's character as "impetuous and disposed to disturbences," a phrase reminiscent of a description by Larrión's agent.[48] These words, enshrined over the king's signature, were a permanent reminder that the Council viewed Baquíjano with distaste.

Disfavor in Madrid, however, did not equate with opprobrium in Lima. There José twice had found enough supporters to mount serious challenges against more senior colleagues. The defeats he had received were unpleasant but only temporary setbacks that he had begun to reverse even before the Council made its final ruling on the contested prima chair.

The trough of Baquíjano's career corresponded very closely to Viceroy Croix's tenure as Peru's chief executive. Handpicked for the post on the basis of zealous prior service and a flexible temperament that was to enable him to work with Visitor General Jorge Escobedo, Croix entered Lima thoroughly apprised of Secretary Gálvez's displeasure with the two preceding viceroys.[49] Moreover, he assumed his position just three days after Jáuregui had sent the box of gathered copies of the *Eulogy* to Spain.[50] To think that the new viceroy did not learn almost immediately about Baquíjano and the unprecedented remission of the *Eulogy* presented to his predecessor strains one's credulity. It is highly probable that almost from the day he reached Lima Croix marked Baquíjano as a man to watch.

Certainly such foresight would have been justified. Croix immediately found himself embroiled in the litigation swirling around Villalta's election as rector of San Marcos. When the winner's term ended, the viceroy then received Baquíjano's protest over his opponent's normally *pro forma* move into the vice-rectorship. The merits of the two cases were still being considered in Madrid when the official rebuke of the *Eulogy* arrived. And scarcely had José expressed contrition before he stirred up the cloister over the prima chair of civil law. When Croix turned over his command to Francisco Gil de Taboada y Lemos in late March 1790, Baquíjano's latest protest had yet to be resolved. The ungovernable professor, in short, had been a nearly constant trial to Croix's administrative skills throughout his tenure.

One looks in vain for evidence that Croix responded to the repeated challenges José posed with less than equanimity. Rather his even-handed and prudent handling of the several cases deserves high marks. José neither could nor did blame the viceroy for his losses in the University. His own style and youth, not viceregal interference, accounted for the defeats. The point, however, is that unlike Guirior and Jáuregui, Croix did nothing to aid Baquíjano in his career. Given the closeness of the elections for both the rectorship and the prima chair, the viceroy's favor might easily have swung the balance to the more youthful candidate. But Croix displayed no partiality and thus allowed Baquíjano to suffer the defeats that a majority of his peers thought he richly deserved.

The arrival of Viceroy Gil in 1790 was critical for the reversal of Baquíjano's fortunes. Gil, a career naval officer, had previously served briefly as Viceroy of New Granada. His view of the divine origin of royal authority was traditional, but his belief that the state should act to improve its wealth and the well-being and prosperity of its people was an axiom of Spanish enlightened despotism. Gil was a practical man who favored the spread of knowledge among the populace. Convinced that the inhabitants of Peru needed to be aroused to appreciate how government-sponsored reforms were in their own interest, he supported men with projects to effect this awakening. The marriage of his nephew Francisco to Josefa Baquíjano, José's widowed sister, added a personal dimension to his relations with the ambitious professor. The viceroy, moreover, had strong support at court in the post-Gálvez years, a great virtue in the eyes of persons anxious for royal favors and offices.[51]

Shortly after Gil reached Lima a florescence of modern thought was evident in the city. Although the ideas presented were not new, the overt patronage Gil bestowed upon their proponents increased their acceptability. In this altered environment Baquíjano's fortunes rose quickly. Unlike the late seventies and early eighties, when viceregal favor nearly ensured the hostility of Visitor General Areche, the political setting in Lima was less complex by 1790. When Escobedo, Areche's successor, left Lima in 1788 to assume a post on the Council of the Indies, the viceroy was again the undisputed leader of civil government, a position that gave added weight to his support.[52]

The passage of time also worked in Baquíjano's favor. Much of his difficulty in San Marcos had originated in the refusal to await his turn in a system permeated by respect for seniority. By the early 1790s his age and experience rendered his ambitions more acceptable. Furthermore, old antagonists were passing from the scene. Antonio José Alvarez de Ron, for example, died in 1785, the Marqués de Sotoflorido in early 1792.[53] Former rector Alvarado would turn seventy in 1793, the year in which Antonio de Boza would die.[54] Age had taken its toll and younger men, many who were themselves in mid-career, were assuming control.

An indication of the altered *ambiente* was Baquíjano's selection in 1791 to be vice-rector and senior counselor of San Marcos. With the notable exception of 1784, when he had successfully opposed Villalta's election, the position routinely passed to the rector's nominee. Thus when rector Tomás José de Orrantia proposed Baquíjano after his own reelection in 1791, the cloister unanimously endorsed the choice.[55] The incident was notable in two respects. Orrantia was a supporter of the *Mercurio peruano*, the new periodical that Gil patronized warmly and in whose pages Baquíjano published several articles. Thus the rector's nomination further testified to the increased prominence of intellectuals attuned to modern currents of thought. Since he was a canon, moreover, Orrantia's action signified a thaw in the long-standing conflict between José and the cathedral chapter, none of whose members opposed his naming.

Baquíjano's accommodation with the cloister in 1791 was further illustrated in his laudatory history of San Marcos that began to appear in the *Mercurio* a week after his election as vice-rector. Briefly he described the University's foundation and curriculum, provision of chairs, and conferment of degrees. In contrast to academic backwardness that allegedly marred many contemporary European universities, Baquíjano declared that San Marcos had never suffered such intellectual debility and had always produced learned and illustrious men. The divergence between this raptuous evaluation and his reference a decade earlier to the University's "cold winter of inactivity" was striking.[56]

The death of the Marqués de Sotoflorido in early 1792 provided both the vacancy that Baquíjano had been awaiting in the prima chair of canon law and additional proof that he had returned from the pale. After posted edicts announced the vacancy, Baquíjano applied with alacrity. In notable contrast to the earlier competition for the prima chair of civil law, no other candidates came forward. The absence of rival claimants was probably due to the belief that the talented and prominent professor was now undefeatable. Not only did he enjoy the support of Gil and Orrantia, but this time, in contrast to the earlier contest with Larrión, he was arguably the next man in the ascenso. Only Francisco Antonio de Oyague might have challenged him on the basis of seniority, for he had taught fifteen years longer. Perhaps because he had reached the *vísperas* chair of canon law three years after Guirior had named Baquíjano to the parallel post in civil law, Oyague refrained from entering the competition.[57] Running unchallenged, Baquíjano was elected without a dissenting vote.[58]

After fifteen years as a professor Baquíjano had reached the peak of his faculty. Within months, however, he revealed that this service had been but a way station on the road to the Audiencia. In early January 1793 he initiated the proceedings that would lead to his retirement in the prima chair.[59] Rector Orrantia supported the request and immediately wrote a letter of endorsement to Charles IV.[60]

While Orrantia was clearly an ally to Baquíjano, the laudatory recommendation later submitted by the cloister requires more explanation. Tactfully the report omitted José's participation in Jáuregui's reception, his abortive campaign for the rectorship, his continued harassment of Villalta, and his refusal to acquiesce in Larrión's election to the prima chair of law. Instead, the statement avowed that since 1778 Baquíjano had provided "irrefutable testimony of his eminent, solid, and almost comprehensive learning in repeated *réplicas*, an excessive number of presidencies, and no few pieces of sublime eloquence." These "glorious monuments" revealed his enlightened taste, continued service to San Marcos, and "brilliant merit." It was also noted in the cloister's recommendation that ample precedents existed for dispensing the constitutional requirement for twenty years of service before retirement. They concluded by stating that José was among the school's most outstanding professors, and his request should be honored.[61]

Such paeans bore little relationship to the vituperation José's opponents had heaped upon him in the previous decade. And neither his triumphs in 1791 and 1792 nor the altered composition of the cloister provides by itself a satisfactory explanation of this notable *volte face*. An additional consideration is that while Baquíjano's friends were willing to support his pretension, his enemies probably perceived the requested retirement as a way to be rid of him. Consequently both groups were willing to bless his proposal. And, as Rector Orrantia noted, the retirement would stimulate the University by creating further opportunity for trial lectures. After Viceroy Gil submitted a concurring statement, Baquíjano shortly received the retirement he desired.⁶²

Baquíjano's years in the University of San Marcos underscored his fiercely aggressive desire for self-advancement. Following a disgraceful return from Spain, the University provided the best opportunities for him to forward his career and when these appeared he sought to use them advantageously. In the *Eulogy* he not only praised Jáuregui but identified himself as a student of modern thought and a potential leader in San Marcos. Anxious to add luster to his record, he contested first the rectorship and then the prima chair of civil law. His refusal to accept defeat revealed unmistakably his concern for personal gain over the well-being of the University.

After finally making peace with his opponents in the cloister, José obtained the vice-rectorship and the proprietary prima chair of sacred canons. These successes stimulated rather than sated him, however, and within months he persuaded the University to name him its representative to the Court, sought support for his retirement, and sailed to Spain. University service had been a means to the bureaucratic career he sought, never an end in itself.

Baquíjano's university activities were important both as a step on the road to an Audiencia appointment and as a testimony to his intellectual ability. The university, however, was not the only forum where men of letters could demonstrate their literary skill. The flow of books and pamphlets from New World presses provided authors and censors alike with space for their ideas. The practice of including dedications before longer publications offered still another opportunity for literary display. In the late eighteenth century the increased prominence of the periodical press, for example, the *Mercurio peruano* in Lima, further enabled numerous occasional writers such as Baquíjano to see their prose in circulation.

Audiencia ministers had long participated in specialized literary activities before and after their appointments. Traditionally they had focused their efforts upon the amplification, clarification, or compilation of legal texts that could increase or justify increased royal authority. The works by Juan de Solórzano, Pedro Frasso, and Antonio Joaquín de Rivadeneira exemplified this professional writing. In the late eighteenth century this historic role expanded to include the advocacy of modern ideas, particularly within the context of the crown-supported economic societies. Prominent royal advisers, notably Melchor de Jovellanos and the Conde de Campomanes, set the pace at court. Letrados in the colonies followed their example and participated in economic societies as well as writing materials of general interest for the periodical press. Such activities, they knew, were favored at court and could enhance their prospects for appointment.

In the late eighteenth century letrados labored within an intellectual environment that emphasized observation, experience, experimentation, and the critical use of reason—in brief the modern approach to knowledge—that permeated the works of Spain's celebrated eclectic, Benedictine Father Benito Feijóo. Between 1726 and 1760 Feijóo published fifteen volumes whose total sales of approximately five hundred thousand copies had been exceeded only by *Don Quixote*.[63] Serving as a Spanish Pierre Bayle, Feijóo, more than any other individual, prepared the way for the bureaucrats and intellectuals who advocated reform in Spain and her colonies.[64]

The torrent of criticism from devoted Aristotelians that greeted the Benedictine's first volume in 1726 had nearly dried up by midcentury. When he named Feijóo a royal counselor in 1748 and prohibited further polemics against him in 1750, Ferdinand VI gave royal endorsement to the cause of modernity.[65] In the following decades, persons who proposed changes in agriculture, economics, and education appealed to the experience and critical use of reason that the prolific publicist had advocated.

Feijóo's enormous popularity spread throughout the empire. Creoles received his books with special enthusiasm for he combated the oft-repeated canard that their intellectual capabilities declined precipitously during a premature old age.[66] American libraries regularly contained the eclectic's works, but by the late eighteenth century the most current writers referred to them only occasionally. By then his emphasis upon experience and reason was common currency, a widely accepted base no longer needing the support of his authority. Familiarity with the Benedictine's works was such that Baquíjano could refer to him with full respect in 1788 simply as "our Feijóo."[67]

The modern approach to knowledge that Feijóo espoused gradually penetrated Peru. Pablo de Olavide and Eusebio Llano de Zapata revealed their modern interests by mid-century. Baquíjano's mentor, Agustín de Gorrichátegui, was an active proponent from at least the 1760s. The Royal Convictory of San Carlos founded in Lima in 1771 was dedicated to developing students' critical faculties through exposure to modern knowledge. Public dissemination of modern ideas continued to expand in the following decades.

There were limits, of course, to what writers could publish. Personal prudence and royal policy combined to rule out attacks on revealed religion. Feijóo had set the direction by specifying that he would not become engaged in theological matters, a subject about which much had already been written. Rather he would concentrate on the less well discussed realm of nature, a realm far more enticing to men dedicated to useful knowledge.[68] The second major limitation was critical discussion of royal authority; with the Crown encouraging intellectual activities and practical knowledge and taking concrete steps to improve prosperity, however, few persons even considered this a restriction. For letrados anxious for high office the road was clear; participation in contemporary intellectual activities was advisable, a way to reveal support for the intellectual underpinnings of "enlightened despotism."

Baquíjano typified the ambitious letrado who participated in popular intellectual undertakings, and historians have correctly perceived that he was one of Peru's most notable adherents of the "Spanish Enlightenment."[69] Accepting this position, however, does not preclude also appreciating that his modernity was fashionable within the high bureaucracy he hoped to enter. José recognized this and repeatedly used intellectual activities as a means to advance his career.

The professor's best-known publications were the *Eulogy* in 1781 and several articles in the *Mercurio peruano* in the early 1790s. In the intervening decade, however, he wrote at least five prefatory comments or recommendations for publication that appeared in two dissertations on the immaculate conception, a sermon, a funeral oration, and a poetic discourse lamenting the death of Charles III.[70] These comments revealed several characteristics present earlier in the *Eulogy:* a self-proclaimed tone of impartial observation, a pretentious display of erudition and familiarity with recent publications, and repeated attacks on scholasticism.

José Baquíjano y Carrillo in the black gown worn while civil judge (*oidor*) on Lima's Audiencia. The original portrait is in the Colegio de Abogados, Lima.

Memorial by Baquíjano requesting consideration for the criminal *fiscalía* of Chile. AGI, Chile 258, Madrid, April 16, 1776.

Para la Camara.

Por Real Decreto de 11 de Marzo de este año se sirvió S.M. crear, entre otras, una plaza de Fiscal Criminal en la Audiencia de Chile, con el sueldo annual de 10860 pesos, mandando que la Camara proponga sugetos para ella de conocida literatura, prudencia, y acreditada conducta, Y en su consequencia hace presente la Secretaria los Sugetos que han ocurrido a solicitarla, acompañando sus respectivas Relaciones de meritos.

1°   El Lic.do D.n Agustin Ignacio de comparan y Orbe

2°   El Lic.do D.n Alonso Gonzalez Baca.

3°   El D.r D.n Alonso Pirez y Guesada.

4°   El Lic.do D.n Ambrosio Cerdan de Simon Pontero.

5°   El Lic.do D.n Antonio Suarez

6°   El Lic.do D.n Antonio de Francia y Vzquiola.

7°   El Lic.do D.n Antonio Lopez Quintana.

8°   El D.r D.n Baltasar Padron.

9°   El Lic.do D.n Basilio Luyando.

10   El Lic.do D.n Benito Gonzalez Jove.

11   D.n Carlos Rafael de Ayesa.

12   El Lic.do D.n Ciriaco Gonzalez de Carbajal.

13   El Lic.do D.n Diego Quiroga y Carinde.

14   D.n Diego de Albear

15   El Lic.do D.n Domingo Diez y Santillana

16   El D.r D.n Domingo Ximenez de la Rebilla.

. . . . .

50   El D.r D.n Josef Baquijano Carrillo

List of *pretendientes* for the criminal *fiscalía* of Chile, edited for presentation. Baquíjano was number 50 of 101. AGI, Chile 258, 1776.

✠ ELOGIO

DEL EXELENTISIMO SEÑOR DON
Aguſtin de Jauregui, y Aldecoa; Caballero del orden de Santiago, Teniente General de los Reales Exercitos, Virrey, Gober-
nador, y Capitan General de los Reynos
del Perú, Chile &c.

Pronunciado

EN EL RECIBIMIENTO, QUE CO-
mo á ſu Vice-Patron, le hizo la Real
Univerſidad de S. Marcos el dia
XXVII. de Agoſto del año
de M. DCC. LXXXI.

Por

EL D. D. JOSEPH BAQUIJANO, Y CAR-
rillo; Fiſcal Protector Interino de los Natu-
rales del diſtrito de eſta Real Audiencia, y Catedratico de Viſpe-
ras de Leyes.

Title page of the *Elogio*. Rare Book Room, Perkins Library, Duke
University.

Exmo. señor.

Muy venerado señor mío. En carta n° 326 dejo ofrecido á Vd. que le remitiría impresa la Oración que se dixo en esta Universidad de San Marcos el día que se recivió el Virrey en ella, cuya ceremonia se debe abolir, como que es un caso de 25 á 30.000 pesos inoportunos, é inutiles por el modo feo con que se gastan; y acavando de salir á la luz pública, incluyo á Vd. dos exemplares que han venido á mis manos.

En esta Oración hallará Vd. la terrible, y execrable Doctrina que en el Templo de las Letras, en el Santuario de la Educación, en el Cielo de la enseñanza pública se da, y recita al primer Gefe del Reyno del Perú; Que este la oye, y que no contento con disimularlo por aquella vez, la permite imprimir, y dar, á que se vean mas de espacio los dicterios con que se negece, no solo á los contribuyentes, y administradores de las rentas de Rl. Hacienda, como á todo el gremio...

First page of Areche's letter to Gálvez condemning the *Elogio*. AGI, Lima 1086, Lima, November 3, 1781.

(✠)

MERCURIO PERUANO

DE HISTORIA, LITERATURA, Y NOTICIAS PÚBLICAS

QUE DA A LUZ

LA SOCIEDAD ACADEMICA
de Amantes de Lima.

Y

EN SU NOMBRE

D. Jacinto Calero y Moreira.

TOMO I.º

QUE COMPREHENDE

LOS MESES DE

Enero, Febrero, Marzo, y Abril
de 1791.

CON SUPERIOR PERMISO

Impreso en Lima: en la Imprenta
Real de los Niños Huérfanos.

Title page of the *Mercurio peruano*, 1791. Facsimile edition at Thomas
Jefferson Library, University of Missouri-St. Louis.

RELACION
DE LOS MERITOS,
Y SERVICIOS
DEL Dr. DON JOSEPH BAQUIXANO
CARRILLO DE CORDOBA,

Caballero de la Real distinguida Orden de Carlos Tercero, Catedrático de Prima de Sagrados Canones en la Universidad de Lima, y Diputado general en esta Corte de la misma Real Universidad, y de aquel ilustre Ayuntamiento.

POR una Relacion que en treinta de Septiembre de mil setecientos ochenta y uno se formó al referido Don Joseph Baquixano en esta Secretaría del Perú, y otros documentos, que posteriormente se han exhibido, consta que es natural de la misma Capital de Lima : de edad de quarenta y dos años cumplidos en trece de Marzo del corriente; y hijo legitimo de Don Juan Bautista Baquixano, y de Doña Maria Ignacia Carrillo de Cordoba, Condes de Vista-Florida, ambos de familias de notoria distincion, y calidad.

En veinte y dos de Abril de mil setecientos sesenta y dos entró con Beca de paga en el Real Seminario Colegio de Santo Toribio de la misma Capital de Lima, y estudió Jurisprudencia con singular aplicacion, y aprovechamiento, manifestado en los regulares examenes de los quatro libros de la Instituta, de que salió aprobado

A   por

Relación de los méritos of Baquíjano, 1793, page one. AGI, Lima 967.

Title of Baquíjano's appointment as *alcalde del crimen*, 1797. Copy in AGS, *Sección 23, Inventario 2, legajo 81, título 42.*

The brief remarks reiterated Baquíjano's identification with the advocates of modernity who enjoyed influence at the time. The dedication he wrote in 1784 to a work by Ignacio de Castro illustrated as well the extent to which José employed the printed word as he tried to further his career.

Baquíjano dedicated Castro's *Second Dissertation* to his powerful nemesis José de Gálvez. The Secretary for the Indies, he fawned, devoted his authority to producing "the happiness and glory of America." Gálvez recognized the importance of merit and "the utility of letters" and that increased enlightenment would instill greater obedience among the king's subjects. Obsequiously, Baquíjano declared that posterity would immortalize the Secretary's name.[71] Such encomiums contrasted markedly with his later denunciation once the Secretary was safely entombed. Having just seen the *Eulogy* shipped to Gálvez, however, Baquíjano transparently sought to ingratiate himself with the man who not only would rule on the ill-fated tract but also wielded extensive power over audiencia appointments.

Baquíjano's flattery failed. Gálvez, who had earlier executed the order to expel the Peruvian from Spain, never favored him. Baquíjano's family recognized the impasse and the Secretary's death in 1787 prompted Juan Agustín to write immediately that José could again hope to obtain a position.[72] In the following decade Baquíjano's sense of personal injury led him to charge inaccurately that Gálvez had initiated a discriminatory policy against Americans who sought audiencia appointments.[73] In the interim, however, failure to gain the Secretary's favor only reinforced the need to accumulate acceptable services—the "merit" he said Gálvez recognized—for which to solicit compensation later. An opportunity arose in 1790 when a small group founded a literary and economic society in Lima, the celebrated Friends of the Country (*Amantes del País*).

From the approval of the Basque Society of Friends of the Country in 1765 until the early nineteenth century, over eighty economic societies were founded in the Spanish world. Dedicated to providing useful knowledge and encouraging practical projects of local utility, these societies testified to the Crown's concern that modern ideas be disseminated. Jovellanos, Campomanes, and Gálvez were particularly notable examples of the government officials who joined economic societies.[74] The Lima Audiencia had

at least three ministers who belonged to the Basque Society to
which Baquíjano had been admitted in the 1780s.[75] Membership
in an economic society substantiated one's support of current
government philosophy, and pretendientes and ministers alike regularly mentioned their affiliation when they solicited favors or
promotions.

The Lima Society of Friends of the Country, the fifth of the
twelve colonial societies, developed in 1790 from a revitalized
salon. More a literary than a true economic society, the group's
principal concern soon became the publication of the *Mercurio
peruano*, a biweekly paper. Charter members numbered only four:
José Rossi y Rubí, the Italian-born president; Hipólito Unanue, the
secretary; Juan Maria Egaña; and Demetrio Guasque.[76] A
challenge from a brash young peninsular, however, spurred a
drive to expand both the membership and its activities.

The Extremaduran Jayme Bausate y Mesa arrived in the City of
Kings in the same year that the Lima Society was established.
Fresh from fifteen month's service as an editor for a daily paper in
Madrid, he noted with astonishment that the Peruvian capital
lacked a newspaper. The possibility of plying his craft whetted
Bausate's pen and soon he took steps to found a paper that would
arouse Lima's learned residents from their "lethargic inactivity."
Viceroy Gil received a favorable report on the proposal and
granted the editor a license to publish the *Diario curioso, erudito,
económico, y comercial de Lima.*[77]

The prospectus that announced the *Diario* goaded the Friends of
the Country into conceiving their own publication. A periodical
would provide an outlet for their literary efforts and simultaneously would enable them to spread useful knowledge to the general
public. Concerted recruitment brought an editor, five other new
members, and two protectors to bolster the Society. According to
Rossi, Baquíjano and Diego Cisneros were foremost among the additions. These men, he wrote several weeks after the first *Mercurio*
reached the public in January 1791, "adorn us with distinction"
and are responsible for "the favor that our work receives from the
public."[78]

The group that established the *Mercurio* included three government officials, four members of religious orders, two professors,
and one lawyer.[79] Participation was thoroughly consonant with
government service and the expection of later preferment, and six

of the ten founders either held or aspired to government posts.[80] Viceroy Gil encouraged the group, recommended its efforts to Charles IV, and even subsidized one of its volumes.[81]

Writers for the *Mercurio* emphasized their kinship with enlightened attitudes; they stressed a self-conscious modernity, considering themselves youthful in age and contemporary in outlook. Of the leaders, Rossi and the editor Jacinto Calero were men in their twenties; Unanue was in his thirties, and Baquíjano turned forty in 1791. *Jovenes* they called themselves as they repeatedly underscored their youth and metaphorically accented their modernity. These men endorsed many of the tremendous intellectual changes initiated since the time of Francis Bacon.[82] Furthermore, they approved the recent reforms implemented by the Crown and supported warmly by Gil.[83] The men of the *Mercurio* were both modern men and government men.

The word *utility* summarized the Society's overriding emphasis as youthful eagerness joined the ideal of the service-minded *philosophe*. The declared intention of the *Mercurio* was to be useful to Peru and the Society took this purpose seriously. Under "utility" was subsumed the desire to become better acquainted with Peru and to provide its inhabitants with greater knowledge about their land as well as to present materials that would give foreigners an accurate image of the viceroyalty.[84] The paper published articles that advocated burial in cemeteries instead of churches, recommended ways to avoid dangers during pregnancy, urged support for more efficient, mechanized mining techniques, and presented modern chemical terms. The authors lauded science for it revealed new, better ways to confront old problems; in short, it was useful. Since the best science required experimentation, observation, and reliance upon verifiable facts, the writers acclaimed Newtonian physics and the intellectual approach of Father Feijóo. Proudly emulating the European example, the Lima Friends of the Country offered prizes for the best essays on a subject of utmost utility—the best and most economical way to improve the roads of Peru.[85]

Baquíjano was intellectually comfortable with a group that venerated utility and stressed a modern approach to knowledge. Moreover, a genuine interest in the ideals and outlook of the Friends of the Country complemented his realization that participation might aid his career, a realization encouraged by Gil's overt patronage of the group. An influential member from the time he joined, Baquíjano contributed actively to the Society's endeavors until his departure for Spain in early 1793. He helped to draft the body's constitution and to solicit royal commendation of its efforts. In addition he introduced three volumes of the *Mercurio*, penned several editorial notes, and published four major historical articles.[86] The Society formally recognized his services and abilities when it elected him its president.[87]

José commanded respectable credentials to write articles on the Audiencia of Lima, the University of San Marcos, the development of the mining center of Potosí, and the commerce of Peru. Interim service on the Audiencia had acquainted him with the tribunal itself and also with problems at Potosí; relatives involved in the Chilean grain trade and his position as a legal adviser for the Lima merchant guild had informed him about commerce; many years' association with the University had given him intimate familiarity with its history, statutes, and operation; and, of course, he had read widely as he had indicated in the *Eulogy* a decade earlier.

Baquíjano wrote about familiar aspects of his immediate surroundings, but grounded his work in careful examination of written materials. Repeatedly he mentioned useful documents rescued from archival dust. Royal cédulas, official reports, codes of law, and university cloister records received citation in footnotes containing references to sources as varied as the impeachable Vulgate *Bible* and the *First Discourse* by the less orthodox Jean Jacques Rousseau.

The best-known article Baquíjano contributed to the *Mercurio* was the "Historical-Political Dissertation on Commerce in Peru."[88] Recently the eminent Venezuelan scholar Eduardo Arcila Farías subjected this lengthy discourse to a detailed analysis and concluded that it was void of originality and made no contribution to the economic thought of the time.[89] These characteristics, however, were far less important for Baquíjano's career than his endorsement of the policy of "free trade" within the empire that Charles III had proclaimed in 1778. This position joined the author's contention that Peruvian miners should employ new techniques to improve silver production in indicating his support for the Crown's economic policies. Such approval conformed to Viceroy Gil's expectation that the *Mercurio* would be useful to Peru and the government.

The potentially most interesting part of Baquíjano's discussion, a promised final section on suggested reforms for improving Peruvian commerce, never appeared. As the editor explained, the material was more appropriate for government consideration than public consumption, and the *Mercurio* might not benefit from its publication.[90] This circumspection was fostered, in part at least, by the vocal opposition that had surfaced by the time the last installment of the "Dissertation" went to press in April 1791.

Baquíjano discussed the *Mercurio*'s adversaries with dismay and rising anger when he introduced its second volume on May 1. He complained about *pseudosabios*, who were inappreciative of the time necessary for a periodical to reach maturity and besieged it on one side. Fluttering on the other were dilettantes who lacked any knowledge beyond that acquired through rapidly devouring a romance, popular tragedy, or some other unscholarly work, but had delegated themselves "universal censors of all the sciences." The detractors surrounded the *Mercurio* like insects and forced its writers to work with "a pen in one hand, an exterminator in the other." Some critics, José commented acerbically, could not distinguish between a periodical and a didactic work; they did not realize that in a periodical "diversity forms its merit and beauty and fulfills the principal end of its publication." The few readers who contributed to the paper had submitted items of deplorable quality. Irregular and tardy payment by subscribers, moreover, threatened the *Mercurio*'s solvency. Frankly, Baquíjano lamented, the Society had not anticipated that such obstacles would hinder its efforts to be useful to Peru.[91]

Critics of the paper hurled more strident invective as time passed. "Nothing has been omitted," Baquíjano reported in September, "that would make us abandon our honest work." Opponents had inveighed against the private lives of Society members as if "being authors of the *Mercurio peruano* were an offense against Religion and the State." Hatred and persecution, of course, were commonplace for spokesmen of advanced thought. Descartes, Newton, Linneaeus, and other noted intellectuals had earlier suffered for their views. The assurance that such reflection gave for eventual acceptance, however, was less pleasant than several more tangible indications of support.[92]

The Amantes del País derived satisfaction from the growth and formal approval of the Society, favorable reports received from other colonies and Europe, the appearance of similar societies with periodicals in other locations, and the continued patronage of Viceroy Gil. With bureaucrats and aspirants to office among its membership, the Society was particularly pleased with Gil's support. The viceroy responded positively to a proposal for a formal constitution for the body that was submitted by Baquíjano, Egaña, Unanue, and Calero. Not only did he approve the plan, but also he granted the Society permission to use the library and large meeting room at the University of San Marcos.[93]

The viceroy's active patronage proved especially useful when a royal order of June 9, 1792 arrived calling for the remission of all issues of a paper that treated "curious subjects of literature, commerce, history, and other sciences."[94] Gil promptly shipped a linen-lined wooden box containing a complete set of the *Mercurio* and penned a covering letter, which detailed that he had protected the paper since its inception, granted the authors access to government documents necessary for their labors, and approved the Society's formal establishment. The publication, he declared, was "very useful and desirable" and the persons who published it deserved commendation.[95]

Ironically Gil's approval of the "Constitution" and the arrival of the royal order hastened the *Mercurio*'s demise. Visions of immediate advancement entered the minds of three of the Society's principal members, and within two months after the order was published an exodus began. Baquíjano, now the first president of the formalized Society, and Calero, the editor, sailed for Spain to seek audiencia appointments.[96] In May 1793, José Rossi, the real inspiration of the organization and a major contributor to the paper, departed to solicit naturalization and an office.[97] Left without these major contributors and suffering from a loss of subscribers, lack of revenue, and the weariness and new interests of the remaining writers, the *Mercurio* faltered and then succumbed in 1795.[98] Its ephemeral existence had demonstrated both the presence of enlightened, practical-minded persons in Lima and the thinness of their ranks.

Baquíjano's contributions to the *Mercurio* demonstrated irrefutably his continued commitment to the spread of modern ideas in Peru. The brevity of his involvement, however, revealed as well that more than intellectual affinity had governed his participation. At bottom the *Mercurio* was but one more means of obtaining royal consideration. Consequently the fact that he had participated as an author and organizer outweighed the content of his articles as an aid to his career. By his efforts in a project encouraged by the viceroy, he had won Gil's support and thus increased the probability of gaining the Audiencia appointment he coveted.

Baquíjano had no doubt that the Crown valued literary activities and participation in economic societies. Thus verification of these efforts accompanied other materials he submitted for incorporation into a revised relación de méritos. The new document contained an entire paragraph relating that José had wanted to promote "application and good taste in the Sciences and Arts" in Peru, had helped to establish the Amantes, had assisted in publishing the royally approved *Mercurio*, and had served as the Society's first president.[99]

The confidence Baquíjano displayed in the worth of his efforts was well-founded. In June 1793 the king ordered Gil to propose the *Mercurio*'s authors for positions according to their abilities.[100] For Baquíjano, Calero, Rossi, Unanue, and Egaña, this order confirmed a legitimate claim upon royal largess that each man subsequently called to the king's attention when seeking appointments and favors.[101]

Even before he heard of this latest sign of royal commendation, Baquíjano was en route to Spain. Heartened by his recent triumphs in the University of San Marcos and the favor of Viceroy Gil, his finances healed following his mother's death, and his spirits raised by the displacement of his detractor Antonio Porlier, Marqués de Bajamar, as Secretary for Grace and Justice, Baquíjano had once more set forth in pursuit of the elusive appointment to the Audiencia of Lima. At last the years of frustration were drawing to a close.

5

An Audiencia Appointment

Baquíjano vigorously sought appointment to the Audiencia of Lima in the mid-1790s. Encouraged by his recent accomplishments and confident in his abilities and family background, he again sailed to Spain to add personal entreaties to written petitions. Within the altered political and administrative context, his approach at last bore fruit. In early 1797 Charles IV designated him an alcalde del crimen for his native court. A quarter-century of effort had culminated in the first direct appointment of a native son to Lima in over four decades.

The tactics Baquíjano employed in his quest for office illustrate the persistence and flexibility common to pretendientes. At the same time his maneuvers provide a glimpse at alterations in appointment procedures since the mid-1770s. Placing his naming within the context of other American appointments will enable appreciating both its routine and unique characteristics. Such an examination, moreover, will manifest the difficulties that Americans faced when they sought high office.

By late 1792 Baquíjano had emerged triumphantly from a decade of disillusion and failure. The king had recently admitted him to the Order of Charles III, an honor customarily reserved for prominent officials after extended or particularly meritorious service. The cloister of the University of San Marcos had elected him its vice-rector and senior counselor and he had won the prima chair of sacred canons. He had written for the *Mercurio*, helped to draft the constitution for the Lima Society of Friends of the Country, and been elected the Society's president.[1] The death of his mother in early 1791, moreover, had strengthened his financial position.[2]

The Condesa's fortune was worth over a million pesos at her death and, although he was one of seven surviving children, José's share was adequate to bolster his credit significantly. Since in 1782 his mother had formally relieved him of the debts left after he had squandered his patrimony in Spain, this new inheritance provided the resources for a renewed pursuit of office.[3] Financial means combined with his recent flurry of professional accomplishments to convince the middle-aged aspirant that the time was right for another trip to Spain. Furthermore, the political setting at court had changed since his initial voyage. With Gálvez dead and Porlier replaced as Secretary for Grace and Justice, Baquíjano believed that the probability of his success had increased substantially.

Residents of the Spanish Empire could not simply pack their bags and board the first ship to Cádiz. Travel was restricted by law to persons with prior authorization by a designated official. Baquíjano's situation was further complicated by his chair at San Marcos. The University *Constitutions* forbade professors to absent themselves for over two months except with viceregal permission and in order to serve either the king or the university. Consequently José had to persuade Viceroy Gil to grant him a leave of absence.[4]

To his delight, Baquíjano experienced no difficulty in securing the necessary travel permit. His approach was first to secure commissions to represent both the Lima city council and the university at court. The two bodies accepted his offers to serve without compensation and in early January 1793 each named him its deputy general.[5] Armed with these charges, Baquíjano then applied for a leave of absence. Viceroy Gil and the Audiencia approved the request without delay and granted him permission for a two-year absence from Lima and his university chair.[6]

Baquíjano's willingness to represent the city council and the university without pay did not spring from selflessness. Rather it reflected his shrewd awareness that such commissions would legitimize his presence at court and facilitate access to persons who might further the true purpose of his trip—obtaining an appoint-

,ment on Lima's Audiencia. Clearly the interested parties in Lima
fully understood what he was doing. Viceroy Gil, the Audiencia,
the rector of San Marcos, and the Lima city council all knew that
he sought an appointment and endorsed him in written recommendations.[7]

Spain had been at peace for nearly a decade when on January
18, 1793, Baquíjano sailed in the frigate *La Liebre* from Callao
toward Panama on the first leg of his journey.[8] The execution of
Louis XVI three days later, however, provoked war with France in
early March. Spanish troops invaded French soil in the following
month, but their limited advances had blunted the initial popular
enthusiasm for conflict by the time José reached the peninsula in
late fall.[9]

Wartime expenditures immediately made inroads on government revenues, and the need for voluntary donations from residents in Spain and the empire expanded apace. Early elation
faded as the government resorted to issuing royal bonds after
French forces launched a counteroffensive and invaded northern
Spain in 1794. Popular opinion welcomed the peace signed in July
1795 but, unfortunately for Spain, the respite was short-lived. An
alliance with France produced conflict with Britain beginning in
October 1796. Faced with a loss of American revenue and trade
as the British blockaded Cádiz and harrassed other Spanish ports,
the Crown expanded its issues of royal bonds and welcomed opportunities to reduce expenditures.[10] War and deteriorating
government finances, save for only a brief reprieve in 1795–96,
thus provided the setting against which one must view José's
solicitations during his second trip to Spain.

Soon after his arrival in Madrid, Baquíjano established quarters
in an upstairs apartment at No. 7, Carrera de San Gerónimo.[11]
The address was one of distinction. Pedro Muñoz de la Torre, a
member of the Cámara of the Indies, Manuel Romero, a councilor
of the Indies, two councilors of Castile, and one of Hacienda resided on the street; within several blocks lived the Marqués de Bajamar, Governor of the Council of the Indies, and a number of
other councilors.[12] Moreover, the apartment was well located with
regard to Madrid's major centers. It took only several minutes to
walk to the Puerta del Sol and was an easy stroll to the Royal
Palace and the Plaza Mayor. José's older brother lived on the Calle
de las Huertas a short distance away, and Jacinto Muñoz y Calero,

a good friend and fellow writer for the *Mercurio peruano* who had also come to court to seek a government office, was close at hand.[13] Given its multiple advantages, the apartment's annual rent of five thousand *reales de vellón* was acceptable.

Furnishing the apartment was an additional expense, but in anticipation of a prolonged residence José did not stint. Soon the sitting and dining rooms, bedroom, and kitchen were suitably arrayed with expensive furniture and fixtures. Walnut was the favored wood and appeared in nearly a dozen arm chairs, an expensive covered desk, and a three-cushioned couch. An elaborate mantle and fireplace stood at one end of the sitting room while a hutch occupied each corner. Costly mirrors and curtains further accented the rooms, while two balconies provided access to the street. A pair of gaming tables of luxurious wood added an unmistakable note of the master's perennial obsession for gambling. In the kitchen was a selection of copper cookware and the proper utensils for preparing the morning chocolate.

Obviously Baquíjano was prepared to entertain extensively, although who his guests were remains unknown. Besides his friends Calero and Rossi y Rubí, a number of Peruvians were eligible candidates. The young infantry captain José Antonio de Lavalle y Zugasti was in Madrid and called upon both José and his brother for testimony when he applied for entry in the Order of Calatrava.[14] José's contemporaries, Andrés and Gabriel Gallo Díaz Calvo, both limeños and fellow caballeros in the Order of Charles III, were also in the capital in the mid-1790s.[15] Gabriel, and limeños colonel Julián de Capetillo and José Taboada y Castilla had earlier testified for José prior to his own admission in the Order of Charles III.[16] Tadeo Bravo de Rivero, who would succeed Baquíjano as deputy for the Lima city council, had been at court from at least 1794 and the Conde de Torre Velarde had been a resident and pretendiente for over a decade.[17] Together these acquaintances, even if not close friends, would have provided José with companionship and information about recent developments at court.

While Madrid was the capital and housed the bureaucracy, Charles IV, his family, selected advisers and officials, and a large number of courtiers regularly welcomed the new seasons from different royal residences. In general terms the court wintered at El Pardo, a short distance from Madrid, spent the spring and early summer at the lovely Bourbon palace of Aranjuez south of the capital, enjoyed the lesser heat of the northern-most palace of San Ildefonso, from August to the end of October, and then spent five or six weeks at the monumental retreat El Escorial before returning to Madrid for the Christmas season. These annual movements dictated that the most ambitious pretendientes, too, spent only part of each year in Madrid.

Baquíjano joined other aspirants in annual pilgrimages from palace to palace. He wrote a petition at El Escorial on December 13, 1793, another two weeks later from Madrid, a third while at Aranjuez the following April, and a fourth from San Ildefonso in August. Similar sojourns followed annually until November 1798 when he paid El Escorial a final visit.[18] The length of time he remained at each palace is unknown, but residences of a month or more seem likely on at least two occasions. Added to the cost of maintaining a fashionable household in Madrid, the excursions increased the drain on his financial resources.

Penurious pretendientes were a fixture in Madrid and at the successive palaces visited by the royal entourage. For centuries the Crown had periodically attempted to rid the capital of their presence.[19] Philip II ordered the Cámara of Castile not to propose as candidates pretendientes who lingered at court.[20] His grandson, Philip IV, clarified that lingering meant spending more than thirty days a year at court.[21] A general effort by Charles IV in 1789 to cleanse the court of place seekers and temporary residents of all sorts was sufficiently threatening that the Conde de Vistaflorida immediately sought an exemption from it on the grounds that he had resided in Madrid for nearly nine years, had substantial investments there, and was engaged in "grave and urgent" affairs.[22] The failure of Charles IV's first attempt was revealed not only by José's lengthy stay but by the decision to issue still another order to expel pretendientes in 1799.[23]

The problem of subsistence without employment was one that spurred applicants to despaired importunings. Jacinto Calero, for example, sorrowfully beseeched the king in 1796 that his "destitution" was such that he could not continue his solicitations.[24] Already in 1795 the Conde de Vistaflorida had been expressing concern over his brother's expenditures.[25] Correctly fearing the worst, he wrote a will in April 1796 that stated that should he die while José was in Spain, his executors could provide his sibling with as much as 20,000 *pesos fuertes* and also pay his travel expenses to Peru.[26]

Family support was, indeed, often crucial for pretendientes who saw no point in leaving the capital without an appointment. And as one year extended to five, ten, and even more, the total bill could be staggering. While living on rents and interest was preferable, it was common for an aspirant to consume a large portion, if not all, of his patrimony and to contract debts as well. It should be noted, however, that creoles who lived off revenues from the New World enjoyed the benefit of relatively higher incomes than their peninsular counterparts. Prices on luxury items in Spain were less than in the colonies and thus Americans who brought pesos from Peru or Mexico found they bought more in Madrid than at home. But aspirants felt keenly the need for costly display and the temptations at court were numerous.[27] One suspects that few if any creole pretendientes returned home without empty pockets. Obtaining an appointment in such circumstances often became necessary to stave off financial disaster.

Baquíjano's first step as he renewed his campaign for office was to seek validation of his credentials as Lima's deputy. This alacrity reflected his awareness that the commission could bring access to influential persons, but unlike his counterpart of a century before, he was not escorted into the royal presence by numerous titled nobles and ranking officials. No Secretary of State greeted him at the palace door crying: "Enter City of Lima, His Majesty awaits you."[28] Instead, José had to maneuver arduously even to gain formal recognition as Lima's representative.

The city council had known that its right to send a representative would be questioned. Although a cédula of 1582 had granted it the privilege and Viceroy Gil had given Baquíjano a two-year license to fulfill the commission's responsibilities, the cabildo had anticipated objections. Consequently its deputy carried evidence to support its claim. When he beseeched Charles IV for recognition, Baquíjano presented a letter from the cabildo that asked his acceptance and included certified copies of his appointment, the 1582 cédula, and an account of the reception accorded the city's representative in the late seventeenth century.[29]

Baquíjano's petition was forwarded in late February 1794 to the Council of the Indies for its recommendation as to whether his claim should be recognized. Following its fiscal's advice, the

Council's second chamber firmly stated that the king should deny the pretension. It cited both a 1621 law that forbade any city in America to send a representative to Spain without a special license from the king, or at least from the viceroy or audiencia, and the recent cédula of 1778 that had ordered all bodies in the colonies to entrust their business to an authorized agent of the Indies.[30]

Informed of this decision, Baquíjano immediately protested that neither the letter nor the spirit of the 1621 law invalidated his request. Noting that the law stated that either the viceroy or the audiencia must grant permission, he argued that both authorities had approved his travel. Moreover, he pointed out that the law's intent had been to save cities the expense of sending representatives. Since he was paying his own way and receiving no compensation, this law was inapplicable. Furthermore, he argued, the later law did not nullify the 1582 cédula, for it did not specifically revoke the earlier concession and "everyone knew" that a general law did not overrule a particular concession unless explicitly stated. Finally, to deny the fiscal's assertion that Lima had not employed the privilege granted by the 1582 cédula, he provided certified testimony showing that the king had accepted and recognized Lima's representative in 1692.[31] To the Peruvian's relief, Charles IV accepted the arguments and granted the recognition he sought.[32]

The Council's recommendation to reject Baquíjano's claim continued a unanimous record of opposing his pretensions regardless of the issue. The king's decision to override its opinion, however, marked a turning point in José's fortunes. Although the nature of his business made contact with the Council unavoidable, he had learned that bypassing it afforded a better chance of success.

Baquíjano's remaining efforts as Lima's deputy demonstrated again that he could expect no support from the Council. Having opposed recognizing José as deputy, José Cistué, the long-serving fiscal for Peruvian affairs, promptly scuttled a speedy resolution to the request for a variety of honorific privileges that the deputy presented on behalf of Lima. In this case José's letters to the king and to Eugenio Llaguno y Amirola, Secretary for Grace and Justice, were fruitless. The Council followed Cistué's proposal and reissued as yet unanswered orders of 1781 that required the viceroy and Audiencia of Lima to inform the king whether he should concede the privileges sought.[33] The decision terminated Baquíjano's efforts for the city council and in 1795 he even considered returning to Lima.[34] His labors had brought no immediate results and not until 1802, years after the cabildo had appointed his successor, did Charles IV grant the city's requests.[35]

Baquíjano welcomed being replaced as Lima's deputy. Once he had been accepted as the city's representative in May 1794, he could gain little more from the commission and, although he petitioned on behalf of the city, he had certainly not extended himself. His more energetic successor, Tadeo Bravo de Rivero, even had to write the cabildo for a duplicate set of instructions because Baquíjano, who had been robbed of the one he had brought, had not bothered to request its replacement.[36] The fact was that Baquíjano was far more interested in furthering his own career than in serving the city, and, not surprisingly, he devoted his best efforts to obtaining personal benefits.

Baquíjano renewed his solicitations during a period when the Crown had relaxed its opposition to naming creoles to the American audiencias. In contrast to the twelve creoles named from 1751 to 1777 (12 percent), fifty Americans (31 percent) initiated their audiencia careers from 1778 to 1808. Although in 1793 José could not know that creole appointments would never return to the nadir of 1776–77, it was apparent to any American who faithfully read the *Gaceta de Madrid* and kept track of appointments that conditions had improved. From the time he submitted his final applications in 1776 until his return to Spain, creoles had received a much higher percentage of audiencia appointments (23 percent) than they had between 1774 and early 1776 (10 percent).[37]

While overall figures reveal plainly the improved creole access to the audiencias since 1777, it must be emphasized that the Crown's willingness to name Americans bore only a tenuous relationship to its willingness to name native sons. Thus while one of the two creoles appointed during Baquíjano's stay at court in the 1770s was a native son, only two other Americans began their service at home before his second sojourn in 1793. Moreover, since all three men were from the audiencia district of Bogotá, their appointments offered little encouragement to men from other regions.[38]

Baquíjano, however, was an optimist. The presence of any

native sons demonstrated that the Crown at least occasionally would yield to their entreaties. The increased number of creoles appointed, moreover, suggested that his petitions would be taken more seriously than before. Finally, the presence of native sons on Lima's court had been so permanent that it was difficult to imagine that it would be eliminated entirely.

When Baquíjano first decided to pursue a judicial career in 1772, seven native sons held seats on the Lima Audiencia. Although but half of the number that held appointments at his birth, those who remained provided visible proof that Peruvians of good family and legal training could reach the pinnacle of the American judiciary. The impact upon Baquíjano of having been a youth at a time when Peruvians enjoyed such prominence continued through the lean years that began when he was first at court.

Lima's Audiencia was the last New World court to experience the Crown's renewed emphasis upon naming peninsular ministers. Initiated after the termination of the sale of audiencia appointments in 1750, the policy was dramatically apparent in new appointments. Between 1751 and 1775 only nine of sixty-eight new men named to the American courts were creoles. For nearly a quarter century, Lima was sheltered from this reinvigoration of royal authority, partly because the presence of young supernumerary appointees in 1750 reduced the opportunities for new appointments. In addition, new ministers normally came from lesser courts in South America, courts heavily supplied with American ministers with personal bonds to Lima. Thus of four ministers who initiated their service from 1751 to 1773, only two were initially without ties to Lima; one of them eventually married Baquíjano's sister.[39]

A flurry of appointments in the mid- and late-1770s, however, shook the comfortable Peruvian influence on the court. Through normal attrition, the expansion of the court in 1776 by a regent, two oidores, and an alcalde del crimen, and the retirements and transfers that resulted from Areche and Jacot's reports, the Audiencia in 1779 had more peninsular than American judges for the first time in four decades. After a brief reversal in the 1780s, peninsular Spaniards held a majority of the positions until Peruvian independence.[40]

The decline in American strength, nonetheless, did not mean the elimination of native sons. Six limeños remained in 1779, a legacy of the Crown's financial embarrassment between 1740 and 1750. The Crown's particular reluctance to name native sons after mid-century, however, meant that limeños who served at home were due for further reduction; when Baquíjano was appointed in 1797 only one still sat on the court.[41]

Baquíjano had to contend not only with the Crown's general reluctance to name native sons, but also with its well-established policy of normally appointing only experienced ministers from lesser tribunals for advancement to Lima. Fellow pretendiente Miguel Díaz de Rivera stated the latter problem clearly when he appealed for support from Secretary Llaguno. The Cámara, Díaz complained, had not even accepted memorials from non-ministers when it prepared to propose candidates for vacant positions of oidor in Lima.[42] This policy reduced the possibility of a direct appointment to the viceregal court. Moreover, appointees to Lima customarily began their service as alcaldes del crimen, a post that frequently led to advancement as an oidor. Of the twenty-four alcaldes del crimen named to Lima between 1774 and 1797, fifteen had served as oidores and four as fiscales on minor audiencias.[43] While Díaz, a peninsular attorney in his mid-thirties, grudgingly accepted the Cámara's policy and requested consideration for vacancies left by men promoted to Lima or Mexico, Baquíjano showed no similar disposition.[44] Although he had applied for openings in Charcas and Chile as well as in Lima during his first trip, he directed his efforts during the second trip solely to initiating his judicial career in Lima. What had seemed reasonable as a young man in his twenties held no appeal as he entered his fifth decade. The unwillingness of the Cámara to consider seriously men without previous judicial experience, however, meant that his strategy had to focus most heavily on gaining an appointment by decree. This means alone offered the possibility of providing the office he sought.

While Baquíjano was at court in the 1770s, José de Gálvez had succeeded Julián de Arriaga as Secretary of State for the Indies. The new Secretary's responsibilities were even broader than his predecessor's had been. Simultaneously Gálvez served as Governor of the Council of the Indies and thus wielded a consolidated authority in matters of judicial patronage. Following his death in 1787, however, his portfolios were divided: Antonio Porlier was named Secretary for Grace and Justice; Antonio Valdés assumed control for war, finance, and commerce; and Francisco Moñino, brother of the powerful Conde de Floridablanca, received the governorship of the Council of the Indies.

This division of responsibilities was short-lived. As a final effort to centralize authority and create uniformity in administration, Charles IV ordered in 1790 the incorporation of Indies' affairs into the functional portfolios earlier established for Spain. In the ensuing shuffle, Antonio Porlier became Secretary of Grace and Justice for Spain and the Indies, one of five secretaries responsible for American as well as Spanish affairs.[45]

The reorganization of the central administration coincided with a reduced role by the Cámara in filling audiencia positions. During Baquíjano's first trip to Spain, the Cámara participated in nearly every audiencia appointment. Once the monarch ordered it to advertise a vacancy, the Cámara initiated the procedures that inexorably resulted in a consulta containing the names of three or more nominees, one of whom the king customarily appointed. Beginning in the late 1780s, however, the Cámara was increasingly bypassed in the appointment procedure. Moreover, the nearly automatic approval of one of its nominees for initial appointments that was visible in the mid-1770s no longer occurred two decades later.

Beginning in 1790 the use of decrees in making audiencia appointments became common for the first time since 1750. Although occasionally men named by decree were the same ones that the camaristas were preparing to recommend, more frequently appointees named by decree had successfully circumvented the Cámara. Appointment by decree, in short, was the naked use of royal patronage without prior recommendation by the Cámara or indeed against its recommendation. Within a single decree one or more men could be promoted or given initial appointments.

The use of *resultas* combined respect for traditional bureaucratic procedures as hallowed in the consulta while giving the monarch the freedom from the Cámara's recommendations that was implicit in the use of decrees. As employed here, the term *resulta* refers to an appointment made in the resolution of a consulta for a higher ranked position; thus the use of resultas was tied to reliance upon the ascenso. For example, the Cámara was ordered to propose candidates for the regency of Mexico in 1794 and its second place nominee, Baltázar Ladrón de Guevara, received the appointment. Without additional consultation, his post of oidor in Mexico was given to Miguel Christóbal de Irisarri. Irisarri's post of alcalde del crimen in Mexico in turn went to Joaquín de Mosquera, whose office of oidor in Bogotá was conferred upon the Conde de Torre Velarde.[46] The critical appointment among these four was that of the Conde de Torre Velarde who obtained the post in Bogotá, his initial audiencia appointment, without a preceding consulta. By the 1790s the use of resultas was sufficiently well established that pretendientes wrote memorials seeking "the resulta" that would be left when a senior position was filled.[47] Administrative files even carried such headings as "pretendientes to the 'resulta' of the Regency of Mexico."[48]

More than just interesting variations on appointment procedure, the three methods of consulta, decree, and resulta provided pretendientes with alternative routes for seeking office. The possibility of soliciting either Cámara support or backing from another source, for example one of the secretaries of state or the powerful favorite Manuel Godoy, made the options important to pretendientes. Miguel Aurioles de la Torre, for example, explicitly requested that he be named directly, without waiting for a recommendation from the Cámara.[49] For Baquíjano, too, the availability of an option to a nomination by the Cámara would prove invaluable.

Two weeks after he requested recognition as deputy for the Lima cabildo, Baquíjano initiated his personal solicitations. To accompany his requests he had available a relación de méritos so new that the ink was scarcely dry.[50] This recounted his accomplishments since the previous version of 1781 as well as the support given him by the viceroy of Peru, the Audiencia of Lima, and the University of San Marcos. A summary of his petitions from Madrid in late December and from Aranjuez the following month will indicate their basic theme and the kind of personal information included in them. The requests reveal, moreover, common techniques employed by pretendientes as they pursued honor and advancement.

Petitioners routinely sought to convince the king that he was obligated to grant their requests either for their own as yet unrewarded services or those of their relatives, or because precedents existed for rewards being conferred in analogous circumstances.

Baquíjano reminded Charles IV of everything that might promote his aims: ancestors in the royal service who had received
special commendation; his own steadfast pursuit of letters; such
rapid advancement in formal education that he had obtained the
doctorate at the age of fourteen; admission as a practicing attorney before the Audiencia of Lima; appointments as legal adviser by the Lima merchant guild and city council; and possession
of different university chairs. He recounted nearly three years of
interim service as protector of the Indians and fiscal del crimen of
the Audiencia, positions that he had served "without salary or any
recompense." Pointing out his importance in the Society of
Friends of the Country, he noted that the king had approved the
Mercurio. More recent signs of confidence were the appointments
as general deputy at court by the city council and university. In
sum, Baquíjano claimed twenty-eight years of faithful service to
the king and public and expressed an ardent desire to receive the
appropriate rewards: retirement as prima professor of sacred canons at San Marcos and an appointment as supernumerary oidor of
the Audiencia of Lima. Observing that Melchor de Santiago Concha held a cédula that exempted him from daily attendance, José
suggested that his appointment in a supernumerary capacity
would conveniently meet the Audiencia's need for a minister when
Santiago Concha was absent. He would even serve without salary
until he occupied the first vacant regular position.[51]

Even before these petitions received consideration, Baquíjano
submitted another so markedly different in tone that it deserves an
extended elaboration.[52] He switched from stressing personal qualifications and years of unrewarded service to advance the argument of the broader question of creoles serving on American
audiencias. His contention was simple and pointed: since Julián de
Arriaga's death in 1776, Peruvians had suffered discrimination
when they sought appointment to the Lima Audiencia. While Arriaga was Secretary for the Indies, officials had never listened to the
"unfounded maxim" that such appointments were poor policy
and had not prohibited the naming of creoles to American tribunals. Arriaga had proceeded with admirable impartiality and
rewarded worthy Americans with audiencia positions; his actions
were a glorious example that his successors should emulate.

The Marqués de Sonora (José de Gálvez), however, had altered
Arriaga's approach and convinced Charles III that naming creoles

was unwise. Yet, Baquíjano related, Sonora himself had known his innovation was ill-conceived and appointed four limeños as oidores in Lima.[53] His successor, the Marqués de Bajamar (Antonio Porlier), had continued the discrimination for personal reasons and applied it invariably against Peruvians.

This policy of exclusion, Baquíjano protested, was not only discriminatory, but unfounded in law. The *Recopilación* contained statutes specifying that natives were not only to be given judicial and administrative offices, but were to be the preferred candidates for positions in their home districts. Descendants of conquistadors were to receive special favor.

The marqueses of Sonora and Bajamar had mistreated the Lima tribunal in another way as well. By their appointments, three brothers-in-law held seats on the court, two serving as oidores and the third as a fiscal.[54] This delayed the administration of justice for the relatives could not hear the same case. Santiago Concha's exemption from attending the Audiencia's sessions further hampered the court. Consequently, the king's "unhappy vassals suffer retarded administration of justice and implore the [justice] of Your Excellency for remedy of these ills."

Baquíjano moved from his condemnation of the existing system to argue for his own appointment as a supernumerary oidor. Beyond summarizing the qualifications and unrewarded services detailed in earlier petitions, he particularly emphasized his ancestors who had been conquistadors, information directly related to the favorable law he had cited. In conclusion he requested a supernumerary position without salary, but with the right to fill the first vacant regular place of oidor.

The vituperative appeal to a golden age of American appointments under Arriaga was, in fact, ill-founded. No more than eight of sixty-four appointees to the American courts during Arriaga's tenure as Secretary from 1754 to 1776 were of New World birth and the number of native sons who held appointment dropped dramatically from nineteen in 1755 to nine at the close of 1775. Gálvez did not reverse his predecessor's policy, rather he brought it to a climax by the end of 1777.[55]

Baquíjano's real concern, however, was native-son appointments to Lima rather than general appointment policy. Ironically, the facts even in this restricted context did not support his contention that Gálvez had reversed Arriaga's policy. Only one native son joined the court during the Arriaga years, and special circumstances attended his naming.[56] In contrast, four limeños received appointments while Gálvez was Secretary. Although it was true that no Peruvians were named to their natal court during Porlier's tenure as Secretary, the brevity of his service made Baquíjano's bald indictment seem strained. Yet despite errors in his description of appointments made during the preceding four decades, Baquíjano had perceived correctly that native-son strength on the court had diminished. And it was against this decline that he had aimed his most vigorous protest.

Baquíjano's condemnation of the appointment policies followed by Sonora and Bajamar should be seen within the context of his own history of frustration as well as the political and administrative structure of the day. Long before he received a title of nobility, José de Gálvez had overseen the Peruvian's expulsion from the peninsula. This extraordinary action, of course, had dashed Baquíjano's hopes for an early appointment and stirred his resentment against the Secretary to such an extent that Areche later commented on it. The fiascos surrounding the *Eulogy* and the rectorship of San Marcos and the visible transformation of the Audiencia of Lima also had taken place during Gálvez's tenure. Understandably Baquíjano loathed the Secretary. His antipathy, moreover, was not unique. Several weeks after his death in June 1787, Gálvez's portfolios were divided between two secretaries, and the governorship of the Council of the Indies passed to a third man. The concentration of power he had enjoyed was at an end.

It was one thing to denounce a feared man who was safely dead, however, and quite another to attack a still exceedingly prominent politician. The facts regarding appointments that José included in his censure of Bajamar were correct, but beneath the surface lay an undercurrent of bitterness based at least in part upon more personal considerations. There can be little doubt that Baquíjano had known Bajamar personally in Lima before his first trip to Spain. At that time the Governor was the untitled Canarian Antonio de Porlier, a minister whose credit had been rescued by his American wife's dowry shortly before he advanced from service on the Audiencia of Charcas to the criminal fiscalía in Lima in 1766.[57] Porlier found service in Lima unsatisfying, however, and his desire to return to Spain was met in 1773 when Charles III named him a fiscal for the Council of the Indies. Designated Secretary of Grace and Justice for the Indies in 1787 and for both Spain and the Indies in the reorganization of 1790, Porlier had risen far from his modest origins. Baquíjano felt the Secretary's hand explicitly during the early 1790s. Three times Porlier peremptorily dismissed his requests for honors of oidor of Lima.[58] In consequence José felt no grief upon hearing that Charles IV had transferred the Secretary to the governorship of the Council of the Indies in July 1792.

Even if one concedes that Baquíjano had grounds for his antipathy toward Bajamar, the unanswered question is why he denounced him so strongly while he remained as Governor of the Council. Unfortunately one must employ conjecture rather than documentation when searching for an explanation. Since only through uncharacteristic naiveté could José have thought that Bajamar would not read his charges, one must discard the idea that he believed Secretary Llaguno would treat the letter confidentially. Conceivably the aspirant thought that Bajamar would oversee his appointment in order to disprove the charges, although this, too, proved a fantasy. It is more probable that Baquíjano had decided immediately to focus his efforts on obtaining an appointment by a decree that would originate in the Secretariat of Grace and Justice and thus had relegated the Cámara to little importance in his plans. By this interpretation the document was designed to inform Llaguno of past inequities and to challenge him to reverse the earlier policies. Regardless of José's motivation when he submitted his memorial, however, the immediate results demonstrated that a censorious approach was not the key to success.

When Antonio Porcel, the man who had evaluated the *Eulogy* nine years earlier, prepared to consider Baquíjano's several requests, he drew from the files material that would provide a more complete picture of the petitioner. The official professed ignorance about Arriaga's procedures in handling appointments, but confirmed Baquíjano's contention that no law in the *Recopilación* prohibited the designation of native sons. Statutes that restricted ministers' personal and economic ties to the district where they served and past experience with native sons, however, had led to a tradition of generally avoiding their appointment. But, as Baquíjano's examples revealed, native sons had been named and, "far from proving the aversion of the ministry toward creoles," their appointments showed "that it was not trying to exclude them absolutely, but to moderate their number." In sum,

Baquíjano's criticism was unjustified. He should notice the repeated examples of creoles promoted within the Audiencia of Lima and "ought to trust that his own merit rather than censure of the ministry would give him equal satisfaction." It seemed strange, moreover, that Baquíjano sought not only to initiate his career in a senior audiencia, but to begin as an oidor rather than as an alcalde del crimen. To put his recent petitions in perspective, Porcel summarized the correspondence concerning the Peruvian's expulsion from Spain in 1776, the unfavorable decision rendered on the "pernicious and subversive" contents of the *Eulogy*, and the three denials recently administered to his solicitations for honors of oidor. Llaguno agreed that José's petition was presumptuous and ordered that he direct his efforts to the Cámara.[59] For the nonce Baquíjano's gamble on the Secretariat for Grace and Justice had failed; both present policy and his past difficulties had weighed against him.

Rejection was never pleasant, but it was an experience that pretendientes knew frequently. As in the 1770s, repeated solicitation and flexibility were normal prerequisites for eventual success. Baquíjano knew the rules from his earlier efforts, and the adverse decision merely stimulated him to further efforts.

A week after the denial of his earlier petitions, José modified his strategy. Instead of seeking both retirement in his university chair and an appointment as a supernumerary oidor, he limited his request to retirement alone.[60] From his perspective retirement at this time offered the advantages of a partial salary and freedom from seeking additional licenses to remain in Spain rather than teaching. When Llaguno forwarded the request to Bajamar for an opinion three months later, however, the response was not surprising.[61]

The governor produced an opinion within ten days that left no doubt where he stood. If Baquíjano's request for retirement before he had completed the prescribed twenty years of service in a proprietary chair were honored, "it would be a very bad example for the future." Since the war had forced the professor to remain in Havana for nearly a year, his license should be extended one more year. As an incentive to get José back to Peru before his permit expired, the chair should be declared vacant should he not have reassumed it by the end of the extension.[62] Once more Bajamar had left Baquíjano empty-handed.

Before Llaguno accepted Bajamar's opinion, however, Baquíjano presented a statement from the University of San Marcos that buttressed his appeal. Faced with this additional information Llaguno ordered Viceroy Gil to provide a report and the file was temporarily closed.[63] In the summer of 1795 a lengthy document arrived from the University that strongly urged concession of the retirement Baquíjano sought. Viceroy Gil endorsed the request and in July Charles IV acceded.[64] As in the earlier question of recognizing Baquíjano as the representative of Lima, the secretariat again had proved critical for the success of his pretensions.

Baquíjano had more than one request under consideration most of the time he was in Spain. In early 1795 not only the question of retirement was pending, for he had memorialized the monarch to confer upon him the honors and seniority of oidor of Lima. He justified this request by an appeal to precedent. Since the four senior professors of civil and canon law at the universities of Alcalá and Valladolid had received the honors of ministers in the Chancellery of Valladolid, as a professor at the equally privileged University of San Marcos he should be so honored as well, particularly since he had not yet been rewarded for his service as an unpaid interim minister of Lima's Audiencia.[65]

No study has yet been made of the phenomenon, but it appears that the reign of Charles IV was marked by an openhanded bestowal of honors that far exceeded that of his father. Officeholders often sought the "honors" of the rank above their own. Thus legal advisers to intendants, for example, sought "honors" of oidor of the audiencia for their district. Long-serving audiencia ministers, in turn, requested honors of the Council of the Indies and the councilors themselves often sought honors of the Cámara.

Law professors too sought the additional prestige that accrued to men who possessed the honors of an audiencia position. And, as Baquíjano had discovered, the Crown had recently begun to consent to their petitions. In 1789, for example, Charles IV granted honors of alcalde del crimen of the Chancellery of Valladolid to Vicente Fernández de Ocampo, the prima professor of Spanish law (*derecho real*) at the University of Salamanca. In the following year Juan José Miranda y Salinas, the prima professor of law at the University of Valladolid received honors of oidor of the same chancellery. Two successive prima professors of canon law at Valladolid were similarly honored in the next three years.[66] By the time Baquíjano entered his request in January 1795, the precedents were well-established. This time his persistence was recompensed. On March 8, 1795, Charles IV granted him the honors of an alcalde del crimen of the Audiencia of Lima.[67]

A man with honors of an alcalde del crimen was entitled to wear the formal judicial robe and to sit with the criminal judges of the court at public ceremonies. His prestige rose accordingly and he had the pleasure of seeing his name printed with the other members of the tribunal in succeeding editions of the *Guía de Forasteros*, the annual handbook that listed high-ranking officials in Spain and America. Honors, however, did not imply a later appointment to an audiencia. Bartolomé de Casabuena, for example, held honors of alcalde del crimen for the Audiencia of Lima for twenty years without ever joining the court. Similarly Antonio de Boza never received a full appointment as alcalde. Indeed, Baquíjano, whose name followed those of Casabuena and Boza in the 1796 *Guía*, was the sole honorary alcalde of the decade who later advanced to an appointment on the court.[68]

Bedecked with his recent sign of royal favor, Baquíjano again showed flexibility when he sought to convince Charles IV to create a new position for him: a joint appointment as appeals judge for Lima's merchant guild and for Peru's mining tribunal. The proposal called for the replacement of the two annually named oidores who served the bodies by commission with one judge. Since the cases were complex, one qualified royal appointee who devoted his entire time to handling them could expedite justice far better than oidores with multiple responsibilities. Although the argument contained some merit, it brought no change to the established system.[69]

In 1795 Baquíjano took stock of his situation and, encouraged by his brother, seriously contemplated returning to Lima.[70] Heavy expenses had produced rewards that were modest at best when compared to his expectations. Instead of a supernumerary appointment to the civil chamber of the Lima Audiencia, he had received only honors of alcalde del crimen. Repeated attempts to obtain the position of appeals judge for the Lima merchant guild and the tribunal of mining had been completely fruitless. Invariably the Council of the Indies had opposed his pretensions. After nearly two years in Spain José, along with his friend Calero, was experiencing the frustration that some creole pretendientes had known for years. The Mexican José Arías de Villafañe, for example, had been an aspirant at court since Baquíjano's trip in the 1770s. Still without a position, Arías de Villafañe, although in his late fifties, was even willing to go to Manila.[71]

The recent appointment of fellow limeño the Conde de Torre Velarde as an oidor for the Audiencia of Bogotá again demonstrated that Americans could obtain audiencia posts, but the circumstances were hardly encouraging. The Conde had been in Spain since at least 1781 and over the years had been included on a number of consultas. When his fortune at last improved, however, it was not merit that brought the change. The Conde owed his appointment to "a pearl remarkable in size" that he presented to Queen María Luisa by the hand of Manuel Godoy, Duque de Alcudía. Soon after Godoy informed Secretary Llaguno that the queen had accepted the pearl and the Conde's pretensions should be considered, the aging limeño received his appointment.[72]

The appointment in September 1795 of a second native son to Chile's court in two years was perhaps what convinced Baquíjano that he should persevere. José Santiago Aldunate was also at court when he obtained an appointment as a supernumerary oidor without salary until he entered one of the four regular positions in Santiago.[73] The terms were precisely those that Baquíjano had sought since 1793. It is possible, too, that receiving word that limeño oidor José de Tagle had died in October encouraged him to further efforts.[74]

José's balance sheet, in any case, was actually far from unsatisfactory. He had been recognized as Lima's representative, gained retirement in his university chair, and obtained honors of alcalde del crimen. Having ceased his efforts for the Lima cabildo, he was now free to solicit personal advancement alone. For the remainder of his trip he single-mindedly pursued his goal.

From El Escorial in early November 1795, Baquíjano once more offered to serve as a supernumerary oidor of Lima without salary. This time he added the honors of alcalde del crimen and university retirement to previously mentioned qualifications. Again invoking precedent he related that previous kings had conferred special favors to two of Lima's representatives. One had been named an oidor; the other had received three corregimientos and an honorific position in the queen's service. Charles IV, however, did not share the pretendiente's conviction that he deserved similar treatment and yet again José left the palace disappointed.[75]

To understand Baquíjano's repeated offers to serve as a supernumerary oidor without salary requires a brief detour into the details of the organization of the Audiencia. The 1776 expansion of the American courts had left Lima with eighteen regular (*número*) judicial positions: a regent, ten oidores, five alcaldes del crimen, and two fiscales. The subsequent creation of the audiencias of Buenos Aires and Cuzco, however, reduced the Lima court to fifteen members and its salary budget from 95,000 pesos to 77,500 pesos.[76] These changes had two implications for Baquíjano. Fewer número positions meant fewer vacancies and thus a reduced possibility of even applying for a regular appointment. Moreover, the reduction of the regent's salary from 10,000 to 7,500 pesos revealed the Crown's concern to hold the line on salary expenditures.

From the time Baquíjano began his solicitation in December 1793 until late 1795 not a single vacancy appeared in the número ranks of Lima's court. Under this circumstance there was no alternative but to apply for a supernumerary appointment. And since no money was budgeted to pay for an extra minister, the post could carry no compensation. In fact the Crown's concern to confine total audiencia salaries was so great that when it retired an audiencia minister it frequently forced his replacement to bear the cost until a still more junior minister was named. For example, when Manuel del Campo y Rivas was named oidor of Guatemala in 1792, he received half salary since the other half went to the recently retired Sebastián de Talavera.[77] Similarly in 1794 José de Santiago Concha received only half salary as oidor in Chile while his father Melchor received the remainder as a retired oidor of Lima. Only upon his father's death would José receive full pay.[78]

The deaths of limeño José de Tagle and New Granadan Nicolás Vélez de Guevara in late 1795 provided Baquíjano with his first opportunity to apply for a número appointment. On July 22, 1796, Llaguno ordered the Cámara to recommend candidates for the vacancies and quickly Baquíjano submitted a relación and an application for both the vacancies and, more realistically, the "resultas." Routinely the camaristas considered the serving alcaldes del crimen and fiscales of Lima for promotion. In addition to these *ex oficio* candidates, eleven pretendientes submitted their applications. Nine of them already held número positions on other audiencias; Baquíjano and fellow American Pedro Vicente Cañete, the legal adviser to the intendent of Potosí and an honorary oidor of the Audiencia of Charcas, were the remaining aspirants. Since persons without audiencia appointments were excluded from all consideration, only the possession of honors of alcalde del crimen gained Baquíjano a place on the list of pretendientes.[79]

As he had discovered years before, Baquíjano found again how long a distance lay between the list of pretendientes and the consulta. The Cámara's unanimous selection for first place for Tagle's post was the senior alcalde del crimen. The votes for places two and three were divided among four serving ministers of other tribunals. For the vacancy left by Vélez de Guevara, the Cámara supported Manuel Pardo, another alcalde del crimen, and Fernando Quadrado, the senior oidor in Quito whom the Cámara had been ordered to consider. Although Cañete received two votes for third place, Baquíjano enjoyed no support. Charles IV resolved the consulta by designating alcalde del crimen Juan del Pino Manrique and Quadrado. For the vacancy Pino left of alcalde, he named Manuel María del Valle del Postigo, the legal adviser (asesor general) to the Viceroy of Peru.[80] The two appointments to oidor emphasized again how important the ascenso had become.

Even before the Cámara provided consultas for the vacancies left by Tagle and Vélez de Guevara, word reached Spain that the Marqués de Corpa, a septuagenarian limeño oidor who had been named to the court as a supernumerary alcalde del crimen nearly a half century before, had died at last. Baquíjano responded from San Ildefonso to this latest piece of news with a memorial to Charles IV. Following the usual summary of his accomplishments, the pretendiente focused on royal policy toward native-son appointments. He would already have been named to the court, he wishfully avowed, had the monarch not continued his father's desire to make the number of American and peninsular ministers more equal. Since the number of native sons on Lima's court had declined so precipituously in the preceding twenty years that only one remained, it was appropriate, Baquíjano claimed, that he be named to fill one of the three recent vacancies.[81] This imaginative interpretation of previous appointment policy failed completely. Faced with the appointments of two candidates recommended by the Cámara, Baquíjano quickly applied for the third vacancy of oidor "or the resulta of alcalde."[82]

José fared no better in the final consulta than he had before. The camaristas headed by the Marqués de Bajamar unanimously supported the senior alcalde del crimen of Lima, Domingo Arnáiz de las Revillas, for first place and divided their votes for the second and third places among five other candidates. Although his status as an honorary alcalde del crimen had once more gotten his name upon the list of pretendientes, Baquíjano received no votes for the position. The advancement of an experienced oidor from the Audiencia of Charcas to the "resulta of alcalde" reiterated the extent to which the ascenso ruled all but initial appointments to American courts at this time.[83] Having been one of but five pretendientes not to have received a single vote on any of the three consultas, the lesson for Baquíjano was harsh but unmistakable—his appointment to Lima could come only from outside the Cámara.

In February 1797, Baquíjano's exertions at last brought an appointment as a número alcalde del crimen. Appropriately his naming enabled another American, Tomás González Calderón, to join his home court as well. González, the son of a wealthy peninsular merchant in Mexico, had been named an oidor in Guatemala in 1775 after Secretary Arriaga had ordered the Cámara to consider him "in attention to his father's services," services that had benefited the Crown more than one million pesos.[84] González found the climate of Guatemala intolerable, however, and eventually sought a transfer to a more pleasant region. When the Crown responded in 1788 by moving him to Lima, this too was unsatisfactory and the new alcalde del crimen assumed his post only with great reluctance. Although promoted to oidor in 1792, he continued to remind the Crown of his father's financial services and to request a transfer to Mexico. On January 10, 1797, his nephew petitioned for González's appointment as a supernumerary oidor in Mexico with salary until one of the ten authorized positions became vacant.[85] This request finally produced the desired result.

The transfer of González to the court in Mexico City had two implications. The Crown would incur an expense of five thousand pesos if it paid both him and a replacement in Lima. Not to replace him, on the other hand, would leave the Lima court under-staffed. Since neither alternative was desirable, the availability of Baquíjano provided a convenient solution.

Baquíjano had offered several times to serve on Lima's court as a supernumerary oidor without pay until a regular position became vacant. Faced with González's petition, Secretary Llaguno recalled these offers and found his answer. On February 12, Charles IV agreed to the transfer that González sought.[86] A decree of February 19 formalized this decision as well as naming Manuel Pardo, the senior alcalde del crimen, to the resulting vacancy. The last phrase of the decision bore the news Baquíjano awaited. "And for the resulta of alcalde del crimen that he [Pardo] has in the same audiencia, the honorary alcalde Don Joseph de Baquíjano y Carrillo, who will serve it without salary until [González] Calderón enters a número position in Mexico."[87]

José's appointment confirmed that he had been correct to seek support from persons other than camaristas. It is important to recognize, however, that candidates named by decree were not necessarily less qualified than those who had been proposed on consultas. That Baquíjano had been persistently pushing his own case and had the luck to be at court when González's petition was granted does not lessen his credentials. Indeed, José was arguably one of the most qualified men to receive his first audiencia appointment during the 1790s. Yet many able pretendientes never succeeded. And so a question lingers. Was it merit or money that turned the scales in his favor?

Beyond dispute Baquíjano's family and professional credentials were solid. His father's wealth and title and the history of service for the Crown by his mother's family combined to give José a social background that few of his competitors could surpass. Higher degrees in canon law from the University of San Marcos and approval to practice law before the Audiencia of Lima provided acceptable qualifications for entry into a university or bureaucratic career, particularly since his early attainment of them testified to unusual intellectual abilities. Service as a legal adviser for both the city of Lima and the Lima merchant guild had given him breadth, while employment as interim protector of the Indians and fiscal del crimen had provided experience in the Audiencia's procedures. Nearly fifteen years as a professor at San Marcos and especially elevation to the prima chair of canon law and the responsibility to teach Spanish law confirmed his abilities in the traditional academic road to an audiencia appointment. By teaching Spanish law, moreover, he belonged to a group of professors that was increasingly benefiting from royal consideration.[88] Activities in Lima's Society of Friends of the Country and the *Mercurio peruano* highlighted his interest in contemporary intellectual pursuits while commissions as general deputy for the Lima cabildo and for San Marcos were additional signs of confidence in his abilities. Finally, the possession of honors of alcalde del crimen for Lima's audiencia set him apart from all other pretendientes in 1797. Merit alone clearly could justify his appointment.

Years later, however, an anonymous critic alleged that Baquíjano had bought his appointment.[89] Since the Conde de Torre Velarde owed his appointment to a pearl, the possibility cannot be dismissed without consideration that Baquíjano also had bribed the queen, Godoy, or perhaps other highly influential persons.

The only available evidence that supports the anonymous charge is the fact that Baquíjano left Spain substantially in debt.[90] His obligations, however, dated after his appointment as an alcalde del crimen. Sketchy evidence, moreover, suggests that Baquíjano lacked the resources at the time he was named to provide a bribe large enough to be noticeable. In fact, unlike some aspirants, he apparently did not even provide a *donativo* for the war effort.[91] Finally, no evidence has been found that even suggests that the Crown was selling audiencia appointments to raise cash in the 1790s. On the contrary, on the advice of the Cámara the Crown rejected two creoles who made offers.[92]

On the basis of current evidence, one must conclude that Baquíjano's merit rather than financial service to the Crown or an extraordinary bribe to a venal official brought his appointment. At the same time, it is worth recalling Porcel's comment that royal policy was not to exclude creoles but to moderate their number. With control over the courts at an acceptable level, the Crown could afford to name Baquíjano to Lima and González Calderón to Mexico. Such appointments were popular in the colonies and, as long as they were limited in number, offered no threat to royal authority.

Comparing Baquíjano's appointment with the other twenty-one

made to new men from the time he had arrived in Spain further highlights the qualifications and features he shared with other appointees. American birth placed José with the minority of seven appointees. Since two were native sons, however, his appointment was rare but not unique. At age forty-five, the limeño was about average for the recent American appointees while a decade older than the average peninsular named. His doctorate placed him with the minority of total appointees, but a majority of the creoles. More importantly, six of the twenty-one men had previously taught in a university, while seven had previous permanent letrado positions in the American bureaucracy. Only three of the men, however, had honors of an audiencia position before their appointments and, unlike Baquíjano, each had received the honors for government rather than university service. The single *caballero* of the Order of Charles III among the twenty-one men was a young relative of the Marqués de Bajamar.[93]

Comparing Baquíjano to the other new appointees is only part of the picture, however. His initial appointment to Lima immediately placed him above nineteen of the twenty-one men. The only other men who began their service on the viceregal tribunals of Lima or Mexico were the two viceregal advisers Rafael Bachiller de Mena and Manuel María de Valle del Postigo. They, like Baquíjano, entered the courts as alcaldes del crimen.

It is within the context of recent appointments of alcaldes del crimen in Lima that Baquíjano's accomplishment can best be judged. From the time he left Spain at the close of 1776 until his appointment in 1797, the Crown selected sixteen alcaldes. Thirteen of this group had experience on other courts, one had been the legal adviser to a viceroy, and another had been part of the general visita to Peru. Only one alcalde, Galician Manuel Pardo, had no previous American experience. The mean age of the alcaldes was thirty-nine years with the youngest appointee twenty-nine and the oldest, forty-eight. By skipping the normal apprenticeship on a lesser court, Baquíjano found himself going to Lima's tribunal at an age not significantly older than his colleagues had been when named.[94]

The most notable feature of Baquíjano's appointment, of course, was that he was a native son, the first named to Lima's court in twenty years and the only one since 1750 who had not purchased his initial audiencia appointment. In a broader perspective, his appointment made him one of only eleven native sons named directly to their home courts between 1751 and 1808.[95]

Baquíjano's title of office, dated March 22, 1797, contained the standard provision that within two months of the date he was to be at a Spanish port prepared to embark for his destination. Failure to do so, the title read, would result in the position being declared vacant.[96] The king's intention in limiting the time new appointees could remain at court was not only to maintain a full complement of officials in the New World, but also to preclude the kind of renewed solicitation to which Baquíjano promptly devoted himself.

Since conflict between Spain and England hindered transatlantic crossings, twice in 1797 José obtained extensions to remain at court. [97] During the time of the first reprieve, he sought to add a potentially lucrative commission to his post of alcalde. In response to a rumor that the king had decided to establish a royal lottery in Lima, José promptly requested to be named its judge, a position that would normally be given to an oidor. Although his gambling experience perhaps gave him exceptional qualifications for the post, this time ambition had led him astray. Charles had not established a lottery in Peru nor, despite Baquíjano's charge that the ministers who currently served as lottery judges by commission were incompetent and negligent, did he name the limeño to replace them. Learning that the viceroy customarily rewarded oidores with the commissions, the king continued this time-honored procedure.[98]

Frustrated but still inventive, José used the time of the second extension to renew his earlier pretension to become an appeals judge for both the Lima merchant guild and Peru's mining tribunal. The influence of Francisco Saavedra, Secretary for the Royal Exchequer, served him well, and Charles conferred the requested appointment.[99] Now that he was an alcalde del crimen, however, Baquíjano buried his 1795 argument that an oidor would be unable to serve adequately both the Audiencia and the commission. Instead, he used his new commission as a lever in a final effort to secure honors and seniority of oidor in Lima.

Baquíjano's request represented a complete rejection of his earlier contention that the responsibilities of the appeals judge for the merchant guild and mining tribunal were so complex and taxing that they required a magistrate's undivided attention. Amid the usual self-adulation and claims of important service and devotion to the king, he now argued shamelessly that since he held positions that previously had been served by oidores, he should at least be given honors of oidor with seniority starting at once and the right to fill the first vacancy.[100]

Gaspar de Jovellanos, the noted author and reformer who had replaced Llaguno as Secretary for Grace and Justice in November 1797, forwarded Baquíjano's latest petition to the Cámara of the Indies for its opinion.[101] Although Jovellanos has been portrayed as one of Baquíjano's influential patrons, this episode displayed no sign of such support.[102] As in every previous matter concerning the vociferous Peruvian, opposition to the request surfaced at once. In a devastating analysis later supported by the Cámara, the fiscal noted Baquíjano's powerful family connections in Peru, the sufficient importance of his post of appeals judge, his apparent desire to push ahead of the presently serving alcaldes, and finally that Charles IV had already rewarded his services adequately. Baquíjano, he noted, was claiming as services the rewards the king had previously granted him.[103]

Baquíjano learned of the fiscal's objections before the Cámara considered them and immediately protested to Jovellanos. Angrily he impugned the fiscal's presentation. Cistué, he contended, had misinterpreted the relevant statues, altered facts to make him look ambitious, and generally misrepresented the petition.[104]

This latest and largely unjustified outburst sent an official of the Secretariat back to Baquíjano's file. Carefully the bureaucrat summarized the alcalde's expulsion from Spain in the 1770s, the consequences of the *Eulogy* in the 1780s, and the more recent accusations of discrimination and mishandling of appointments to the Audiencia of Lima.[105] Before the Secretary presented a recommendation to the king, however, he sought an evaluation by camarista Jorge Escobedo, the former visitor general of Peru.[106] The assignment could not have been a pleasant one for Escobedo. He had known José in Lima, served with his brother-in-law on the Audiencia of Charcas, and since 1795 had owed a substantial debt to his brother the Conde de Vistaflorida.[107] To his credit, however, Escobedo did not allow these personal relationships to obscure the weakness of Baquíjano's case. In a moderately toned report the camarista supported the fiscal's major contentions.[108] Charles IV confirmed the recommended denial of Baquíjano's pretension and the alcalde at last prepared to depart from Madrid.[109] In October he obtained a passport and six months later he reached Cádiz.[110]

As his debts mounted, Baquíjano spent a year awaiting an opportunity to sail home. Although he finally embarked aboard *La Providencia* on April 3, 1800, the British seized the entire Spanish convoy, temporarily imprisoned him, and sequestered his valuable library and personal possessions.[111] Returned to Cádiz once more, Baquíjano initiated a round of petitions in which he sought the commencement of his salary as alcalde and the first vacant position of oidor in Lima. The king, he observed hopefully, had been generous to other ministers trapped in similar circumstances.[112] Repeatedly he instructed his agent in Madrid how best to secure his salary. The treasury, however, was suffering under the unrelenting burden of prolonged war and the uncertain timing of remissions from the Americas. In this setting Baquíjano's pleas did not bring him half-pay until January 1802, long after González Calderón had moved into a regular seat as oidor in Mexico.[113] The assured early advancement as oidor that Baquíjano had sought was never forthcoming.

Baquíjano's second detention in epidemic-ridden Cádiz continued until early 1802. At last, however, he found passage on the warship *Rufina* and again set sail for America.[114] He reached Lima at mid-year and on July 1 the city provided fiestas in honor of his return. A poetic eulogy that accompanied the gala event rhapsodized that the new criminal judge, Lima's son and now her protector, was a man of great sentiments and noble spirit who had spread Peru's fame widely.[115] A week later Baquíjano informed the Secretary of Grace and Justice that he had officially assumed his seat on the Audiencia.[116] Success had culminated the long, tortuous struggle to reach the tribunal.

The fiestas that honored Baquíjano's return to Lima revealed both respect for his accomplishments and, more importantly, the city's pride that another native son had joined the Audiencia. José was not only the first new native son in two decades, but also just the sixth Peruvian named to any American tribunal since the middle of the eighteenth century. When one considers that seventy-three had been named between 1687 and 1750, his appointment gains additional significance.[117]

Baquíjano's success highlighted the difficulty native sons experienced in gaining appointment in the second half of the eighteenth century. His family's economic and social standing, his intellectual gifts and attainments, and a youth spent in a unique environment for stimulating bureaucratic ambition made him expect appointment to the Lima court. Yet the way was long and strewn with unanticipated hurdles. Unlike numerous earlier limeños who had secured their posts while in their twenties, Baquíjano was in his mid-forties when named and over fifty when he finally assumed office. The difficulties he faced despite his advantages crushed men of lesser means and persistence; the frustration he voiced at repeated failure reflected a more general concern.

From New Granada, New Spain, and Peru appeared petitions that called for native-son appointments after 1770.[118] Together they formed an empire-wide response to the Crown's reinvigorated policy of limiting American participation in general and native-son participitation in particular on the New World tribunals. Nowhere was the protest more anguished than in Lima. José's plea for his own appointment mirrored the city council's instructions that he seek a quota for native sons.[119] Both José and the Lima cabildo sought a return to an earlier appointment policy. Despite the discrimination that the sale of appointments to native sons before 1750 had implied, prominent Peruvians looked back nostalgically to the local influence in government that they had provided for a century.

6

Anticlimax

After nearly five years of service as alcalde del crimen, on April 2, 1807, Baquíjano assumed a seat as oidor on Lima's Audiencia.[1] This advancement was free from the plaintive solicitation that had preceded his earlier appointment. Acting upon the Cámara's recommendation for the vacant regency in Chile in September 1806, Charles IV named an oidor of Lima and for the resulta routinely appointed José, the senior alcalde.[2] Thirty-five years after deciding to pursue a judicial career, the new oidor had finally realized his ambition. The attainment was more impressive than he could have originally anticipated, for in his youth limeños had comprised over half of the court; in 1807 he was the tribunal's single native son.

The uniqueness of Baquíjano's position reflected the Crown's success in controlling audiencia appointments during his lifetime. Faced with numerous native sons in Lima and elsewhere in 1750 as a consequence of sales, it had deliberately named few subsequently as part of a general appointment policy of favoring peninsulares for high office. After earlier intermittent protest, Americans vented their hostility to this policy in chorus following Napoleon's invasion of Spain and the abdications of Charles IV and Ferdinand VII in 1808.

The well-known list of American grievances presented to the Cortes of Cádiz in December 1810 explicitly called for native sons to receive half of all New World positions.[3] Although the Cortes never acceded, one consequence of such pressure in the midst of imperial disruption was an unprecedented effort to recruit Americans for highly responsible positions in Spain. Baquíjano's service as oidor quickly identified him as a logical candidate for one of the six American places on the new Council of State.

The Cortes overwhelmingly elected Baquíjano to the Council on February 4, 1812.[4] The selection was appropriate for he was a native son and the ranking creole on Lima's Audiencia. As a limeño with substantial government experience, he could provide detailed knowledge of Peruvian affairs. Moreover, naming the titled creole (he became the third Conde de Vistaflorida in 1809) would certainly be well-received in the viceroyalty for he had been the most popular candidate in its elections for deputy to the Junta Central in 1809.[5] His election also complemented superbly the previous choice of Melchor de Foncerrada, a Mexican who also served as oidor in his home audiencia.

Baquíjano's election not only made sense politically, but was justified by the quality of his service during the preceding decade. As an alcalde he had performed the normal judicial duties, hearing cases that varied from assault to homicide to female impersonation. At one point the Viceroy, the Marqués de Avilés, commissioned him to prevent the docking and unloading of a ship from Cádiz feared contaminated with the plague and to oversee fumigation of the ship, its cargo, and its crew. Additionally he served as the government's overseer for the University of San Marcos from 1804 to 1812. Once named oidor, Baquíjano received more commissions from Viceroy José Fernando Abascal. Among other responsibilities, he became protector of the Royal Convictory of San Carlos, president of the sanitation committee, a member of the committee that watched over the government pension system in Lima, and promoter of the patriotic subscription to support wartime expenses. Throughout his years on the court he continued as appeals judge for the Lima merchant guild and the mining tribunal.[6]

The judge's service satisfied nearly everyone.[7] Lima citizens praised his ability to temper justice with clemency.[8] Abascal wrote confidentially in 1808 that, although Baquíjano was "passionately fond of gambling," he had " a great deal of talent, literature, and instruction," and was "honest, just, and laborious."[9] The special representative from the Junta Central related the following year that Baquíjano was one of only four ministers he considered "excellent," the remainder being either indolent or excessively involved with local business interests.[10]

Baquíjano learned of his appointment to the Council of State on June 28, 1812.[11] Unaware until then of the Council's creation, Lima's inhabitants were jubilant upon receiving the news and celebrated for days.[12] The recipient's own reaction was mixed and he accepted the unsolicited honor only on August 8.[13]

Baquíjano had hesitated for several reasons. Spain's condition was clearly precarious and whether the government at Cádiz could successfully resist the French was questionable. The prospect of a long, difficult trip held little appeal to the aging minister, particularly since the new position required him to abandon a comfortable life as a rich, respected judge and local noble serving at home. In Spain he would receive uncertain appreciation for his efforts while facing severe winters and torrid summers. The cold weather, moreover, would aggravate his gout. Since the ailment forced him to remain abed until late each morning, he was uncertain that he could serve the Council satisfactorily. Learning that it would meet only three days a week at ten o'clock in the morning, however, relieved his worries and he resolved to sacrifice personal comfort in order to serve the king.[14] Yet selfless loyalty alone did not determine his final decision. Due to the deaths of several executors, the Conde envisioned gaining control over his deceased brother's immense fortune in Spain, a potential gain he considered worth the loss of a secure income in Lima and the expense of escorted travel.[15]

The Conde and his secretary finally left Callao in May 1813.[16] Following a warm welcome in Panama, they sailed toward Jamaica, looking for English protection from the insurgent corsairs of Cartagena.[17] After an extended, trying, and costly voyage, they finally reached Cádiz on January 16, 1814.[18] Discomfort from gout and difficulty in obtaining suitable transport delayed his arrival in Madrid and not until March 14 did the Conde swear the oath of his new office.[19] Ten days later Ferdinand VII returned to Spanish soil. On May 4 he abrogated the Constitution of 1812 and a month later disbanded the Council of State and left Baquíjano without a position.[20]

Although he provided occasional advice subsequently, Baquíjano's government service effectively ended with the Council's abolition.[21] When Ferdinand VII reestablished the Council of the Indies on July 2, 1814 and named him to one of the places designated for Americans, the aged Peruvian declined. Recounting his long and faithful service, he protested that continuing bad health made it impossible to serve. As requested, Ferdinand accepted the renunciation.[22]

Baquíjano's decision did not mean he wanted to return to Lima empty-handed. On October 4, 1814, he petitioned for honors of Councilor of State and appointment as superintendent of Jesuit properties for Peru. Ten days later Ferdinand granted him a "key of gentleman of the [king's] chamber, with entrance," but denied the desired honors and position.[23]

With customary persistence, Baquíjano personally presented a memorial to the king the following January.[24] The contents are unknown, but probably he again sought honors of the Council of State and the superintendency of Jesuit properties, requests he repeated in February. Finally he received the long-sought honors, and it seemed that an appointment as subdelegate of Jesuit properties for Peru was imminent.[25] But on August 5, 1815, Ferdinand refused to sign the decree, noting that the revenues of the Jesuit properties had already been placed in order and thus the position was unnecessary.[26]

Two months later Baquíjano reached Seville, where he had been confined by a royal order that apparently resulted from intrigue surrounding the contested control over his brother's estate.[27] Vigorous correspondence with his agent in Madrid over possession of the inheritance brought no reversal before his death in Seville on January 24, 1817.[28]

Baquíjano died loyal to the Spanish monarchy at a time when the colonies were rife with rebellion. He was not blind to the monarchy's shortcomings, but argued for accommodation and reform, not revolution. The appointment of more native sons to audiencias and all other institutions he considered an important measure for effecting reconciliation. His own experience, of course, had intensified his concern in this area. Although ultimately successful, his course had been fraught with difficulties, difficulties that many Americans had undergone to no avail.

José Baquíjano devoted twenty-five years to securing an appointment to the Audiencia of Lima, but then served scarcely a decade. Unlike native sons Antonio de Querejazu and José de Tagle Bracho, who were judges at the time of his birth and still held their posts as the 1790s opened, Baquíjano had comparatively little time to savor his triumph. In monetary terms, the salary of a decade was far less than his expenditures during the two trips he made to Spain in quest of his goal.

The brevity of his tenure, however, should not obscure the fact that contemporaries considered José's appointment alone ample cause for celebration. And well they might, given the uncommonness of native-son appointments in the years after 1750. In contrast to Pedro Vázquez de Noboa, Antonio Alvarez de Ron, Jacinto Muñoz Calero, and numerous other frustrated limeño pretendientes, Baquíjano had been successful. As only the sixth Peruvian to obtain an initial audiencia appointment since 1750, and the first since then to join·the Lima court without prior experience on a lesser tribunal, his naming distinguished him from his peers.

Baquíjano's appointment as an alcalde del crimen in 1797 was unusual from both imperial and Peruvian perspectives. His career too had distinctive features, scars left by a strong and ambitious personality. Within the uniqueness of his individual case, however, one can discover features common to pretendientes as a group as well as appreciate the importance of alterations in policy and personnel at the highest ranks of government.

José enjoyed the inestimable advantage of being born into a wealthy and prominent family. Like most Americans, he had a maternal tie to the region of his birth. The peninsular origin of his father, however, placed him among "first-generation" creoles, a group distinguished by its avidity for success. Although his academic record was extraordinary, like nearly every formally educated creole Baquíjano received degrees from a New World university. Subsequent training enabled him to qualify as an attorney, a routine step for men who aspired to high judicial office.

Baquíjano decided to pursue an Audiencia appointment even before his age made him eligible. In regard to this requisite, as in the number of native sons, the Lima environment had misled him. By the time he reached court in 1773, the Crown had been requiring more stringent professional standards for over two decades. Largely because of the earlier sale of appointments and attendant entry of young limeños into the Audiencia, Peruvians did not appreciate how singular its composition was. At any given time, however, personal solicitation increased the odds of gaining an office.

Baquíjano was one of a steady trickle of Americans who sailed to Spain to seek appointment. As his fellow pretendientes, he soon discovered that the pursuit was time-consuming and costly and the goal elusive. In contrast to other office seekers, however, neither an appointment nor personal choice determined his departure. In a measure as rare as it was devastating, Charles III expelled José from Spain and ordered him to return to Peru.

Failure to obtain an office joined this ignominious expulsion in emphasizing the need to establish solid professional credentials based upon public service as a base for future solicitation. Pretendientes for audiencia appointments normally followed the paths of university or government service and Baquíjano, as many other aspirants, engaged in both. Aided by Viceroy Guirior's favor, he became second professor of civil law and an interim protector of the Indians and fiscal of the Audiencia. His ascent visibly underway, he prepared to resume his efforts to secure an office.

Ironically, the very university and government activities that buoyed his hopes also led to a major reversal of his fortunes. Selected by the rector of San Marcos to eulogize Viceroy Jáuregui, he aroused Visitor General Areche's ire as a result of the oration's content, the site of its delivery, and his government position. The proscription of the *Eulogy* and defeats for the university rectorship and first chair of civil law engraved Baquíjano's name as a trouble-maker in the minds of camaristas and bureaucrats at court and removed the Cámara as a potential source for support.

The replacement of Viceroy Croix by Gil in 1790 and the sudden improvement in José's record is a reminder of the value that viceregal favor could hold for pretendientes. Less than three years after Gil's arrival, Baquíjano thought his newly invigorated vita justified a return to Spain. Within the altered political setting he largely focused his solicitations on the Secretary for Grace and Justice. Having thoughtfully obtained a commission as the Lima city council's representative, he proceeded to gain entry to the court, entry undoubtedly facilitated by his brother's financial and personal ties in Madrid. Artfully building upon each favor received, José finally won the office he had coveted so long. Persistence, presence at court, a willingness to serve initially without compensation, and a relación de méritos that carefully omitted reference to the stains in his past combined to make him an acceptable solution to the problem raised by González Calderón's desire to transfer from Lima to Mexico City. José, as scores of other pretendientes, had correctly perceived that in the 1790s the road to success led through the Secretary not the Cámara.

The tortuous course of Baquíjano's career reveals clearly, almost pathetically, both the intensity with which Americans sought office and the regional focus of their efforts. His life represents the extent to which the seemingly boundless desire for signs of prominence and preeminence, high position, and honorific splendor permeated creole society. For Americans with modest resources, however, the time and money Baquíjano committed to his quarter-century campaign were unthinkable. And it was their ranks that more quickly produced insurgents in the years after 1808.

APPENDIX A

Native Sons Appointed to the Audiencia
of Lima, 1687-1750

This appendix provides professional, family, and appointment information about the thirty-eight native sons named to the Audiencia of Lima from 1687 to 1750.

Explanation of Categories and Abbreviations:

1. Post: Initial post received on the Audiencia of Lima. Abbreviations are:

   AC: alcalde del crimen
   AF: alcalde del crimen futurario
   AX: alcalde del crimen supernumerario
   FR: fiscal del crimen
   OD: oidor
   OF: oidor futurario
   OS: oidor supernumerario

2. Purchase: A dollar sign ($) indicates that the initial post was purchased.

3. Year: Year in which the royal title (título) of office was issued. Successive appointees within each year are listed in order by month and day of the title.

129

4. Travel: An asterisk indicates that the appointee was in Spain prior to receiving his initial audiencia appointment. A blank indicates that no evidence has been found for such travel.

5. Name: Common spelling has been employed. Titles of nobility are included to facilitate identification even if not held at the date of appointment.

6. First Generation Creole: *X* means that one or more of an appointee's parents had been born in Spain. *N* means that neither parent had been born in Spain. *?* indicates inadequate evidence to determine parents' place of birth.

7. Age: Approximate age at the time of appointment to the Audiencia of Lima.

8. University: University affiliation is listed regardless of whether attendance, receipt of a degree, or incorporation of a degree was involved. Abbreviations employed are *AL:* Alcalá de Henares; *LI:* Lima (University of San Marcos); *SA:* Salamanca; *SI:* Siguenza.

9. Colegio: *SF* represents membership in the Colegio of San Felipe in Lima; *SM* represents attendance at the Colegio of San Martín in Lima.

10. Degree: The degree listed is the highest for which reference has been found. *D:* doctorate; *L:* licentiate; *B:* bachelor.

11. Abogado: Tribunals to which a man had been admitted to practice law. *LI:* Lima; *RC:* Royal Councils.

12. Previous Post: The upper letters indicate the post, the lower ones the audiencia district of service. Abbreviations are: (upper) *AG:* asesor general; *FI:* fiscal; *FR:* fiscal del crimen; *OD:* oidor; *PI:* protector of the Indians; *PR:* president; *X-:* service in a non-audiencia position. (lower) *CH:* Chile; *CS:* Charcas; *LI:* Lima; *SF:* Santa Fe de Bogotá.

13. University Service: *CA:* catedrático (professor); *OP:* opositor; *SU:* substitute.

14. Fathers: The following abbreviations are employed. to indicate employment and membership in military orders:

   AB: position in the royal bureaucracy in America, e.g., contador, corregidor
   AL: knight of the Order of Alcántara
   CA: knight of the Order of Calatrava
   FI: fiscal of an audiencia

HM: military rank of colonel, maestre de campo, or general
M: merchant (wholesale)
OD: oidor
PR: president of an audiencia
SA: knight of the Order of Santiago
XX: minor or local office in Spain or America (e.g., alcalde
        ordinario) or military rank below colonel

APPENDIX A

Native Sons Appointed to the Audiencia of Lima 1687–1750[1]

Post	Purchase	Year	Travel	Name	First Generation Creole	Age	University	Colegio	Degree	Abogado	Previous Post	University Service	Fathers
AC	$	1687		NUÑEZ de SANABRIA, Miguel	X	42	LI	SM	D		AG LI	CA	XX
FR		1688	*	GARCIA de SALAZAR, Sancho	X	50	LI	SM	D	LI	OD CH	CA	OD
FR		1688	*	JARAVA y BUITRON, Francisco	?		LI	SF	L		FI CS		AB
FR		1690	*	VASQUEZ de VELASCO, Pablo	X	39	LI	SM	L		FR CH		PR
AF	$	1693	*	PEREZ de URQUIZU, Juan de	X	38			D	LI			XX
AF	$	1693	*	SANTIAGO CONCHA, José de (Marqués de Casa Concha)	X	26	LI SA	SM	L	LI	X- LI	SU	AB
OF	$	1694		PAREDES y ARMENDARIZ, Nicolás de	N	20	LI SA	SM	D			OP	FI
AX	$	1699	*	VASQUEZ de VELASCO, Pedro	N	31	LI	SM	L				HM
AX	$	1699	*	ARANBURU y MUÑOZ, Vicente de	X	42	LI	SM	L	RC		OP	AB
AF	$	1699		ROJAS y ACEVEDO, Francisco	N	48	LI	SM	D		AG LI		FI

OS	$		1700	VILLAVICENCIO y CISNEROS, Pedro de	?	36	LI	SM	L	LI			HM
OS	$		1704	CANAL, Pedro Gregorio de la	X	30	LI	SM	D	LI			XX
OS	$		1704	PERALTA y SANABRIA, Juan	?	56	LI	SM	D		PI LI	CA	XX
AX	$		1707	SANTOS y CUENTAS, Francisco Antonio de los	X	51	LI		B	LI	X- LI		XX
AX	$	*	1708	MENA CABALLERO, Juan Antonio de	X	24	LI	SF	L				XX, M
OS	$	*	1708	ECHAVARRIA ZULOAGA, Juan Bautista de (Marqués de Sotohermoso)	X	25	LI	SM	D				M, SA
AC	$	*	1708	MUNARRIZ, Bartolomé de	X	22	LI	SM	L			OP	AB, M.SA
OS	$		1710	ECHAVE y ROJAS, Pedro Antonio	X	30	LI			LI			HM, SA
OS	$	*	1711	CAVERO de FRANCIA, Alvaro	N	26	LI	SM	D	LI		SU	XX, CA
AC		*	1721	GOMENDIO URRUTIA, Miguel de	X	51	SI AL		L		FI CH	SU	AB
OD²		*	1729	NUÑEZ de ROJAS, Gregorio	N	55	LI	SM	D		OD CS		OD
FR			1730	ORTIZ de FORONDA, Francisco	N	24	LI	SM	D				HM, M.SA
OS	$	*	1733	BRAVO de RIVERO, Pedro	X	32	LI	SM SF	D	LI			HM

APPENDIX A (continued)
Native Sons Appointed to the Audiencia of Lima 1687–1750[1]

Post	Purchase	Year	Travel	Name	First Generation Creole	Age	University	Colegio	Degree	Abogado	Previous Post	University Service	Fathers
OS		1735		SALAZAR, Tomás de	?	60	LI		D	LI	OD SF	CA	
OS		1736		SAGARDIA y PALENCIA, Francisco	X	45	LI	SM	D	LI	OD CS		AB, X
AX	$	1736		BORDA y ECHEVARRIA, Manuel Antonio de	X	25	LI	SM	D	LI			HM, M,SA
AX		1738		VILLALTA y NUÑEZ, José Antonio	X	39	LI	SM	D	LI	OD CS		HM, SA
OS	$	1740	*	URQUIZU IBAÑEZ, Gaspar	N	27	LI	SM	D	LI	PI CS		OD
OS	$	1741		TAGLE BRACHO, José de	X	24	LI	SM	D		OD CS		AB, M
OS	$	1744		OLAVIDE, Pablo Antonio de	X	19	LI	SM	D	LI	X-LI	CA	AB
OS		1744		QUEREJAZU y MOLLINEDO, Antonio Hermenegildo de	X	33	LI	SM	D		PR CS		HM, M,SA

OS	$	1745	*	ZURBARAN y ALLENDE, Manuel	X	29	LI	SM	D	LI	OD CS	CA	
OS	$	1746		BRAVO de CASTILLA, Pedro José	N	44	LI	SM SF	D	LI	AG LI	CA	HM
AX	$	1747		PUENTE y IBAÑEZ, Juan José de la (Marqués de Corpa)	N	23	LI	SM SF	D	LI			HM, M,AL
OS	$	1748	*	MIRONES y BENAVENTE, Manuel Isidro de	X	57	LI	SM	D	LI	OD CS		XX
OS	$	1749	*	ORRANTIA, Domingo de	X	21	LI	SM	D	LI		OP	XX, M,SA
AX	$	1749	*	ORBEA y ARANDIA, Diego José de	X	37	LI	SM	D	LI			HM
AX	$	1750		MANSILLA ARIAS de SAAVEDRA, Manuel de	N	25	LI	SM SF	D	LI		CA	AB

¹Adapted from Burkholder and Chandler, *From Impotence to Authority*, Appendix X with later additions.

²Núñez de Rojas purchased his original appointment to the Audiencia of Charcas.

APPENDIX B

Oidores Appointed to the Audiencia
of Lima, 1751-1808

This appendix provides professional and appointment information for the thirty-two men named oidores of the Audiencia of Lima from 1751 to 1808. The organization is by date of selection.

Explanation of Categories and Abbreviations:

1. Date: Date on which the appointee was selected. Each date is for either the consulta or decree that determined the selection.
2. Form of Appointment. *C* indicates that the appointment was made following a consulta and the person named was listed on the consulta. *D* indicates that the appointment was made by a royal decree. *R* indicates that the appointment was made by *resulta*. *X* indicates that a consulta was made for the position but the appointee was not listed on it.
3. Name: Common spelling has been employed. Titles of nobility are included to facilitate identification even if not held at the date of appointment. An asterisk before the name indicates the appointee never served.
4. Birthplace: *S* stands for birth in Spain or the Canary Islands. For Americans, identification is by audiencia district of birth. The abbreviations are: *CH:* Chile; *LI:* Lima; *ME:* Mexico; *SF:* Santa Fe de Bogotá.
5. Age: Approximate age at the time of appointment.
6. University: University affiliation is listed regardless of

whether attendance, receipt of a degree, or incorporation of a degree was involved. Abbreviations employed are:

AL: Alcalá de Henares
AV: Avila
BO: Bologna
BZ: Baeza
CH: Chile
GR: Granada
LI: Lima
OM: Osma
OR: Orihuela
SA: Salamanca
SE: Sevilla
SF: Santa Fe de Bogotá
SI: Siguenza
SN: Santiago
VD: Valladolid

7. Degree: Highest degree received. D: doctorate; L: licentiate; B: bachelor.
8. Abogado: Tribunals to which a man had been admitted to practice law.
GA: Galicia
GR: Granada
LI: Lima
ME: Mexico
RC: Royal Councils
SE: Sevilla
SF: Santa Fe de Bogotá
VA: Valencia
VD: Valladolid

9. University Service: CA: catedrático (professor); OP: opositor; SU: substitute.
10. Previous Post:
AC: alcalde del crimen
AG: asesor general
AX: alcalde del crimen supernumerario
FV: fiscal de lo civil
OD: oidor
X-LI: service in Lima in a non-audiencia position
(lower) CH: Chile; GT: Guatemala; LI: Lima; QU: Quito; SF: Santa Fe de Bogotá.

APPENDIX B

Oidores Appointed to the Audiencia of Lima, 1751–1808[1]

Date	Form of Appointment	Name	Birthplace	Age	University	Degree	Abogado	University Service	Previous Post
15-12-1755	D	MESIA y MUNIVE, Cristóbal (Conde de Sierrabella)	CH	38	LI	D	LI	CA	X- LI
25-6-1763	C	*CASAL y MONTENEGRO, Benito de	S	60	AV SN	D	GA	OP	OD SF
22-2-1770	D	MANSILLA ARIAS de SAAVEDRA, Manuel de	LI	44	LI	D	LI	CA	AX LI
23-1-1775	C	RUEDAS MORALES, Gerónimo Manuel de	S		OM SA	D		CA	FV LI
23-5-1775	C	*CARRION y MORCILLO, Alfonso	S						AC LI
6-9-1775	C	*VILLALTA y NÚÑEZ, José Antonio	LI	77	LI	D	LI		AC LI
14-6-1776	C	*BORDA y ECHEVARRIA, Manuel Antonio de	LI	65	LI	D	LI		AX LI
14-6-1776	C	*TRASLAVIÑA y OYAGUE, José Clemente de	LI		LI	D	LI		OD CH

Date	Class	Name		Age					
7-8-1777	D	PUENTE y IBAÑEZ, Juan José de la (Marqués de Corpa)	LI	53	LI	D	LI		OD CH
7-9-1778	C	FERRER de la PUENTE, José	S		OR	D	VA RC	OP	OD QU
23-10-1778	C	MATA LINARES, Benito María de la	S	29	AL SA	B			OD CH
23-10-1778	C	RIVERA y PEÑA, Ramón de	S	48	SN	D	GA	CA	AC LI
27-1-1779	C	SANTIAGO CONCHA, Melchor de	LI	63	LI	L	LI		AC LI
7-9-1778	X	ARREDONDO y PELEGRIN, Manuel Antonio (Marqués de San Juan Nepomuceno)	S	41	SA	B	RC		OD GT
1-17-1779	X	ESCOBEDO ALARCON, Jorge	S	38	GR SA	B		OP	AC LI
27-9-1784	C	CERDAN y PONTERO, Ambrosio	S		SI AL	L	RC		AC LI
28-9-1785	X	PORTILLA y GALVEZ, José de la	S		GR	D	GR		AG LI
28-9-1785	X	MORENO y ESCANDON, Francisco Antonio de	SF	49	SF	D	SF	CA	FV LI
2-5-1787	C	VELEZ de GUEVARA, Nicolás	SF		SF	D	SF	CA	AC LI
28-1-1789	C	MARQUEZ de la PLATA, Fernando	S	49	SE	D			AC LI

APPENDIX B (continued)
Oidores Appointed to the Audiencia of Lima, 1751–1808[1]

Date	Form of Appointment	Name	Birthplace	Age	University	Degree	Abogado	University Service	Previous Post
24-9-1792	C	GONZALEZ CALDERON, Tomás	ME	52	ME	D	ME	SU	AC LI
20-6-1794	R	RODRIGUEZ BALLESTEROS, Juan	S	56	GR SE	B	SE RC		OD CH
16-11-1794	D	GARCIA de la PLATA, Manuel	S	44	GR	L	RC		AC LI
2-5-1796	R	MUÑOZ y CUBERO, Lucas	S	62	GR	L	GR	CA	OD QU
5-9-1796	C	PINO MANRIQUE de LARA, Juan del	S	49	GR				AC LI
5-9-1796	C	QUADRADO y VALDENEBRO, Fernando	S	60	VD SA	B			OD QU
28-11-1796	C	ARNAIZ de las REVILLAS, Domingo	S	47	CH VD	D	VD	CA	AC LI
19-2-1797	D	PARDO RIVADENEYRA, Manuel	S	37					AC LI

			SF	49	SF OM,VD SA	D	RC	SU	AC LI
12-10-1800	R	MORENO y ESCANDON, Francisco Xavier de	SF	49	SF OM,VD SA	D	RC		AC LI
25-3-1804	D	VALLE del POSTIGO, Manuel María de	S	50	BZ GR	B	SE RC		AC LI
18-12-1805	D	PALOMEQUE, Tomás Ignacio	S	49	AL BO	B		CA	AC LI
12-8-1806	R	BAQUIJANO y CARRILLO, José Xavier (Conde de Vistaflorida)	LI	55	LI	D	LI	CA	AC LI

[1] Adapted from Burkholder and Chandler, *From Impotence to Authority*, Appendix X with later additions.

APPENDIX C

Alcaldes del Crimen Appointed to the Audiencia of Lima, 1751-1808

This appendix provides professional and appointment information for the thirty men named alcaldes del crimen for the Audiencia of Lima from 1751 to 1808. The organization is by date of selection.

Explanation of Categories and Abbreviations:

1-7. See Appendix B for the categories and abbreviations employed.

8. Abogado: The abbreviations employed are the same as for Appendix B except that no appointee was an abogado of Valencia (VA).

9. University Service: See Appendix B.

10. Previous Post: The upper letters indicate the post, the lower ones the audiencia district of service. Abbreviations are: (upper) AG: asesor general; FR: fiscal del crimen; OD: oidor; PI: protector of the Indians; X: service in a non-audiencia position. (lower) CH: Chile; CS: Charcas; GT: Guatemala; LI: Lima; MA: Manila; QU: Quito; SF: Santa Fe de Bogotá.

APPENDIX C

Alcaldes del Crimen Appointed to the Audiencia of Lima, 1751–1808[1]

Date	Form of Appointment	Name	Birthplace	Age	University	Degree	Abogado	University Service	Previous Post
6-9-1775	C	*TRASLAVIÑA y OYAGUE, José Clemente de	LI		LI	D	LI		OD CH
29-11-1775	C	TAGLE BRACHO, Pedro de	LI	54	LI	D	LI		OD CS
11-3-1776	D	*MIER y TRESPALACIOS, Cosme Antonio de	S	31	OM VD	D		SU	PI LI
6-6-1776	D	*VERDUGO del CASTILLO, Juan Antonio	CH	74	LI		LI	SU	OD CH
14-6-1776	R	*MARTINEZ de ALDUNATE, Domingo de	CH	69	CH LI	D	LI	CA	OD CH
16-12-1776	C	RIVERA y PEÑA, Ramón de	S	47	SN	D	GA	CA	OD CS
16-12-1776	C	SANTIAGO CONCHA, Melchor de	LI	61	LI	L	LI		OD CH
11-3-1778	C	CABEZA ENRIQUEZ, José	S		VD SA	L	RC	SU	OD QU

APPENDIX C (continued)

Alcaldes del Crimen Appointed to the Audiencia of Lima, 1751–1808[1]

Date	Form of Appointment	Name	Birthplace	Age	University	Degree	Abogado	University Service	Previous Post
23-10-1778	C	ESCOBEDO ALARCON, Jorge	S	36	GR SA	B		OP	OD CS
3-2-1779	R?	CERDAN y PONTERO, Ambrosio	S		SI AL	L	RC		FR CH
21-4-1779	C	VELEZ de GUEVARA, Nicolás	SF		SF	D	SF	CA	OD QU
21-4-1779	C	*POSADA y SOTO, Ramón de	S	29	AV VD	L	RC	SU	OD GT
6-3-1780	C	REZABAL y UGARTE, José de	S	33	GR SA	B		SU	OD CH
15-3-1780	C	MARQUEZ de la PLATA, Fernando	S	41	SE	D			FR CS
9-3-1785	X	BOETO, Antonio	S						X- LI
20-10-1786	C	GONZALEZ CALDERON, Tomás	ME	48	ME	D	ME	SU	OD GT

Date		Name							
2-5-1787	R	GARCIA de la PLATA, Manuel	S	37	GR	L	RC		OD CS
28-7-1788	X	PINO MANRIQUE de LARA, Juan del	S	41	GR				FR CS
28-1-1789	R	ARNAIZ de las REVILLAS, Domingo	S	39	OM VD	D	VD	CA	FR CS
24-9-1792	R	PARDO RIVADENEYRA, Manuel	S	33					
16-11-1794	D	MORENO y ESCANDON, Francisco Xavier de	SF	43	SF OM,SA VD	D	RC	SU	OD MA
5-9-1796	R	VALLE del POSTIGO, Manuel Maria de	S	42	BZ GR	B	SE RC		AG LI
28-11-1796	R	PALOMEQUE, Tomás Ignacio	S	41	AL BO	B		CA	OD CS
19-2-1797	D	BAQUIJANO y CARRILLO, José Xavier (Conde de Vistaflorida)	LI	45	LI	D	LI	CA	X- LI
22-10-1800	R	CISNEROS de la OLIVA, Felipe	S	63	OR	B	GR RC		OD MA
28-6-1802	C?	MORENO AVENDAÑO, Juan de	S	59	OS GR	B	SE RC		OD QU
25-3-1804	D	ESTERRIPA, Francisco Xavier	S	41	AL	D			OD SF
15-12-1806	D	OSMA y TRICIO, Gaspar Antonio de	S	31	VD AL	B	RC		OD SF

APPENDIX C (continued)

Alcaldes del Crimen Appointed to the Audiencia of Lima, 1751–1808[1]

Date	Form of Appointment	Name	Birthplace	Age	University	Degree	Abogado	University Service	Previous Post
12-8-1806	R	*SANTIAGO CONCHA JIMENEZ LOBATON, José	CH	46	LI	B	LI		OD CH
9-8-1807	D	IGLESIA y HUGUES, José de la	S	68	SE	D	SE RC		OD CS

[1] Adopted from Burkholder and Chandler, *From Impotence to Authority*, Appendix X with later additions.

Notes

1

1. *Actas de las sesiones secretas de las cortes generales extraordinarias de la nación español.* . . . (Madrid, 1874), p. 554.

2. José Antonio Miralla, *Breve descripción de las fiestas celebradas en la capital de los Reyes del Perú con motivo de la promoción del Excmo. Señor D.D. José Baquíjano y Carrillo.* . . . (Lima, 1812), p. 4.

3. The photograph in the illustration section is that portrait, which is reproduced in Guillermo Lohmann Villena *Los ministros de la audiencia de Lima en el reinado de los Borbones (1700–1821)* (Sevilla, 1974), p. 8; José de la Riva-Agüero's description can be found conveniently in *Historia del Perú: Selección* 2 vols. (Lima, 1953), 2:71.

4. Preston E. James, *Latin America*, rev. ed. (New York, 1950), p. 167; James Lockhart, *Spanish Peru, 1532-1560* (Madison, 1968).

5. Rubén Vargas Ugarte, *Historia general del Perú* 6 vols. (Lima, 1966), 3:11; "Reflexiones históricas y políticas sobre el estado de la población de esta capital, que se acompaña por suplemento," *Mercurio peruano* (Lima), 1:10 (February 3, 1791):90–97.

6. Juan Bromley and José Barbagelata, *Evolución urbana de la ciudad de Lima* (Lima, 1945), plates 1 and 3.

7. For mining production see D. A. Brading and Harry E. Cross, "Colonial Silver Mining: Mexico and Peru," *Hispanic American Historical Review* (hereafter *HAHR*) 52:4 (November 1972):569, 575 and J. R. Fisher, *Silver Mines and Silver Miners in Colonial Peru, 1776-1824* (Liverpool, 1977), pp. 2–6.

8. Woodrow Borah, *Early Colonial Trade and Navigation Between Mexico and Peru* (Berkeley and Los Angeles, 1954), p. 127; Michael T. Hamerly, *Historia social y económica de la antigua provincia de Guayaquil 1763-1842* (Guayaquil, 1973), p. 123; Demetrio Ramos, *Trigo chileno, navieros del Callao y hacendados limeños entre la crisis agrícola del siglo XVII y la comercial de la primera mitad del XVIII* (Madrid, 1967); Sergio Villalobos R., *El comercio y la crisis colonial* (Santiago, Chile, 1968), chaps. I–III.

9. See Oscar Febres Villarroel, "La crisis agrícola del Perú en el último tercio del siglo XVIII," *Revista histórica* (Lima) 27 (1964):102–99.

10. Jorge Juan and Antonio de Ulloa, *A Voyage to South America*, The John Adams Translation, abridged and edited by Irving A. Leonard (New York, 1964), p. 230.

11. Tadeo Haënke, *Descripción del Perú* (Lima, 1901), pp. 15–16.

12. Conde Bertrando del Balzo, "Familias nobles y destacadas del Perú en los informes secretos de un virrey napolitano (1715–1725)," *Revista del instituto peruano de investigaciones genealógicas* (Lima) 14 (1965):108–10; Juan and Ulloa, *A Voyage to South America*, p. 193; "Plan demonstrativo de la población comprehendida en el recinto de la Cuidad de Lima. . . ," *Mercurio peruano* 1:10 (February 3, 1791):follows p. 97.

13. Luis de Izcue, *La nobleza titulada en el Perú colonial*, second edition (Lima, 1929).

14. For titled nobles in New Spain, see Doris M. Ladd, *The Mexican Nobility at In-dependence 1780–1826* (Austin, 1976), pp. 15–17.

15. Juan Bromley y Seminario, "Alcaldes de la ciudad de Lima en el siglo XVIII," *Revista histórica* 25 (1960–1961):342; Archivo General de Indias (hereafter AGI), Audiencia de Lima (hereafter Lima), legajo 941, expediente 32, "Relación de los méritos, y servicios del Doctor Don Joseph Baquíjano, Carrillo de Córdoba, Regente de la Cátedra de Instituta en la Universidad de Lima, y Abogado de aquella Real Audiencia," Madrid, September 30, 1781 (hereafter Relación de méritos, 1781).

16. Archivo Nacional del Perú (hereafter ANP), Sección de Protocolos (hereafter Protocolos), Azcarrunz, Orencio de, legajo 81, (1759–1760), fol. 144 v. to 146 v. "Poder para testar. El Sʳ Conde de Vistaflorida a la Sᵃ Condesa de Vistaflorida y otros," Lima, June 1, 1759; George Robertson Dilg, "The Collapse of the Portobelo Fairs: A Study in Spanish Commercial Reform, 1720–1740," (Ph.D. dissertation, Indiana University, 1975), Appendix C; Archivo Histórico del Ministerio de Hacienda, No. 0610, "Quaderno de juntas desde el año de 1731 hasta el de 1739," fol. 502–03 v.

17. The inventories of his property are in ANP, Protocolos, Ascarrunz, Orencio de, legajo 81 (1759–1760).

18. *Ibid.*

19. *Ibid.*, p. 326; legajo 77 (1751–1752), fol. 475.

20. *Ibid.*, legajo 74 (1739–1746), pp. 407–09.

21. *Ibid.*, legajo 81 (1759–1760), p. 144 v. to 146 v.

22. Archivo Histórico Nacional, Madrid (hereafter AHN), Sección de Ordenes Militares (hereafter Ordenes), Santiago, expediente 827, Pruebas de Caballeros, Juan Agustín de Baquíjano y Carrillo, 1784. Royal cédula to the Viceroy of Peru, Valladolid, December 4, 1601.

23. Juan Luis Espejo, *Nobiliario de la Capitanía General de Chile* (Santiago, 1967), pp. 219–22, 526–29.

24. AGI, Lima, legajo 941, expediente 32, Relación de méritos, 1781; Bromley y Seminario, "Alcaldes de la ciudad de Lima," pp. 309–10.

25. Archivo General de Simancas, Simancas (hereafter AGS), Sección XXIII, Dirección General del Tesoro (hereafter Sección XXIII), Inventario 2, legajo 9, título 11. Agustín Carrillo de Córdoba regente de tribunal de la contaduría mayor de cuentas de Lima, Zaragoza, April 27, 1711; AGI, Lima, legajo 941, expediente 32, Relación de méritos, 1781; AGI, Indiferente General, legajo 525, "Año de 1746, Relación de los empleos de justicia, políticos, y de real hacienda de los dominios de el Perú, que se han concedido por servizio pecuniario desde el año de 1700 al de 1746."

26. AGI, Lima, legajo 605, letter by Viceroy Marqués de Villa García to the King, Lima, April 9, 1737.

27. AHN, Sección de Códices y Cartularios (hereafter Códices), legajo 239B. "Memorias académicas para la historia de la insigne Universidad de Lima, y de los tres Rˢ Colegˢ de Sⁿ Felipe, San Martín, y Santo Torivio: Que escribía un limeño aficionado á las antigüedades de su patria, año de 1786." AGI, Lima, legajo 941, Josephus de Baquíjano, et Carrillo, *Relectio extemporanea ad explanationem Legis Pamphilo XXXIX. . . .* (Lima, 1788); AGI, Lima legajo 993, letter by Manuel de Gorrichátegui (for José Gómez Carrillo) to the King, San Ildefonso, August 26, 1771.

28. Espejo, *Nobiliario*, pp. 175, 65.

29. AGS, Sección XXIII, Inventario 24, legajo 183, título 113. Conde de Vistaflorida, traslado del título de tal Conde a Dⁿ Juan Bauptista de Baquíjano para sí y sus herederos, y subcesores, Madrid, July 30, 1755; Izcue, *La Nobleza*, p. 10D.

30. AHN, Sección de Estado, Ordenes Civiles, Carlos III, expediente 579, copy of death certificate, Lima, June 12, 1759; Felipe Barreda Laos, *Vida intelectual del virreynato del Perú* (Buenos Aires, 1937), p. 286; AGI, Lima, legajo 699, expediente 95, will of the Condesa de Vistaflorida, Lima, February 13, 1791.

31. *Ibid.*

32. AGI, Lima, legajo 970, expediente 17, memorial de Josefa Baquíjano y Carrillo [1798].

33. AGI, Lima, legajo 699, expediente 95, will of the Condesa de Vistaflorida, Lima, February 13, 1791.

34. AGI, Lima, legajo 1003, "La Condesa de Vistaflorida y demás consortes, vecinos de la ciudad de Lima supp^can no se admitan las instancias que haga D^n Manuel Lorenzo de Léon y Encalada, en solicitud de moratoria," July 29, 1790.

35. Bromley y Seminario, "Alcaldes de la ciudad de Lima," p. 349; Espejo, *Nobiliario*, p. 28.

36. AGI, Lima, legajo 699, expediente 95, will of the Condesa de Vistaflorida, Lima, February 13, 1791; Luis Antonio Eguiguren, *Diccionario* histórico cronológico de la Real y Pontificia Universidad de San Marcos y sus colegios. Crónica é investigación, 3 vols. (Lima, 1940-1951), 2:247.

37. Domingo Amunátegui Solar, *Mayorazgos i títulos de Castilla*, 3 vols. (Santiago, 1901-1904), 3:363-64; Espejo, *Nobiliario*, p. 341; AGS, Sección XXIII, Inventario 24, legajo 685, título 27, Conde de San Xavier y Casa Laredo, Aranjuez, May 28, 1763.

38. AGI, Lima, legajo 997, letter by the Condesa de San Xavier y Casa Laredo to Exmo. Señor, Lima, December 27, 1783; AGS, Sección XXIII, Inventario 2, legajo 92, título 73, Conde de San Xavier, regent, Audiencia of Charcas, Seville, November 30, 1809; *ibid.*, legajo 94, título 32, Gaspar Ramírez de Laredo, regent, Audiencia of Lima, Cádiz, July 18, 1813; *ibid.*, legajo 98, título 55, Gaspar Ramírez de Laredo, minister, Council of the Indies, Madrid, April 19, 1817.

39. AGI, Lima, legajo 997, letter by the Condesa de San Xavier y Casa Laredo to Exmo. Señor, Lima, December 27, 1783; *ibid.*, legajo 914, expediente 73, report by Gregorio Guido; *ibid.*, letter by Nicolás Fernández Rivera (for Ambrosio Fernández Cruz), Madrid, August 22, 1785.

40. AGI, Lima, legajo 997, letter by the Condesa de San Xavier y Casa Laredo to Exmo. Señor, Lima, December 27, 1783; *ibid.*, legajo 914, expediente 73; *ibid.*, legajo 698, note to Antonio Valdés, San Lorenzo, November 21, 1785.

41. AHN, Sección de Consejos Suprimidos (hereafter Consejos), Castilla, legajo 27537, expediente 8, pieza 7a; J. R. Fisher, *Government and Society in Colonial Peru: The Intendant System 1784-1814* (London, 1970), p. 242.

42. Lohmann Villena, *Los ministros de la audiencia de Lima*, p. lxxxi.

43. AGI, Lima, legajo 877, expediente 15, *súplica* by Gerónimo Manuel Ruedas Morales, Lima, June 26, 1775; *ibid.*, legajo 597, extract by the Cámara of the Indies, May 13, 1767; AGS, Sección XXIII, Inventario 2, legajo 60, título 285, Gerónimo Manuel de Ruedas, regent, Audiencia of Charcas, San Lorenzo, November 14, 1776. For his membership on the university committee, see *Constituciones para la Real Universidad, cuyos treinta y tres capítulos abrazan la reforma de los principales abusos que en ella se habían introducido con el transcurso del tiempo . . .* (Lima, 1771). (Hereafter *Constituciones para la Real Universidad, 1771*). Printed in Daniel Valcárcel, *Reforma de San Marcos en la época de Amat* (Lima, 1955), pp. 31-45.

44. AHN, Ordenes, Calatrava, legajo 299, 1855-1856, Gaspar de Osma Ramírez de Arellano, no. 8; *ibid.*, legajo 2149, Pruebas de caballeros, Domingo Ramírez de Arellano. Approved August 27, 1776; *ibid.*, Consejos, Castilla, legajo 27537, expediente 8, pieza 7a, will of Domingo Ramírez de Arellano, May 13, 1811; Manuel de Mendiburu, *Diccionario histórico-biográfico del Perú*, 8 vols. (Lima, 1874-1890), 8:450; Leon G. Campbell, *The Military and Society in Colonial Peru 1750-1810* (Philadelphia, 1978), p. 37.

45. AHN, Estado, Ordenes Civiles, Carlos III, expediente 579, copy of the baptismal certificate of Juan Agustín Manuel Baquíjano y Carrillo, Lima, June 24, 1748; *ibid.*, Sección de Universidades y Colegios, Signatura 1304-F. He entered the Seminary of Nobles on October 26, 1762 and left it on November 26, 1764. AGI, Lima, legajo 618, letter by the Con-

de de Vistaflorida to the King, San Ildefonso, August 3, 1783; note of January 19, 1784. The proofs of *limpieza de sangre* are in AHN, Ordenes, Santiago, expediente 827. Pruebas de Caballeros, Juan Agustín de Baquíjano y Carrillo, 1784. Bromley y Seminario, "Alcaldes de la ciudad de Lima," p. 342.

46. Numerous examples are in Guillermo Lohmann Villena, *Los americanos en las ordenes nobiliarias (1529–1900)*, 2 vols. (Madrid, 1947).

47. AHN, Consejos, Castilla, legajo 27537, expediente 8, testamentaria del S.D. Juan Agustín de Baquíjano, Madrid, April 15, 1796.

48. *Ibid.*

49. *Ibid.*, Consejos, Castilla, legajo 21730, letter by the Conde de Vistaflorida, Madrid, December 19, 1789. A minister of the Council of the Indies received a salary of fifty-five thousand *reales*.

50. AHN, Estado, Ordenes Civiles, Carlos III, expediente 579, Pruebas de Don José Javier de Baquíjano Conde de Vistaflorida, partida de bautismo, May 30, 1751. The original of this document, found in the Archivo Parroquial del Sagrario, Lima, has been published by Miguel Maticorena Estrada, "Nuevas noticias y documentos de don José Baquíjano y Carrillo, Conde de Vista-Florida," in Pontificia Universidad Católica del Perú, *La causa de la emancipación del Perú: Testimonios de la época precursora 1780–1820* (Lima, 1960), p. 207. On Zelayeta see AGI, Lima, legajo 699, expediente 95, will of the Condesa de Vistaflorida, Lima, February 13, 1791; and Mendiburu, *Diccionario*, 11:380.

51. ANP, Protocolos, Azcarrunz, Orencio de, legajo 81 (1759–1760), "Ymventario de los vienes del Conde de Vistaflorida," Lima, November 7, 1759, pp. 326–28.

52. AGI, Lima, legajo 941, expediente 32, Relación de méritos, 1781.

53. Paul Bentley Ganster, "A Social History of the Secular Clergy of Lima During the Middle Decades of the Eighteenth Century," (Ph.D. dissertation, University of California, Los Angeles, 1974), pp. 65–68.

54. Joseph de Baquíjano y Carrillo, *Alegato que en la oposición a la cátedra de prima de leyes de la Real Universidad de San Marcos de Lima . . .* (Lima, 1788).

55. Biblioteca de la Real Academia de la Historia (Madrid), Colección de Manuscriptos de D. Benito de la Mata y Linares, tomo 80, no. 5, Toribio Rodríguez de Mendoza and Mariano Rivero, "Plan de estudios," Lima, December 30, 1791; Ignacio de Castro, *Oración panegírica, que á la feliz llegada del ilustrísimo señor doctor don Agustín de Gorrichátegui . . .* (Lima, 1771), pp. 10–11.

56. Miguel Maticorena E. [Estrada], "Documentos para la historia de la Universidad Nacional Mayor de San Marcos," *Boletín bibliográfico* (Lima), 19:1–2 (July, 1949):140; AGI, Lima, legajo 866, expediente 2, informe by Diego Antonio, Archbishop of Lima, Lima, March 31, 1773.

57. AGI, Lima, legajo 941, expediente 32, Relación de méritos, 1781; Maticorena, "Documentos," p. 141.

58. Baquíjano, *Alegato*; AGI, Lima, legajo 866, expediente 2, informe by the Iglesia Metropolitana, Lima, March 29, 1773; informe by Diego Antonio, Archbishop of Lima, Lima, March 24, 1773; informe by Agustín, Bishop of Cuzco, Lima, April 4, 1773; Maticorena, "Documentos," p. 141.

59. AGI, Lima, legajo 941, expediente 32, Relación de méritos, 1781.

60. Unless otherwise indicated, support for statements about audiencia personnel can be found in Mark A. Burkholder and D. S. Chandler, *From Impotence to Authority: The Spanish Crown and the American Audiencias, 1687–1808* (Columbia, 1977). See especially Appendix IX.

61. AGI, Lima, legajo 993, letter by Manuel de Gorrichátegui to the King, Madrid, September 9, 1771; *ibid.*, legajo 866, expediente 2, informe by Agustín, Bishop of Cuzco, Lima, April 4, 1773.

62. Baquíjano, *Alegato.* In 1812 Gerónimo de Calatayud y Borda, first professor of sacred theology at the University of San Marcos, stated that Baquíjano had provided him with a detailed, superb statement concerning a point under discussion at the Council. Gerónimo de Calatayud y Borda, *Elogio del excmo. señor D. José Baquíjano . . .* (Lima, 1813), p. 17.

63. See John Leddy Phelan, *The People and the King: The Comunero Revolution in Colombia, 1781* (Madison, 1978), chapter 1 and Burkholder and Chandler, *From Impotence to Authority.*

64. *Recopilación de leyes de los Reynos de las Indias* (4 vols., Madrid, 1681; reprinted 1973), libro III, título ii, xiiii.

65. *Ibid.*, libro II, título xvi, numerous laws.

66. See, for example, AGS, Gracia y Justicia, legajo 163 (antiguo); the question of native sons in Spain warrants detailed examination.

67. See Burkholder and Chandler, *From Impotence to Authority*, pp. 6–8, 75.

68. Figures for the period 1687–1750 are from Burkholder and Chandler, *From Impotence to Authority*, Appendixes IX and X. Earlier figures derive from a variety of sources; the most valuable are Antonine Tibesar, O.F.M., *Franciscan Beginnings in Colonial Peru* (Washington, D.C., 1953), Appendix IV; Eguiguren, *Diccionario*, 1:523–30 and 2:135–205; Mendiburu, *Diccionario*; Lohmann Villena, *Los americanos*; Lohmann Villena, *Los ministros*; Espejo, *Nobiliario*; José María Restrepo Sáenz, *Biografías de los mandatarios y ministros de la real audiencia* (1671 a 1819) (Bogotá, 1952); and Abraham de Silva i Molina, *Oidores de la real audiencia de Santiago de Chile durante el siglo XVII* (Santiago, Chile, 1903). Further investigation might increase the figures for Peruvians and other Americans.

69. See Appendix A; Burkholder and Chandler, *From Impotence to Authority*, Part One and Appendixes III, IX, and X and sources cited there, for information employed in this and the following discussion.

70. Antonio Hermenegildo de Querejazu y Mollinedo.

71. Miguel Núñez de Sanabria, Francisco Rojas y Acevedo, and Pedro José Bravo de Castilla.

72. Juan Peralta y Sanabria (Lima) and Gaspar Urquizu y Ibáñez (Charcas).

73. José de Santiago Concha and Pablo Antonio José de Olavide.

74. Francisco Antonio de los Santos y Cuentas.

75. Querejazu is the possible exception.

76. Miguel Núñez de Sanabria, Sancho García de Salazar, Pablo Vásquez de Velasco, Juan de Pérez de Urquizu, José de Santiago Concha, Vicente de Aranburu y Muñoz, Pedro Gregorio de la Canal, Francisco Antonio de los Santos y Cuentas, Juan Antonio de Mena Caballero, Juan Bautista de Echavarría Zuloaga, Bartolomé de Munárriz, Pedro Antonio Echave y Rojas, Miguel de Gomendio Urrutia, Pedro Bravo de Rivero, Francisco Sagardia y Palencia, Manuel Antonio de Borda y Echevarría, José Antonio Villalta y Núñez, José de Tagle Bracho, Pablo Antonio José de Olavide, Antonio Hermenegildo de Querejazu y Mollinedo, Manuel Zurbarán y Allende, Manuel Isidro de Mirones y Benavente, Domingo de Orrantia, and Diego José de Orbea y Arandia.

77. Those with non-Peruvian mothers were Núñez, Vásquez, and Aranburu. Place of birth for the mothers of García and Munárriz is unknown. Among the remaining nineteen mothers, all but those for Mena and Gomendio were from Lima.

78. From Alava: García and Aranburu; from Guipúzcoa: Echavarría, Echave, Querejazu, and Orbea; from Vizcaya: Pérez, Gomendio, Zurbarán, Mirones, and Orrantia; from Navarre: Munárriz, Sagardia, Borda, and Olavide; from Santander: Santiago Concha and Tagle.

79. García and Vásquez.

80. Mena, Echavarría, Munárriz, Sagardia, Borda, Tagle, Querejazu, and Orrantia.

81. The seven fathers all belonged to the Order of Santiago: Echavarría, Munárriz, Echave, Borda, Villalta, Querejazu, and Orrantia.

82. This number includes Manuel Mansilla who held an appointment but did not assume a seat as a result of his failure to pay the balance of the agreed upon purchase price until after a second appointment in 1770.

2

1. AGI, Lima, legajo 941, expediente 32, Relación de méritos, 1781.

2. Guillermo Céspedes del Castillo, *Lima y Buenos Aires* (Sevilla, 1947) sets forth the economic repercussions on Peru. J. R. Fisher, *Silver Mines*, demonstrates a late eighteenth-century mining boom within Peru, an important reminder that it is necessary to follow the Peruvian economy closely over time.

3. AGI, Lima, legajo 599, letter by Baquíjano to the King, San Lorenzo, November 1, 1798.

4. Archivo Municipal (Lima), "Libro 36 de los cavildos de esta Ciudad que comiensa en el año de 1756. Y demas años," pp. 196 v.–197.

5. *Ibid.*; pages 410–11 provide a list of the asesores.

6. AGI, Lima, legajo 866, expediente 2, informe by the Cabildo, Lima, March 24, 1773.

7. AGI, Lima, legajo 620, letter by Manuel de Gorrichátegui to Julián de Arriaga, Madrid, November 24, 1774; José de la Riva-Agüero, "Don José Baquíjano de Beascoa y Carrillo de Córdoba, tercer conde de Vistaflorida en el Perú (1751–1818)," *Revista de archivos, bibliotecas y museos* (Madrid), 3º Epoca, 46 (1925):473; M. Défourneaux, "Pablo de Olavide, L'Homme et le Mythe," *Cahiers de monde hispanique et luso-brésilien* (Toulouse, 1966), p. 173.

8. Burkholder and Chandler, *From Impotence to Authority*, Appendix III.

9. AGI, Lima, legajo 620, letter by Manuel de Gorrichátegui to Julián de Arriaga, Madrid, November 24, 1774.

10. A rare example of the announcement posted can be found in AGI, Audiencia of Quito (hereafter Quito), legajo 358, expediente 9, cartel, Madrid, March 16, 1796.

11. For example, see AGI, Lima, legajo 892, expediente 34.

12. For example, AGI, Charcas, legajo 501, expediente 48, note on memorial and relación de méritos of Juan de Dios Calvo.

13. AGS, Sección XXIII, Inventario 13, legajo 8, título 556, Phelipe de Arco Riba Herrera, plaza de capa y espada, Council of the Indies, San Ildefonso, July 25, 1744; *ibid.*, legajo 9, título 564, Phelipe de Arco Riva Herrera, plaza de la Cámara, San Ildefonso, September 27, 1770.

14. AGS, Sección XXIII, Inventario 13, legajo 8, título 406, Marcos Ximeno, ministro togado, Council of the Indies, Buen Retiro, February 20, 1764; *ibid.*, título 399, Marcos Ximeno, plaza de la Cámara, El Pardo, March 18, 1767.

15. AGS, Sección XXIII, Inventario 13, legajo 9, título 466, Domingo de Trespalacios y Escandón, ministro togado, Council of the Indies, San Ildefonso, September 20, 1764; *ibid.*, título 465, Domingo de Trespalacios y Escandón, plaza de la Cámara, Palacio, April 14, 1767.

16. AGS, Sección XXIII, Inventario 13, legajo 8, título 150, Josef de Gálvez, ministro togado, Council and Cámara of the Indies, Madrid, July 7, 1772.

17. AGS, Gracia y Justicia, legajo 815 (antiguo), royal order, August 15, 1751.

18. This order of voting was set forth for the Council of Castile in the fourteenth century and continued in other bodies as well. *Novísima recopilación de las leyes de España*, 6 vols. (Madrid, 1805; reprinted, Madrid, 1976), libro IV, título viii, ley 1.

19. For example, see AGI, Quito, legajo 302, consulta, November 27, 1775.

20. These figures are derived from an examination of the memoriales and lists of pretendientes available for these years in the Archivo General de Indias.

21. Memoriales from Moreno, Gorospe, Saravia, Talavera, Calvo, and López are in AGI, Chile, legajo 258. One from Bodega is in AGI, Lima, legajo 292, expediente 34. Villafañe indicated that he was at court during these years in a memorial of July 2, 1797, found in AGI, Audiencia de Filipinas, legajo 366. For González Calderón see AGI, Audiencia of Guatemala, legajo 409.

22. AGI, Chile, legajo 258 has memoriales by the agents for López, Guzmán, and Vázquez. One for Alvarez de Ron is in AGI, Lima, legajo 892, expediente 34.

23. Alonso de Guzmán received an appointment to the Audiencia of Santa Fe de Bogotá, but refused to serve it. His efforts to obtain an appointment to his home tribunal of Chile never succeeded.

24. AGI, Lima, legajo 876, expediente 77, memorial by Manuel de Aganza (for Baquíjano) to the King, Madrid, December 1, 1773.

25. AGI, Lima, legajo 876, expediente 77.

26. AGI, Audiencia of Mexico (hereafter Mexico), legajo 1639, consulta of June 18, 1763. The ascenso is set forth in *Recopilación*, libro II, título ii, ley xxxiiii.

27. AGI, Lima, legajo 877, expediente 18, memorial by Baquíjano to the King, Madrid, May 1775; *ibid.*, Audiencia of Chile (hereafter Chile), legajo 258, memorial by Baquíjano to the King, Madrid, April 16, 1776; *ibid.*, Charcas, legajo 510, memorial by Baquíjano to the King, Madrid, October 3, 1775; *ibid.*, Lima, legajo 877, memorial by Baquíjano to the King, Madrid, October 19, 1775.

28. AGI, Lima, legajo 877, expediente 18, memorial by Baquíjano to the King, Madrid, July 3, 1775.

29. *Ibid.*, consulta, September 6, 1775. José Clemente de Traslaviña y Oyague received the appointment.

30. AGI, Charcas, legajo 423, consulta, November 29, 1775.

31. AGI, Mexico, legajo 1641, royal decree to the Conde de Valdellano, El Pardo, March 11, 1776. The decree was published in the *Gaceta de Madrid* on March 19, 1776. I want to thank the Interlibrary Loan Department of Thomas Jefferson Library, University of Missouri-St. Louis for securing microfilm of the *Gaceta* for me.

32. AGI, Chile, legajo 258, memorial by Baquíjano to the King, Madrid, April 16, 1776.

33. *Ibid.*, list of pretendientes for fiscal del crimen.

34. The following three paragraphs are drawn from the memoriales submitted by the pretendientes in *ibid.*

35. Gerónimo de Revenga y Alvarez.

36. Systematic presentation of pretendientes' marital state was required in 1773. AGI, Indiferente General, legajo 10, "Nota para la Secretaría," Madrid, July 7, 1773.

37. AGI, Chile, legajo 258, memorial by Ambrosio Cerdán de Simón Pontero, Madrid, April 16, 1776; AGI, Audiencia of Guadalajara, legajo 304, consulta, September 13, 1773; AGI, Lima, legajo 877, expediente 18.

38. Ciriaco González Carbajal and Gerónimo Revenga y Alvarez.

39. Between December 1773 and July 1776 the Cámara provided consultas for the following positions: fiscal-Guadalajara, fiscal-Charcas, oidor supernumerario-Manila, oidor-Guadalajara, oidor-Guatemala, oidor-Guadalajara, oidor-Quito, fiscal-Guatemala, oidor-Guatemala, fiscal-Charcas, oidor-Quito, oidor-Chile, oidor-Bogotá, oidor-Charcas, fiscal de lo civil-Manila, oidor-Quito, fiscal de lo civil-Chile, fiscal del crimen-Chile. There were also consultas for oidor-Manila (filled by Félix Díez Quijada y Ovejero) and oidor-Santo Domingo (filled by José Bernardo Osorio Pardo y Llamas), but these have not been located.

40. Gregorio Ignacio Hurtado de Mendoza, Conde de Cumbres Altas, was named to fill

one of the vacancies although not proposed by the Cámara. He had held a purchased appointment as a supernumerary oidor on the Audiencia of Quito since 1750. AGI, Quito, legajo 302, consulta, July 5, 1775.

41. In the order listed in Burkholder and Chandler, *From Impotence to Authority*, the thirty-two men were: Miguel de Martínez Escobar, Emetrio Cacho Calderón de la Barca, Juan Antonio Mon y Velarde, Ramón de Posada y Soto, Tomás González Calderón, Francisco de Saavedra y Carvajal, Modesto de Salcedo y Somodevilla, José Castilla Cavallero, José Cabeza Enríquez, Fernando Márquez de la Plata, Cosme Antonio de Mier y Trespalacios, Francisco Antonio de Moreno y Escandón, Joaquín Basco y Vargas, Jorge Escobedo Alarcón, Benito María de la Mata Linares, Juan Alvarez Valcárcel, Lorenzo Blanco Cicerón, Ambrosio Cerdán y Pontero, Joaquín de Gacitua Gómez de la Torre, José Gorvea Vadillo, Nicolás de Merida y Segura, José de Rezabal y Ugarte, Estanislao Joaquín de Andino, Luis de Chaves y Mendoza, Agustín Ignacio Emparán y Orbe, Miguel Cristóbal de Irisarri y Domínguez, Ciriaco González Carbajal, José Ortiz de la Peña, José Benito Rodríguez de Quiroga, Joaquín José Inclan y Arango, Julián Díaz de Saravia, and Domingo Arnáiz de las Revillas.

42. The six men were: Tomás Adan Martínez, Carlos Rafael de Ayerdi, Francisco Xavier de Gorospe y Padilla, Nicolás Piferrer, Estanislao Saravia y Rueda, and Felipe de Vergara. Carbonel was named Juez de Apelaciones (oidor) in 1784.

43. Tomás González Calderón and Francisco Antonio de Moreno y Escandón.

44. AGI, Lima, legajo 900, expediente 47, consulta, February 23, 1780.

45. AGI, Lima, legajo 620, letter by Manuel de Gorrichátegui to Julián de Arriaga, Madrid, November 24, 1774. Carlos Deustua Pimentel has published this letter in "Nuevos datos sobre José Baquíjano y Carrillo," *La Causa,* pp. 143–44, but incorrectly places it in AGI, Lima, legajo 624. ANP, Protocolos, Torres Preziado, Valentín de, legajo 1072 (1782–83), fol. 291v–293. "Declarac^n, La Condesa de Vistaflorida," Lima, April 24, 1782.

46. Gerónimo de Calatayud y Borda, *Elogio del excmo. señor D. José Baquíjano y Carrillo . . .* (Lima, 1813), p. 20.

47. Joseph de Baquíjano y Carrillo, *Alegato que en la oposición a la cátedra de prima de leyes . . .* (Lima, 1788).

48. AGI, Lima, legajo 620, *mesa* report, February 19, 1794.

49. *Ibid.*, royal order, Aranjuez, April 21, 1776.

50. *Ibid.*, letter by Baquíjano to Gálvez, Cádiz, May 31, 1776; AGI, Sección de la Casa de Contratación de las Indias, legajo 5522, expediente 33, letter by Baquíjano to President Francisco Manjón, Cádiz, December 23, 1776.

3

1. Jacot's gambling is reported in AGS, Gracia y Justicia, legajo 161 (antiguo), consulta, December 19, 1774.

2. John Lynch, *Spain under the Habsburgs* 2 vols. (New York, 1964–1969), 2:267. For further discussion see Richard L. Kagan, *Students and Society in Early Modern Spain* (Baltimore, 1974), particularly Part II.

3. Vicente Palacio Atard, *Los españoles de la ilustración* (Madrid, 1964), p. 133.

4. For example, see AGI, Audiencia of Panama, legajo 124, list of pretendientes for post left vacant by the death of Andrés Martínez de Amileta.

5. Olavide had served the chair of Maestro de las Sentencias. Luis Antonio Eguiguren, *Catálogo histórico del claustro de la Universidad de San Marcos 1576–1800* (Lima, 1912), pp. 21, 27, 28.

6. Burkholder and Chandler, *From Impotence to Authority*, Appendix X.

7. AGI, Lima, legajo 967, expediente 24. "Relación de los méritos, y servicios del Dr. Don Joseph Baquíjano Carrillo de Córdoba . . . ," Madrid, December 4, 1793 (hereafter Relación de méritos, 1793).

8. *Constituciones para la Real Universidad,* . . . (Lima, 1771). See also Daniel Valcárcel, *Reforma de San Marcos en la época de Amat* (Lima, 1955).

9. *Constituciones para la Real Universidad,* constituciones 2, 9, 10, 16, 12, 17, 30, 18.

10. *Relaciones de los vireyes y audiencias que han gobernado el Perú,* 3 vols. (vol. I, Lima, 1867, vols. II and III, Madrid, 1871–1872), 3:16, 133.

11. AGI, Lima, legajo 958, "Copia de la instrucción reserbada que el Sor D^n Josef Antonio de Areche, Visitador Gral. q^e fué del reyno del Perú entregó en consequencia de lo prevenido en la real orn. de 8 de septiembre a D^n Fernando Márquez de la Plata," Lima, February 1, 1783; *Relaciones de los vireyes,* 3:16–17.

12. The decree was dated July 13, 1780. The cloister received it on July 20, the day Jáuregui replaced Guirior as viceroy. Areche later accused Guirior of pre-dating the decree. Eguiguren, *Diccionario,* III, 19–20; AGI, Lima, legajo 967, expediente 24, Relación de méritos, 1793; *ibid.,* legajo 958, "Copia de la instrucción," Lima, February 1, 1783.

13. AGI, Lima, legajo 967, expediente 24, Baquíjano to the King, Aranjuez, April 30, 1798.

14. *Relaciones de los vireyes,* 3:16.

15. George M. Addy, *The Enlightenment in the University of Salamanca* (Durham, 1966), pp. 108, 279–87.

16. AHN, Códices, legajo 239B. "Memorias académicas."

17. *Constituciones,* título I, constituciones ix, v. The *Constituciones* are reprinted in David Rubio, *La Universidad de San Marcos de Lima durante la colonización española (datos para su historia)* (Madrid, 1933), pp. 43–216.

18. *Relaciones de los vireyes,* 3:134, Eguiguren, *Diccionario,* 3:65–68.

19. Decree by Jáuregui, Lima, May 31, 1781. Printed in Eguiguren, *Diccionario,* 3:68.

20. Delay had an additional advantage in that his interim appointment to the Audiencia rendered his eligibility uncertain. See *Constituciones,* título I, constitución xi.

21. *Constituciones,* título VI, constituciones xv, lxxi; Eguiguren, *Diccionario,* 3:19–20; AGI, Lima, legajo 1004, letter by Tomás José de Orrantia, Lima, May 19, 1792.

22. AGI, Lima, legajo 941, expediente 32, Relación de méritos, 1781.

23. *Ibid.*

24. For example, AGS, Sección XXIII, Inventario 2, legajo 18, título 260, Tomás Brun, protector of the Indians, San Lorenzo, August 30, 1720.

25. AGI, Lima, legajo 792, letter by Melchor de Jacot to Gálvez, Lima, February 20, 1778.

26. AGI, Lima, legajo 1082, royal order to Areche, San Ildefonso, September 24, 1778; *ibid.,* legajo 995, letter by Joaquín de Galdeano to Gálvez, Lima, October 5, 1778; *ibid.,* legajo 1083, letter 74 by Areche to Gálvez, Lima, February 20, 1779; *ibid.,* legajo 598, confidential letter by Gálvez to Areche, San Ildefonso, August 1, 1779.

27. AGI, Lima, legajo 941, expediente 32, Relación de méritos, 1781.

28. AGI, Lima, legajo 621, letter by Baquíjano to the King, San Ildefonso, December 7, 1796; *ibid.,* legajo 620, extract of a letter by Baquíjano, Madrid, December 27, 1793.

29. AGI, Lima, legajo 599, informe by the Audiencia of Lima, Lima, January 7, 1793.

30. AGI, Lima, legajo 1548, Baquíjano to the King, San Ildefonso, September 2, 1795; Baquíjano, *Alegato.*

31. ANP, Real Audiencia, procedimientos Penales, legajo 37, año 1779, "Autos que sigue D^n Jossef Bernuy contra Manuel Cartagena sobre exsesos año de 1779."

32. *Ibid.,* legajo 39, año 1780, "Quad^{no} 3° Yncidencia de la causa criminal seg^{da} de oficio cont^a Pablo Sipion Cusisoli . . . ."

33. "Exposición que hace el Dr. José Baquíjano abogado y protector general de tem-

poralidades, de los bienes dejados en Arequipa por la Compañía de Jesús y su aplicación para Universidad y otros fines," Lima, December 6, 1779. Printed in Víctor M. Barriga, *Documentos para la historia de la Universidad de Arequipa 1765–1828* (Arequipa, 1953), pp. 60–73.

34. Opinion by Baquíjano, Lima, August 22, 1780. Printed in Luis Antonio Eguiguren, *Guerra separatista (1777–1780)* (Lima, 1942), pp. 19–28, 52–65.

35. ANP, Real Audiencia, Procedimientos Penales, legajo 38, año 1779, "Autos criminales que siguen cont^a Pedro Jph Soria alias Piñita. . . ," 1779.

36. Baquíjano, *Alegato*.

37. AGI, Mexico, legajo 1641, royal decree to the Conde de Valdellano, El Pardo, March 11, 1776.

38. AGI, Lima, legajo 941, expediente 32, Relación de méritos, 1781.

39. The traditional interpretation is best stated by José de la Riva-Agüero who considered the *Eulogy* "the remote omen of Independence." For his ground-breaking biographical study see "Don José Baquíjano y Carrillo," *El Ateneo de Lima*, VII, No. 38 (1905), 1946–79 and VII, No. 39 (1906), 5–47. See also Carlos Deustua Pimentel, *José Baquíjano y Carrillo* (Biblioteca Hombres del Perú, Primera edición, Primera serie, VII: Lima, 1964). Fredrick B. Pike has brought the accepted Peruvian perspective into English in *The Modern History of Peru* (New York, 1967), pp. 34–35. For a discussion of Baquíjano in historical thought see Mark Alan Burkholder, "José Baquíjano and the Audiencia of Lima," (Ph.D. diss., Duke University, 1970), Chapter I.

40. AGI, Lima, legajo 1445, letter by Areche to Gálvez, Lima, June 20, 1777; *ibid.*, Lima 1088, letter by Areche to Gálvez, Lima, June 26, 1782.

41. Vicente Palacio Atard, *Areche y Guirior. Observaciones sobre el fracaso de una visita al Perú* (Seville, 1946) has set forth the conflict between Areche and Guirior but does not discuss Jacot.

42. AGI, Lima, legajo 655, letter 104 by Guirior to Gálvez, Lima, January 20, 1777; *ibid.*, legajo 654, letter 19 by Guirior to Gálvez, Lima, September 20, 1776.

43. AGI, Lima, legajo 792, letters by Jacot to Gálvez, Lima, June 20, 1777 and July 20, 1777.

44. *Ibid.*, August 20, 1777.

45. *Ibid.*, September 20, 1777.

46. *Ibid.*, and letter by Jacot to Gálvez, Lima, November 20, 1777.

47. AGI, Lima, legajo 891, expediente 18; *ibid.*, legajo 645A, letter 383 by Guirior to Gálvez, Lima, December 20, 1778, and Antonio de Porlier to Gálvez, Madrid, September 24, 1779; *ibid.*, legajo 645B contains examples of later letters by Guirior about Jacot.

48. AGI, Lima, legajo 1445, letter by Areche to Gálvez, Lima, June 20, 1777; *ibid.*, legajo 792, letter 3 by Jacot to Gálvez, Lima, May 28, 1782.

49. The instructions to Areche can be found in AGI, Lima, legajo 1082.

50. Palacio Atard discusses the controversies briefly in *Areche y Guirior*, particularly pages 31–45.

51. AGI, Lima, legajo 792, letter by Jacot to Gálvez, Lima, June 5, 1780. On June 20, 1780, Jáuregui replaced Guirior as viceroy.

52. AGI, Lima, legajo 1087, letter 432 by Areche to Gálvez, Lima, May 3, 1782; Palacio Atard, *Areche y Guirior*, p. 27.

53. AGI, Lima, legajo 598, royal order to Guirior, Madrid, July 31, 1778; *ibid.*, legajo 931, letter by Guirior, Lima, April 3, 1779.

54. AGI, Indiferente General, legajo 513, título for Agustín de Jáuregui, Viceroy of Peru, El Pardo, January 10, 1780.

55. AGI, Lima, legajo 640, highly confidential letter to Teodoro de Croix, El Pardo, March 28, 1783.

56. AGI, Lima, legajo 958, "Actuaciones reservadas, Concluye el Núm. 68," royal order by Gálvez to Fernando Márquez de la Plata, San Ildefonso, September 8, 1781.

57. AGI, Lima, legajo 780, letter by Guirior to the King, Lima, August 24, 1780; Palacio Atard, *Areche y Guirior*, p. 47.

58. For a full discussion, see Mark A. Burkholder, "From Creole to *Peninsular:* The Transformation of the Audiencia of Lima," *HAHR*, 52:3 (August 1972), 395–415. See also Leon G. Campbell, "A Colonial Establishment: Creole Domination of the Audiencia of Lima During the Late Eighteenth Century," *ibid.*, 52:1 (February 1972), 1–25.

59. AGI, Lima, legajo 1085, letter 289 by Areche to Gálvez, Cuzco, June 12, 1781.

60. AGI, Indiferente General, legajo 513, "Despacho de Virreyes Peru desde 13 de Octu^{re} de 1761 hasta 14 de Jul^{o} de 1800," title of Agustín de Jáuregui, Viceroy of Peru, El Pardo, January 10, 1780.

61. AGI, Lima, legajo 1085, letter 277 by Areche to Gálvez, Cuzco, April 30, 1781; letter 278 by Areche to Gálvez, Cuzco, April 30, 1781; letter 289 by Areche to Gálvez, Cuzco, June 12, 1781.

62. *Ibid.*, letter 278 by Areche to Gálvez, Cuzco, April 30, 1781.

63. AGI, Lima, legajo 1085, letter 278 by Areche to Gálvez, April 30, 1781; confidential letter 295 by Areche to Gálvez, Cuzco, July 17, 1781; letter 263 by Areche to Gálvez, Cuzco, March 1, 1781.

64. AGI, Lima, legajo 958, "Copia de la instrucción," Lima, February 1, 1783.

65. Eguiguren, *Diccionario*, 3:325–26. The total cost of the reception was 23,064 pesos.

66. Joseph de Baquíjano y Carrillo, *Elogio del excelentisimo Señor Don Agustín de Jáuregui, y Aldecoa. . . .* (Lima, 1781). For a more detailed examination of the *Eulogy* and the reaction to it, see Burkholder, "José Baquíjano and the Audiencia of Lima," Chapter V.

67. Jefferson Rea Spell, *Rousseau in the Spanish World Before 1833. A Study in Franco-Spanish Literary Relations* (Austin, 1938), p. 136.

68. Eguiguren, *Diccionario*, 3:326. For sake of clarity, I employ *Eulogy* to refer to the printed version of the speech and "eulogy" for the oral presentation.

69. See Burkholder, "José Baquíjano and the Audiencia of Lima," pp. 130–31.

70. AGI, Lima, legajo 996, confidential royal order to Jáuregui and Escobedo, Aranjuez, April 24, 1782.

71. AGI, Lima, legajo 1086, letter 326 by Areche to Gálvez, Lima, November 3, 1781. Carlos Deustua Pimentel has also perceived the importance of Areche's criticism for the fate of the *Elogio*. See "El Visitador Areche y el 'Elogio' de don José Baquíjano y Carrillo," *Boletín del Instituto Riva-Agüero (Lima)*, 8 (1969–1971):124–34.

72. AGI, Lima, legajo 1086, letter 341 by Areche to Gálvez, Lima, November 22, 1781. Although letter 341 was dated November 22, the documents it cited were not completed and consequently it was not sent with letters numbered 322 to 344 on November 23. *Ibid.*, "Yndice de las cartas de oficio que en esta fha. dirige el Visitador Genl del Perú al Exmo. Señor D. Joseph de Gálvez," Lima, November 23, 1781.

73. AGI, Lima, legajo 1000, expediente 356, mesa report.

74. This and the following seven paragraphs come from AGI, Lima, legajo 1086, letter 341 by Areche to Gálvez, Lima, November 3, 1781.

75. In Buenos Aires Juan Baltasar Maziel, a creole educator, commented at length on the Elogio, but no evidence has been found that his criticisms ever reached Gálvez. See Juan Probst, *Juan Baltasar Maziel el maestro de la generación de mayo* (Buenos Aires, 1946), pp. 203–18. The *Reflexiones sobre la famosa arenga, pronunciada en Lima por un individuo de la Universidad de San Marcos . . .* is printed in *ibid.*, pp. 389–456.

76. AGI, Lima, legajo 958, "Respuesta de Sor. Fiscal," Madrid, December 18, 1784.

77. AGI, Lima, legajo 1000, confidential letter 8 by Jáuregui to Gálvez, Lima, January

16, 1783; *ibid.*, marginal note; confidential royal orders to Jáuregui and Escobedo, San Ildefonso, August 1, 1783.

78. AGI, Lima, legajo 1000, expediente 356, order by Jáuregui to Juan María de Gálvez, Lima, January 31, 1784; Juan María de Gálvez to Jáuregui, Lima, April 1, 1784; Jáuregui to Gálvez, Lima, April 1, 1784.

79. Porcel's response in the following four paragraphs is from AGI, Lima, legajo 1000, expediente 356, mesa report.

80. *Ibid.*, royal orders to Croix and Escobedo, San Ildefonso, August 10, 1785.

81. AGI, Lima, legajo 1000, letter 563 by Croix to the Marqués de Sonora, Lima, February 28, 1787.

82. *Ibid.*, expediente 563, memorial by Baquíjano, Lima, n.d.; Miguel Maticorena Estrada has published this document in "Nuevas noticias y documentos de don José Baquíjano y Carrillo, Conde de Vista-Florida," *La causa*, pp. 164–66. For him, as for Deustua Pimentel, however, the "real" Baquíjano is the one who wrote the *Eulogy*, not the memorial. See Miguel Maticorena Estrada, "José Baquíjano y Carrillo, reformista peruano del siglo XVIII," *Revista de estudios americanos* (Seville), 15:76–77. (January-February, 1958) 55–56 and Carlos Deustua Pimentel, *José Baquíjano y Carrillo*, pp. 22–24.

83. AGI, Lima, legajo 1000, letter 563 by Croix to the Marqués de Sonora, Lima, February 28, 1787.

84. AGI, Lima, legajo 599, "Consulta de la Cámara en vista de la solicitud de Dn. José Baquíjano á honores de oydor de Lima con antiguedad y obción en la primera vacante: Pretensión del interesado al mismo efecto, y noticias de su anterior conducta."

4

1. Eguiguren, *Diccionario*, 3:83–85.

2. *Ibid.*

3. AGI, Lima, legajo 914, expediente 70, no. 1, interrogatory, p. 8v; petition by Baquíjano, pp. 34v–39.

4. *Ibid.*, p. 8; Burkholder and Chandler, *From Impotence to Authority*, Appendix X; Bromley, "Alcaldes de la Ciudad de Lima," p. 352.

5. Eguiguren, *Diccionario*, 1:539; AGI, Lima, legajo 914, expediente 70, no. 1, p. 43v.

6. See AGI, Lima, legajo 914, expediente 70.

7. *Ibid.*, statement by Antonio Alvarez de Ron, August 27, 1783.

8. Eguiguren, *Diccionario*, 2:246.

9. AGI, Lima, legajo 770, letter by José María Boza and Diego Boza, n.d. See also, AGI, Lima, legajo 914, expediente 70, memorial by Antonio Alvarez de Ron, p. 12.

10. *Ibid.*, interrogatory, pp. 7v–8v.

11. AGI, Lima, legajo 998, letter 348 by Escobedo to Gálvez, Lima, September 20, 1784; legajo 941, expediente 32, opinion of the viceroy's legal adviser (asesor general), Lima, July 30, 1785.

12. AGI, Lima, legajo 914, expediente 70, vista fiscal, Madrid, August 6, 1786.

13. AGI, Lima, legajo 914, expediente 70, no. 1, diligencia, Lima, August 5, 1783, pp. 28v–29.

14. *Ibid.*, certification by José Antonio Gimeno y Amarita, Lima, August 6, 1783, p. 2.

15. *Ibid.*, vista fiscal, Madrid, August 6, 1786; memorial by Baquíjano, n.d.

16. *Ibid.*, p. 41.

17. AGI, Lima, legajo 914, expediente 70, no. 2, decrees by Croix, Lima, June 17 and June 25, 1784, pp. 2v, 5.

18. AGI, Lima, legajo 914, expediente 70, vista fiscal, Madrid, August 6, 1786.

19. *Ibid.*, consejo pleno de dos salas, October 26, 1786.

20. AGI, Lima, legajo 998, letter 348 by Escobedo to Gálvez, Lima, September 20, 1784.

21. *Ibid.*

22. Representation by Baquíjano, Lima, n.d. Printed in Eguiguren, *Diccionario*, 3:110–13. Jáuregui passed it to the cloister on January 16, 1784.

23. *Ibid.*, p. 110.

24. *Ibid.*, p. 126.

25. AGI, Lima, legajo 941, expediente 32.

26. Previous students of Baquíjano's university activities have emphasized that the conflict with Villalta for the rectorship was fought over the issue of university reform, particularly in the matter of curriculum. A close reading of the hundreds of pages of testimony growing out of the controversy does not support this interpretation.

27. The chair was filled by Francisco Antonio Ruíz Cano y Galeano, Marqués de Sotoflorido. See Eguiguren, *Catálogo*, p. 25.

28. AGI, Lima, legajo 941, expediente 32, certification by Cortijo, Lima, August 1, 1788.

29. *Ibid.*, Pedro Díaz Ybáñez and Narciso Francisco Blázquez (for Baquíjano) to Señor, Madrid, March 4, 1789.

30. *Ibid.*, representation by the ecclesiastical cabildo of Lima to Croix, Lima, October 27, 1788.

31. AGI, Lima, legajo 1002, letter by Manuel Estanislao García Vargas y Ribera to Antonio Porlier, Lima, May 20, 1788.

32. AGI, Lima, legajo 941, expediente 32, Estevan Bueno Ruimonte (for Larrión), to Señor, Madrid, March 30, 1789.

33. *Ibid.*, and Antonio Luis Guazo and Juan Escolano (for Larrión) to Señor, Madrid, May 15, 1792.

34. *Ibid.*, Nicolas Fernández Rivera (for Villalta), Madrid, February 13, 1787.

35. *Ibid.*, Estevan Bueno Ruimonte (for Larrión) to Señor, Madrid, March 30, 1789.

36. AGI, Lima, legajo 886, informe by Diego Antonio, Archbishop of Lima, Lima, June 18, 1776; Eguiguren, *Catálogo*, pp. 34, 40, 42.

37. AGI, Lima, legajo 941, expediente 32, Estevan Bueno Ruimonte (for Larrión) to Señor, Madrid, March 30, 1789.

38. AGI, Lima, legajo 770, letter by José María Boza and Diego Boza, n.d.

39. AGI, Lima, legajo 941, expediente 32, certification by Cortijo, Lima, August 1, 1788. Each voter cast several ballots, the number varying with his rank and faculty.

40. *Ibid.*, Estevan Bueno Ruimonte (for Larrión) to Señor, Madrid, March 30, 1789.

41. *Ibid.*, Croix to Señor, Lima, October 5, 1788.

42. *Ibid.*, Baquíjano to Excelentísimo Señor, Lima, July 14, 1788.

43. *Ibid.*, auto, Lima, July 21, 1788.

44. *Ibid.*, Croix to Señor, Lima, October 5, 1788.

45. For example, see *ibid.*, Pedro Díaz Ybáñez and Narciso Francisco Blázquez (for Baquíjano) to Señor, Madrid, March 4, 1789 and Ruimonte (for Larrión) to Señor, Madrid, March 30, 1789.

46. *Ibid.*, opinion by the fiscal, Madrid, October 27, 1790.

47. *Ibid.*, confirmation by the Council of the Indies, Madrid, February 23, 1791.

48. *Ibid.*, cédula, April 19, 1791.

49. AGI, Lima, legajo 640, highly confidential instructions to D. Teodoro de Croix, El Pardo, March 28, 1783.

50. Croix assumed his office on April 4, 1784.

51. Richard Konetzke, "Ideas políticas del Virrey Francisco Gil de Taboada," *Mar del*

sur (Lima), 7:20 (March/April, 1952), 44–55; Allan J. Kuethe, *Military Reform and Society in New Granada, 1773–1808* (Gainesville, 1978), pp. 145–58.

52. AGI, Lima, legajo 1000, letter 7, Croix to Porlier, Lima, February 27, 1788. Escobedo and his family left Callao on the frigate *La Concordia* on February 27.

53. Eguiguren, *Diccionario*, 3:725.

54. *Ibid.*, 2:238; Lohmann Villena, *Los ministros*, p. 17.

55. Eguiguren, Diccionario, 3:298–99; AGI, Lima, legajo 967, expediente 24, Relación de méritos, 1793. It is worth recalling that Orrantia's father, an oidor of Lima, was a witness at Baquíjano's baptism.

56. "Historia de la fundación, progresos, y actual estado de la Real Universidad de San Marcos de Lima," *Mercurio peruano*, 1:53–56. (July 7-July 17, 1791), 166–204; Baquíjano, *Elogio*.

57. Consideration of possible opposition based upon Eguiguren, *Catálogo*.

58. AGI, Lima, legajo 967, expediente 24, Relación de méritos, 1793.

59. AGI, Lima, legajo 620, letter by Tomás Joseph de Orrantia to Excmo. Señor, Lima, January 8, 1793.

60. *Ibid.*, letter by Thomas Joseph de Orrantia y Alberro and Mariano de Llano y Cortijo to Señor, Lima, January 19, 1793.

61. AGI, Lima, legajo 710, expediente 19. "In Spanish universities, making *réplica* was generally the same as 'making an opposition' or objection to the respondent, who maintained his thesis against the difficulties proposed." John Tate Lanning, *The University in the Kingdom of Guatemala* (Ithaca, 1955), p. 318.

62. AGI, Lima, legajo 710, expediente 19, oficio by Christóbal Montaño to Gil, Lima, January 14, 1795 and letter 19 by Gil to Llaguno, Lima, January 23, 1795.

63. Gregorio Marañón, *Las ideas biológicas del Padre Feijóo* (3rd ed.; Madrid, 1954), p. 17 gives the figure 420,000. Vicente Palacio Atard, "La influencia del P. Feijóo in América," in *Simposio sobre el Padre Feijóo y su siglo* (Oviedo, 1966), p. 22 provides the figure 528,000 volumes.

64. See John Tate Lanning, *The Eighteenth-Century Enlightenment in the University of San Carlos de Guatemala* (Ithaca, 1956), pp. 158–60 and Arturo Ardao, *La filosofía polémica de Feijóo* (Buenos Aires, 1962), p. 15, 18.

65. Agustín Millares Carlos, "Prólogo," in *Clasicos Castellanos* (Madrid, 1923), 48:10, 40.

66. For example, see Joseph Mariano Gregorio de Elizalde Ita y Parra, "Parecer" in Benito Gerónymo Feijóo, *Theatro crítico universal, o discursos varios en todo género de materias, para desengaño de errores comunes*, 8 vols. (Madrid, 1753), 4.

67. Baquíjano, *Alegato*.

68. Feijóo, *Theatro crítico universal*, 1:1, "Voz del pueblo."

69. An effort to analyze Baquíjano's thought systematically is José Ignacio López Soria, "El pensamiento de José Baquíjano y Carrillo," *Historia y cultura* (Lima), 5 (1971): 94–185.

70. Ignacio de Castro, *Disertación sobre la concepción de Nra. Sra.* (Lima, 1782); Ignacio de Castro, *Segunda disertación* (Lima, 1784); José Manuel Bermúdez, *Sermon predicado el día de la santísima trinidad*, . . . (Lima, 1781); Gerónimo de Calatayud y Borda, *Oración Fúnebre que en las solemnes exequias de la R.M. María Antonio de San Joseph, Larrea, Arispe, de los Reyes* . . . (Lima, 1782); Estevan de Terralla y Landa, *Lamento métrico general llanto funesto, y gemido triste . . . Carlos III . . .* (Lima, 1790).

71. Castro, *Segunda disertación*.

72. Letter by the Conde de Vistaflorida to Domingo Ramírez de Arellano, Madrid, June 27, 1787, quoted in Riva-Agüero, "Don José Baquíjano de Beascoa," *Revista de archivos*, p. 82, fn. 3.

73. See below, p. 144.

74. See Robert Jones Shafer, *The Economic Societies in the Spanish World (1763-1821)* (Syracuse, 1958), pp. 55, 262-67, 345 and 71 and fn. 138.

75. José Cabeza Enríquez, Benito María de la Mata Linares, and Francisco Xavier de Moreno y Escandón. Moreno was also director of the Economic Society in Manila before his advancement to Lima.

76. Shafer, *Economic Societies*, pp. 145 and 157; "Historia de la Sociedad Académica de Amantes del País y principios del *Mercurio peruano*," *Mercurio peruano* 1:7 (January 23, 1791):49-52. Secondary material on the *Mercurio* and its participants is growing. In addition to Shafer's brief treatment in *Economic Societies*, pp. 157-68, William Pratt Dale provided an anlysis of the *Mercurio* in "The Cultural Revolution in Peru, 1750-1820," (Ph.D. diss., Duke University, 1941), pp. 99-122. Throughout this dissertation Dale emphasized cultural and scientific concern by Society members. John E. Woodham examined the ideas of the principal contributor of scientific materials, Hipólito Unanue, in "Hipólito Unanue and the Enlightenment in Peru," (Ph.D. diss., Duke University, 1964). More recently, Josefina C. Tiryakian has focused upon the periodical in terms of economic developments in Peru during the eighteenth century in "The *Mercurio peruano*: Herald of the Modernization of Peru in the Eighteenth Century," (Ph.D. diss., Harvard University, 1969). She emphasized the *Mercurio* as an advocate of modern economic reforms decreed by the Spanish government after 1776.

77. AGI, Lima, legajo 1004, representation by Jayme Bausate y Mesa, Lima, March 16, 1791; letter by Bausate to Señor, Lima, August 5, 1791.

78. "Historia de la Sociedad Académica," pp. 49-52.

79. José Rossi y Rubí, José María Egaña, Demetrio Guasque; Father Francisco Romero, Father Francisco González Laguna, Father Tomás de Méndez y Lachica, Fray Diego Cisneros; José Baquíjano, Hipólito Unanue; Jacinto Calero y Moreira.

80. Rossi, Egaña, Guasque, Baquíjano, Unanue, Calero.

81. AGI, Lima, legajo 708, letter 140 by Gil to the Marqués de Bajamar, Lima, November 5, 1792; Francisco Gil de Taboada y Lemos, *Memoria*, Vol. VI: *Memorias de los vireyes que han gobernado el Perú, durante el tiempo del coloniaje español*, 6 vols. (Lima, 1859):94-95.

82. "Historia de la Sociedad Académica," pp. 49-50; "Introducción al tomo VII del *Mercurio peruano*," *Mercurio peruano* 7:209 (January 3, 1793):13; "Proyectos literarios," *ibid.*, 3:91 (November 17, 1791):196-99; "Análisis del curso filosófico del Padre Celis, publicado en la *Gazeta de literatura de México* al núm. 17," *ibid.*, 9:293 (October 24, 1793):125.

83. Tiryakian, "The *Mercurio peruano*," p. 326.

84. Jacinto Calero y Moreira, *Prospecto del papel periódico intitulado Mercurio peruano . . .* [Lima, 1790.]

85. "Propuesta de unos premios para las disertaciones en que se proponga el método más económico, fácil, y permanente para mejorar los caminos del reyno," *Mercurio peruano* 3:74 (September 18, 1791):41-45.

86. Citations to these writings are in Burkholder, "José Baquíjano," p. 200, n. 2.

87. AGI, Lima, legajo 967, expediente 24, Relación de méritos, 1793.

88. "Disertación histórica y política sobre el comercio del Perú," *Mercurio peruano* 1:23-31 (March 20, 1791-April 17, 1791):209-89.

89. Eduardo Arcila Farías, *El pensamiento económico hispano-americano en Baquíjano y Carrillo* (Caracas, 1976), pp. 60-61.

90. For a discussion of Baquíjano's heavy reliance upon a 1790 "Informe" by the merchant guild of Lima, see Tiryakian, "The *Mercurio peruano*," pp. 336-37 and Josefina Cintrón Tiryakian, "La Disertación de José Baquíjano y Carrillo: plagio o parelelismo," *Latinoamérica* (Mexico, 1973), 65-83. "Apéndice de la Sociedad," *Mercurio peruano* 1:31 (April 17, 1791), 289.

91. "Introducción al tomo II," *Mercurio peruano* 2:35 (May 1, 1791):1-6.

92. "Introducción al tomo III," *Mercurio peruano* 3:69 (September 1, 1791):318-22.

93. "No. 23. Exped^te en copia certificada sre. la formalización de la Sociedad de Amantes del País para el *Mercurio peruano*," Yale University Library. Also see "Progresos y estado actual de la Sociedad de Amantes del País," *Mercurio peruano* 10:329-30 (February 27, 1794-March 2, 1794):135-50.

94. AGI, Lima, legajo 647, royal order, Aranjuez, June 9, 1791. Printed in "Introducción al tomo VII. del *Mercurio peruano*," *Mercurio peruano* 7:209 (January 3, 1793):6.

95. AGI, Lima, legajo 708, letter 140 by Gil to the Marqués de Bajamar, Lima, November 5, 1792.

96. Baquíjano sailed on January 18, 1793. AHN, Sección de Inquisición, legajo 2216, expediente 4, Lima, cartas al Consejo, 1793, letter by the Lima Inquisition, February 7, 1793. Calero left on January 17, 1793. AGI, Lima, legajo 599, Relación de los méritos y servicios de Don Jacinto Muñoz Calero, Madrid, January 17, 1794; supplication by Calero to Señor, San Lorenzo, September 30, 1796.

97. AGI, Lima, legajo 599, letter by José Rossi y Rubí to Señor, Aranjuez, April 16, 1794; "Progresos y estado actual de la Sociedad de Amantes del País," p. 143. The Society gave Rossi the title of "Founder" for his services.

98. For a succinct statement of the difficulties of the *Mercurio*, see "Introducción al tomo X del *Mercurio peruano*," *Mercurio peruano* 10:313 (January 2, 1794):1-5.

99. AGI, Lima, legajo 967, expediente 24, Relación de méritos, 1793.

100. AGI, Lima, legajo 708, note on the extract of letter 140 by Gil to Bajamar, Lima, November 5, 1792.

101. AGI, Lima, legajo 599, memorial by Calero to Señor, San Lorenzo, September 30, 1796; *ibid.*, letter by Rossi to Señor, Aranjuez, April 16, 1794; *ibid.*, legajo 1008, undated letter by Unanue accompanying letter 123 by Viceroy Marqués de Osorno to Caballero, Lima, July 23, 1800; *ibid.*, legajo 728, memorial by Egaña, Lima, January 28, 1793.

5

1. He had entered the Order of Charles III on December 8, 1791, perhaps with the aid of his brother, a Knight of Santiago. Baquíjano's activities through 1792 are summarized in AGI, Lima, legajo 967, expediente 24, Relación de méritos, 1793.

2. The Condesa de Vistaflorida died in Lima in February 14, 1791. AGI, Lima, legajo 699, expediente 95.

3. ANP, Protocolos, Torres Preziado, Valentín de, legajo 1072 (1782-83), p. 291v-93, declaration by the Condesa de Vistaflorida, Lima, April 24, 1782; Riva-Agüero, "Don José de Beascoa," p. 173.

4. AGI, Lima, legajo 620, letter by Baquíjano to Gil, n.d.; *Constituciones*, título VI, constitución lxxiii.

5. AGI, Lima, legajo 599, letter by Baquíjano to Señor, Aranjuez, April 23, 1794; *ibid.*, legajo 949, expediente 15, cabildo of Lima, January 17, 1793; *ibid.*, legajo 967, expediente 24, Relación de méritos, 1793.

6. AGI, Lima, legajo 620, approval by Gil on a letter by Tomás Joseph de Orrantia, Lima, January 8, 1793; legajo 599, letter by Baquíjano to Señor, Aranjuez, April 23, 1794.

7. AGI, Lima, legajo 599, informe by the Audiencia of Lima to Señor, Lima, January 7, 1793; *ibid.*, legajo 620, letter by Orrantia to Señor, Lima, January 9, 1793; *ibid.*, legajo 949, expediente 15, copy of the minutes of the cabildo meeting, Lima, January 2, 1793.

8. AHN, Inquisición, legajo 2216, expediente 4, Lima, cartas al Consejo, 1793, letter from Inquisition of Lima, Lima, February 7, 1793.

9. Richard Herr, *The Eighteenth-Century Revolution in Spain* (Princeton, 1958), pp. 282, 285–6, 312–13.

10. *Ibid.*, pp. 314, 335, 376–97.

11. Information on Baquíjano's apartment in this and the following paragraph is from the Hispanic Society of America, New York, Salazar y Baquíjano, Manuel, Conde de Vistaflorida. Correspondencia de Joseph Baquíjano y Manuel Salazar y Baquíjano con Miguel de Nájera, su agente en la corte de Madrid (v.p.) 1799–1827. MS HC418/403/1. I want to thank Dr. César Pacheco Vélez for granting me permission to use this material and the Hispanic Society of America for providing me with microfilm of these documents. Some of the materials have been published with an introduction by Pacheco Vélez in "José Baquíjano y Carrillo en Cádiz (1799–1802)," *Quinto Congreso Internacional de Historia de América*, 5 vols. (Lima, 1972), 2:531–93.

12. Addresses are from *Kalendario manual, y guía de forasteros en Madrid, para el año de 1793* (Madrid 1793). Locations were determined using Charles E. Kany, *Life and Manners in Madrid 1750–1800* (Berkeley, 1932), illustrations 19, 65.

13. Lohmann Villena, *Los americanos* 2:326, 425. Calero also lived on Carrera de San Gerónimo, quite likely in Baquíjano's apartment.

14. *Ibid.*, pp. 61–62.

15. *Ibid.*, AHN, Estado, expediente 579, pruebas de Don José Javier de Baquíjano, Conde de Vistaflorida.

16. *Ibid.*

17. Lohmann Villena, *Los americanos* 2:62; AGS, Gracia y Justicia, legajo 163 (antiguo), consulta, May 9, 1781.

18. AGI, Lima, legajo 599, extract, Madrid, December 13, 1793; *ibid.*, legajo 620, extract, Madrid, December 27, 1793; *ibid.*, legajo 599, Baquíjano to Señor, Aranjuez, April 23, 1794; *ibid.*, legajo 620, Baquíjano to Señora, San Ildefonso, August 16, 1794; *ibid.*, legajo 599, Baquíjano to Señor, San Lorenzo, November 1, 1798.

19. *Novísima recopilación*, libro III, título xxii.

20. *Ibid.*, ley ii.

21. *Ibid.*, ley v.

22. AHN, Consejo de Castilla, legajo 21730, Conde de Vistaflorida to Excmo. Señor, Madrid, December 19, 1789.

23. *Novísima recopilación*, libro III, título xxii, ley xvi.

24. AGI, Lima, legajo 599, súplica by Jacinto Muñoz Calero to Señor, San Lorenzo, September 30, 1796. The claim was obviously exaggerated since he remained for several more years.

25. José de la Riva-Agüero, "Un capítulo inédito de la nueva biografía de Baquíjano y Carrillo," *Boletín del Museo Bolivariano* (Lima) 1:12 (August 1929), 496.

26. AHN, Consejo de Castilla, legajo 27537, expediente 8.

27. See Kany, *Life and Manners.*

28. AGI, Lima, legajo 599, copy of certification by Pedro de Lerma, Madrid, June 23, 1692.

29. AGI, Lima, legajo 949, expediente 15, letter by Baquíjano to Señor, El Escorial, December 13, 1793.

30. AGI, Lima, legajo 620, report by the fiscal of the Council of the Indies.

31. *Ibid.*, letter by Baquíjano to Señor, Aranjuez, April 23, 1794.

32. AGI, Lima, legajo 949, expediente 15, "De parte á 26 de abril de 1794."

33. AGI, Lima, legajo 600.

34. Riva-Agüero, "Un capítulo inédito," p. 496.

35. AGI, Lima, legajo 600, mesa report, note of March 16, 1802.

36. Archivo Municipal (Lima), Libro de cabildo 39, pp. 139–146b.

37. Burkholder and Chandler, *From Impotence to Authority*, Appendixes I and IX.

38. Francisco Antonio de Moreno y Escandón, Joaquín de Mosquera y Figueroa, and José Antonio Berrio y Guzmán.

39. José Casimiro Gómez García was Baquíjano's uncle. Cristóbal Mesía y Munive had been educated in Lima and married a Peruvian wife. Antonio de Porlier and Gerónimo Manuel de Ruedas Morales were peninsulars without initial ties, but Ruedas married Baquíjano's sister. Benito de Casal y Montenegro was named to the Audiencia but never served, and limeño Manuel de Mansilla received his initial appointment in 1750 although he did not assume a seat until after a second appointment in 1770. Both of these men have been omitted from the figures.

40. This dramatic change has been treated at length in Burkholder, "From Creole to *Peninsular.*"

41. Manuel de Mansilla.

42. AGI, Lima, legajo 599, memorial by Miguel Díaz Rivera to Eugenio de Llaguno, Madrid, September 7, 1796.

43. See Appendix C.

44. AGI, Lima, legajo 599, memorial by Miguel Díaz Rivera to Eugenio de Llaguno, Madrid, September 7, 1796.

45. Jacques A. Barbier, "The Culmination of the Bourbon Reforms, 1787–1792," *HAHR*, 57:1 (February, 1977), 56–58.

46. AGI, Mexico, legajo 1642, consulta, January 28, 1795.

47. *Ibid.*, memorial by Pedro Joseph de Torres, 1786; AGI, Lima, legajo 599, memorial by Miguel Díaz Rivera to Eugenio de Llaguno, Madrid, September 7, 1796.

48. AGI, Mexico, legajo 1642.

49. AGI, Audiencia of Caracas, legajo 16, memorial by Aurioles.

50. AGI, Lima, legajo 967, expediente 24, Relación de méritos, 1793.

51. AGI, Lima, legajo 620, memorials by Baquíjano to Señor, Madrid, December 27, 1793 and Aranjuez, January 28, 1794.

52. *Ibid.*, memorial by Baquíjano, n.d. A marginal note is dated February 10, 1794. This and the following four paragraphs are based upon this document.

53. Marqués de Corpa, José Clemente Traslaviña, Melchor de Santiago Concha, and Pedro Tagle y Bracho. Bracho, in fact, had been an alcalde del crimen.

54. Ambrosio Cerdán y Pontero, Fernando Márquez de la Plata, and José Gorvea y Vadillo.

55. See Burkholder and Chandler, *From Impotence to Authority*, pp. 89–106.

56. Manuel de Mansilla who had earlier purchased an appointment but never completed the payment for it.

57. AGI, Indiferente General, legajo 871, expediente Porlier.

58. AGI, Lima, legajo 620, mesa report to February 19, 1794.

59. *Ibid.* On February 23, 1794, Llaguno ordered Baquíjano's petitions sent to the Cámara.

60. *Ibid.*, Baquíjano to Señor, Aranjuez, February 26, 1794.

61. *Ibid.*, Llaguno to the Governor of the Council of the Indies, Aranjuez, May 28, 1794.

62. *Ibid.*, Bajamar to Llaguno, Madrid, June 6, 1794.

63. *Ibid.*, mesa report, notes of June 22, 1794 and June 30, 1794.

64. *Ibid.*, extract of letter 19 by Gil, Lima, January 23, 1795; AGI, Lima, legajo 710, letter 19, Gil to Llaguno, Lima, January 23, 1795 and accompanying documents.

65. AGI, Lima, legajo 620, Baquíjano to Señor, Aranjuez, January 19, 1795.

66. AHN, Consejos, legajo 13533.

67. AGS, Sección XXIII, Inventario 2, legajo 79, título 96, José Baquíjano y Carrillo, honorary alcalde del crimen, Audiencia of Lima, Aranjuez, April 3, 1795.

68. *Kalendario manual y guía de forasteros en Madrid para el año de 1796* (Madrid 1796), p. 154.

69. AGI, Lima, legajo 621, petition by Baquíjano to Señor, Aranjuez, April 4, 1795.

70. Archivo Municipal (Lima), Libro de cabildo 39, p. 73; Riva-Agüero, "Un capítulo inédito," pp. 495–96.

71. AGI, Filipinas, legajo 366, memorial by Josef de Villafañe, Madrid, July 2, 1797.

72. AGI, Mexico, legajo 1642, El Duque de Alcudía to Llaguno, San Lorenzo, December 10, 1794; *ibid.*, consulta, January 28, 1795.

73. AGS, Sección XXIII, Inventario 2, legajo 79, título 227, Josef Santiago Aldunate, oidor supernumerario, Audiencia of Chile, San Lorenzo, October 8, 1795.

74. AGI, Lima, legajo 621, Gil to Llaguno, Lima, October 23, 1795.

75. AGI, Lima, legajo 621, memorial by Baquíjano to Señor, San Lorenzo, November 2, 1795.

76. The new *reglamento* of March 27, 1788 is in AGI, Audiencia of Cuzco, legajo 4.

77. AGS, Sección XXIII, Inventario 2, legajo 76, título 171, Manuel del Campo y Rivas, oidor, Audiencia of Guatemala, San Ildefonso, August 17, 1792.

78. *Ibid.*, legajo 78, título 169, Josef Santiago Concha, oidor, Audiencia of Chile, San Lorenzo, November 26, 1794.

79. AGI, Lima, legajo 959, expediente 28.

80. *Ibid.*, consultas, September 5, 1796.

81. AGI, Lima, legajo 621, Baquíjano to Señor, Ildefonso, September 7, 1796.

82. AGI, Lima, legajo 964, expediente 30, Baquíjano to Señor, Madrid, September 19, 1796.

83. AGI, Lima, legajo 964, expediente 30, consulta, November 28, 1796.

84. AGI, Audiencia of Guatemala (hereafter Guatemala), legajo 409, extract, April 27, 1774.

85. AGI, Guatemala, legajo 411, extract of memorial by González Calderón, April 13, 1785; AGI, Lima, legajo 621, expediente on the transfer of Tomás González Calderón, 1797.

86. *Ibid.*, extract of memorial by González Calderón, January 10, 1797.

87. *Ibid.*, royal decree, February 19, 1797.

88. Based upon an examination of appointments to Spanish courts in the late eighteenth century.

89. AGI, Indife.ente General, legajo 1568, letter by "La muy noble y leal ciudad de Lima" to Señor, Lima, August 10, 1810.

90. AHN, Consejo de Castilla, legajo 27537, expediente 8; AGI, Lima, legajo 734, letter 574 by Viceroy Avilés.

91. AGI, Indiferente General, legajo 1573.

92. Diego Miguel Bravo de Rivero and the hapless José de Arias de Villafañe.

93. See Burkholder and Chandler, *From Impotence to Authority*, Appendix IX. Francisco de Nava Grimón was the caballero.

94. See Appendix B.

95. The previous native son was Melchor de Santiago Concha who was named an alcalde del crimen in 1777. For the other native sons see Burkholder and Chandler, *From Impotence to Authority*, Appendix X.

96. AGS, Sección XXIII, Inventario 2, legajo 81, título 42, José Baquíjano y Carrillo, alcalde del crimen, Audiencia of Lima, Aranjuez, March 17, 1797.

97. AGI, Lima, legajo 595, "Yndice alfabético de este ynventario de consultas del negociado de Lima."

98. AGI, Lima, legajo 1456, Baquíjano to Señor, Aranjuez, June 4, 1797 and mesa report.

99. AGI, Lima, legajo 1548; *ibid.*, legajo 772, Conde de Vistaflorida to Francisco Saavedra, Lima, October 30, 1810. Unfortunately the reason for Saavedra's support is unknown.

100. AGI, Lima, legajo 967, expediente 24, Baquíjano to (Jovellanos), Aranjuez, April 30, 1798.

101. *Ibid.*, Jovellanos to the Governor of the Council of the Indies, Aranjuez, May 4, 1798.

102. Pacheco Vélez, "José Baquíjano y Carrillo en Cádiz," p. 557.

103. AGI, Lima, legajo 967, expediente 24, report by the fiscal, Madrid, May 31, 1798; *de oficio* by the Cámara, June 27, 1798.

104. AGI, Lima, legajo 599, Baquíjano to (Jovellanos), Aranjuez, June 18, 1798.

105. *Ibid.*, mesa report to June 27, 1798.

106. *Ibid.*, royal order to Escobedo, San Ildefonso, August 8, 1798.

107. AHN, Consejos, Castilla, legajo 27537, expediente 8.

108. AGI, Lima, legajo 599, Escobedo to Caballero, Madrid, August 24, 1798.

109. *Ibid.*, mesa report to June 27, 1798; note of September 16, 1798.

110. AGI, Lima, legajo 1526, petition by Baquíjano, San Lorenzo, October 24, 1798; passport for Baquíjano, San Lorenzo, October 27, 1798.

111. AGI, Lima, legajo 1008, Baquíjano to Señor, Cádiz, August 1, 1800.

112. *Ibid.*

113. See Pacheco Vélez, "José Baquíjano y Carrillo en Cádiz," AGI, Lima, legajo 1009, petition by Miguel de Naxera (for Baquíjano) to Señor, Madrid, January 5, 1802; royal order to Miguel Cayetano Soler, Aranjuez, January 22, 1802.

114. *Ibid.*, Baquíjano to Caballero, Lima, July 8, 1802.

115. Eguiguren, *Diccionario*, 3:785–86.

116. AGI, Lima, legajo 1009, Baquíjano to Caballero, Lima, July 8, 1802.

117. Burkholder and Chandler, *From Impotence to Authority*, Appendix II.

118. See *ibid.*, p. 118.

119. Archivo Municipal (Lima), Libro de Cabildo 39, pp. 139–146v.

6

1. Biblioteca Nacional (Chile), Sala Diego Barros Arana, piso 2, estante 25, tabla 2, número del volumen 16, obra número 52, "Libro de acuerdos. S^s Min^s de la R^l Aud^a de Lima desde el mes de Junio de 1799 hasta al año de 1807."

2. AGI, Chile, legajo 173, consulta, August 12, 1806. Baquíjano's appointment by resulta continued his record of appointment without support from the Cámara.

3. "Proposiciones que hacen al Congreso Nacional los Diputados de América y Asia," Isla de Leon, December 16, 1810. Lilly Library, Indiana University, Latin American Mss.—Peru Manuscripts Department. See also Nettie Lee Benson (ed.), *Mexico and the Spanish Cortes, 1810–1822: Eight Essays* (Austin and London, 1966), particularly W. Woodrow Anderson, "Reform as a Means to Quell Revolution," pp. 185–207.

4. *Actas de las sesiones secretas*, p. 554. He received 107 votes; his nearest rival received fourteen.

5. AGI, Lima, legajo 772, Conde de Vistaflorida to Francisco Saavedra, Lima, October 30, 1810. The election results for each city council as well as the final selection are in AHN, Estado, legajo 58, expediente F.

6. Burkholder, "José Baquíjano," pp. 267–70.

7. The exception is seen in an anonymous letter that accused Baquíjano of being a "declared Protestant," "perpetual gambler," and a "perfidious man." AGI, Indiferente

General, legajo 1568, letter from "La muy noble y leal ciudad de Lima" to Señor, Lima, August 10, 1810.

8. Calatayud, *Elogio del . . . José Baquíjano*; José Salia, *Elogio del excmo. señor don José Baquíjano y Carrillo . . .* (Lima, 1813).

9. AGI, Lima, legajo 737, confidential letter 55 by Abascal to Caballero, Lima, May 23, 1808.

10. AGI, Lima, legajo 771, letter by José Manuel de Goyeneche to Conde de Floridablanca, Lima, April 22, 1809.

11. AHN, Estado, legajo 879, expediente 82, no. 10, letter by Vistaflorida to Ignacio de la Pezuela, Lima, August 8, 1812; AGI, Indiferente General, legajo 873, letter by Vistaflorida to Señor, Madrid, July 11, 1814.

12. José Antonio Miralla, *Breve descripción de las fiestas celebradas en la capital de los reyes del Perú con motivo de la promoción del excmo. señor D.D. José Baquíjano y Carrillo . . .* (Lima, 1812).

13. AHN, Estado, legajo 879, expediente 82, no. 10, letter by Vistaflorida to Pezuela, Lima, August 8, 1812.

14. AGI, Indiferente General, legajo 873, Vistaflorida to Señor, Madrid, July 11, 1814.

15. AHN, Consejo de Castilla, legajo 27537, expediente 8.

16. AGI, Lima, legajo 873, Vistaflorida to Señor, Madrid, July 11, 1814; J. Ponte Domínguez (ed.), *José Antonio Miralla y sus trabajos* (Publicaciones del Archivo Nacional de Cuba, LII; Havana, 1960), p. 9.

17. *Ibid.*, pp. 9–10.

18. AGI, Indiferente, legajo 873, Vistaflorida to Señor, Madrid, July 11, 1814.

19. *Ibid.*; AHN, Estado, legajo 877, caja 2, note, Madrid, March 16, 1814.

20. *Ibid.*, legajo 883, caja 2, royal decree to the Duque de San Carlos, Palace, June 3, 1814.

21. AGI, Sección de Estado, legajo 87 has Baquíjano's report on the state of America. Maticorena discusses the report in "Nuevas noticias y documentos," pp. 151–55 and reprints it with related correspondence on pp. 170–206.

22. AGI, Indiferente General, legajo 873, Vistaflorida to Señor, Madrid, July 11, 1814 and note of July 23, 1814.

23. AGI, Indiferente General, legajo 3085, Vistaflorida to Señor, Madrid, October 4, 1814; AHN, Estado, legajo 883, caja 2, expediente 46, note of October 14, 1814.

24. Archivo del Patrimonio Nacional (Madrid), Sección de Registros, Registro 3237, "Lista ó índice alfabético de los memoriales que diariamente se entregan al Rey Nro. Señor en audiencia ó fuera de ella, desde 21 de junio de 1814 con expresión del núm[o], nombre del pretendiente, secretaría ó ramo donde corresponde, fecha de remisión, resolución de S. M. si la huviese, ó recomendaci[n]."

25. I have been unable to find when he received these honors, but there are references to his having them as early as August 30, 1815. AHN, Consejos, Castilla, legajo 27537, expediente 8, pieza 6[a].

26. AGI, Indiferente General, legajo 3084, "Expedientes sobre el nombram[to] del Conde de Vistaflorida p[a] superintend[te] subdeleg[do] de temporalidades del reyno del Perú," note of August 5, 1815, on undated decree to Miguel de Lardizábal y Uribe.

27. See the correspondence in the Hispanic Society of America, MS: HC418/403/1.

28. AHN, Consejos, Castilla, legajo 27537, expediente 8, pieza 6[a] has a copy of the death certificate. Maticorena has published this document in "Nuevas noticias y documentos," pp. 206–7.

Glossary of Spanish Terms Used

abogado   a lawyer, attorney, or advocate

alcalde del crimen   a criminal judge on the viceregal tribunals of Mexico and Lima and also in some of the Spanish courts

alcalde ordinario   a city magistrate

ascenso   the recognized ladder of career advancement through the stages of a bureaucratic hierarchy

asesor   an adviser or counselor; one who renders legal opinions; *asesor general*, one who performed this function for a viceroy

audiencia   high court of justice, exercising some administrative and executive functions

beneficio   here, the purchase of a position from the government

caballero   a gentleman or knight of a military or civil order

cabildo   corporation of a town, or *cabildo eclesiástico*, the chapter of a cathedral

cámara   chamber or cabinet; *camarista*, member of such a body

capa y espada   literally cape and sword; distinguishes non-lawyers from *letrados* on high councils of state

caraqueño   native of Caracas

casta   person with partial Negro ancestry, illegitimate descent, or suspected of having either

cátedra   academic chair or professorship; *catedrático*, the holder of such a position

cédula   royal decree issued by council over the king's signature

chacra   small landholding used for gardening

charqueña, charqueño   native of the province of Charcas

chino   descendant of an Indian and a zambo

colegial   member of a *colegio*

colegio mayor   prestigious residence hall and confraternity associated with certain Spanish and Spanish American universities

conde   count

168

consulado   merchant guild and tribunal of commerce

consulta   a report or brief for the king in Council

contador   accountant

corregimiento   administrative district; *corregidor*, the magistrate or chief officer of such a district

criolla, criollo   a Spaniard born in America; a white

decano   senior member of a court or council

derecho   law, justice; *derecho patrio* or *real*, national or Spanish law

donativo   a contribution, forced loan, or gift

encomienda   grant or authority over groups of Indians, carrying obligation to Christianize and protect them in exchange for labor or tribute

escribano   scribe, notary

estado soltero y libre (de)   bachelor

fiscal   crown attorney to an audiencia or council; *fiscalía*, office held by a fiscal

hacendado   the owner of a large estate or plantation

hidalgo   gentry, lesser nobility

informe   report, recommendation, information

ladrón   thief

lanzas   literally "lances"; a form of taxation assessed on titled nobles

legajo   bundle of documents

letrado   a university-trained lawyer or holder of a legal degree

licenciado   a higher degree in a Spanish or Spanish American university, and the person who has taken that degree; also a title given to lawyers

limeño   native of Lima

limpieza de sangre   purity of blood, racial purity

malagueño   native of Málaga

maldicientes   defamers, bad-mouthers

media anata   tax of one-half of the first year's salary for a position

memorial   petition, request for consideration

mesa   here, "table" or entity within an administrative unit charged with some particular function, in the sense of "the Latin American desk" of the Department of State

mestizo   offspring of a Spaniard and an Indian

número   here, a "regular" or statutory position on an audiencia or other body; opposed to a *supernumerario*, which was temporary and above legal limits

oficial   officer, official;   *oficial real*   treasury official

oidor   judge on an audiencia; on viceregal tribunals, possessing civil functions only

oposición   formal hearing by which academic chairs are filled

pasquinades   lampoons

peso   unit of money, usually silver and containing 272 maravedís or eight *reales de plata* or twenty *reales de vellón*

por vía de   by way of

pretendiente   here, a job applicant or candidate, office seeker, pretender

prima   term referring to the senior academic chair in a particular faculty; opposed to *vísperas*, the junior chair

pseudosabios   ill-educated persons masquerading as if wise and learned

quintal   a hundredweight

real acuerdo   a meeting of an executive with his audiencia in an advisory or cabinet capacity; the viceroy-in-council

real, reales   unit of money, either silver or vellón, containing 34 *maravedís*

regente   regent; presiding officer over an audiencia, a position created in 1776; temporary teaching appointment at a university

reglamento   regulation, ordinance

relación de méritos   a document attesting to personal qualities and accomplishments presented in support of an appeal for a position or favor; a vita

repartimiento   partition or division; in Peru, forced sale of merchandise to Indians

réplica   in universities, the same as making an opposition

residencia   formal inquiry conducted at the end of an official's term of office

resulta   here, position filled after its incumbent had been promoted via a consulta without a subsequent consulta or the use of a decree

sala   chamber

sierra   mountains

sisa   excise tax on foodstuffs

solares   here, urban lots

supernumerario   a supernumerary or official occupying a temporary or unauthorized extra position on a tribunal; may or may not be salaried

súplica   supplication, request

título   title of office; letter of appointment; also, a title of nobility

vellón   a type of money used in Spain consisting of a mixture of silver and copper

visita   official inspection into the conduct of officials

vísperas   term referring to the junior academic chair in a particular faculty

yerba maté   Paraguayan tea

zambo   person of mixed Indian and Negro ancestry

Bibliography

PRIMARY SOURCES

Manuscripts

Archivo General de Indias, Seville
   Audiencia de Lima. Legajos 595, 597, 598, 599, 600, 605, 618, 620, 621, 640, 645A,
   645B, 647, 654, 655, 698, 699, 708, 710, 728, 734, 737, 770, 771, 780, 792, 866, 876,
   877, 886, 891, 892, 900, 914, 931, 941, 949, 958, 959, 964, 967, 970, 993, 995, 996,
   997, 998, 1000, 1002, 1003, 1004, 1008, 1009, 1082, 1083, 1085, 1086, 1087, 1445,
   1456, 1526, 1548
   Audiencia de México. Legajos 1639, 1641, 1642
   Audiencia de Charcas. Legajos 423, 501, 510
   Audiencia de Chile. Legajos 173, 258
   Audiencia de Quito. Legajos 302, 358
   Audiencia de Guatemala. Legajos 409, 411
   Audiencia de Panama. Legajo 124
   Audiencia de Cuzco. Legajo 4
   Audiencia de Caracas. Legajo 16
   Indiferente General. Legajos 10, 513, 525, 871, 873, 1568, 1573, 3084, 3085
   Estado. Legajo 879
   Casa de Contratación. Legajo 5522
Archivo General de Simancas, Simancas
   Sección XXIII, Dirección General del Tesoro
      Inventario 2. Legajos 9, 18, 60, 76, 78, 79, 81, 92, 94, 98
      Inventario 13. Legajos 8, 9
      Inventario 24. Legajos 183, 185
   Sección de Gracia y Justicia. Legajos 161, 163, 815 (antiguos)
Archivo Histórico Nacional, Madrid
   Sección de Consejos Suprimidos, Castilla. Legajos 13533, 21730, 27537
   Sección de Códices y Cartularios. Legajo 239B
   Sección de Universidades y Colegios, Signatura 1304-F
   Sección de Ordenes Militares
      Santiago. Expediente 827
      Calatrava. Legajos 299, 2149
   Sección de Inquisición. Legajo 2216
   Sección de Estado. Legajos 883, 877
   Sección de Estado. Ordenes Civiles, Carlos III. Expediente 579
Archivo del Patrimonio Nacional, Madrid
   Sección de Registros. Registro 3237

Biblioteca de la Real Academia de la Historia, Madrid
   Colección de Manuscriptos de D. Benito de la Mata y Linares. Tomo 80
Archivo Nacional del Perú, Lima
   Sección de Protocolos
      Azcarrunz, Orencio de. Legajos 74 (1739–1746), 77 (1751–52), 81 (1759–60)
      Torres Preziado, Valentín de. Legajo 1072 (1782–83)
      Sección de Real Audiencia, Procedimientos Penales. Legajos 37 (1779), 38 (1779), 39
      (1780)
Archivo Municipal, Lima
   Libro de Cabildo 39
Archivo Histórico del Ministerio de Hacienda, Lima
   No. 0610. "Quaderno de Juntas desde el año de 1731 hasta el de 1739"
Biblioteca Nacional, Santiago, Chile
   Sala Diego Barros Arana. Piso 2, estante 25, tabla 2, número del volumen 16, obra
   número 52. "Libro de acuerdos." (1799–1807)
Lilly Library, Indiana University, Bloomington, Indiana
   Latin American Mss.—Peru Manuscripts Department. "Proposiciones que hacen al Con-
   greso Nacional los Diputados de América y Asia." Isla de Leon, December 16, 1810
Hispanic Society of America, New York
   MS HC418/403/1 (microfilm)
Yale University Library, New Haven
   No. 23 Exped^te en copia certificada sre. la formalización de la Sociedad de Amantes del
   País para el *Mercurio peruano*

Printed Documents

Actas de las sesiones secretas de las cortes generales extraordinarias de la nación española
   . . . . Madrid, 1874.
Baquíjano y Carrillo, Joseph de. *Alegato que en la oposición á la cátedra de prima de leyes
   de la Real Universidad de San Marcos de Lima dixó el Dr. D. Joseph Baquíjano y Carrillo*
   . . . . Lima, 1788.
———. *Elogio del Excelentísimo Señor Don Agustín de Jáuregui, y Aldecoa* . . . . Lima,
   1788.
———. *Relectio extemporanea ad explanationem legis pamphilo XXXXIX* . . . . Lima,
   1788.
Barriga, Víctor M. *Documentos para la historia de la Universidad de Arequipa 1765–1828.*
   Arequipa, 1953.
Bermúdez, José Manuel. *Sermón predicado el día de la santísima trinidad, X de junio de
   M.DCC.LXXXI* . . . . Lima, 1781.
Calatayud y Borda, Gerónimo de. *Elogio del excmo. Señor D. José Baquíjano y Carrillo,
   Conde de Vista Florida, de la Real y Distinguida Orden de Carlos III, consejero de
   estado, &c.* Lima, 1813.
———. *Oración fúnebre que en las solemnes exequias de la R.M. María Antonio de San
   Joseph, Larrea, Arispe, de los Reyes* . . . . Lima, 1782.
Calero y Moreira, Jacinto. *Prospecto del papel periódico intitulado Mercurio peruano de
   historia, literatura, y noticias públicas, que á nombre de una Sociedad de Amantes del
   País, y como uno de ellos promete dar á luz Don Jacinto Calero y Moreira.* Lima, 1790.
Castro, Ignacio de. *Disertación sobre la concepción de Nra. Sra.* Lima, 1782.
———. *Oración panegírica, que á la feliz llegada del ilustrísimo señor doctor don Agustín
   de Gorrichátegui, del consejo de su magestad, dignísimo obispo del Cuzco, á la capital
   de su diocésis, dixó el doctor don Ignacio de Castro, cura y vicario de la doctrina de*

Checa en la provincia de Tinta de la jurisdicción del Cuzco, examinador synodal de aquel obispado. Lima, 1771.

———. *Segunda disertación.* Lima, 1784.

Constituciones para la Real Universidad, cuyos treinta y tres capítulos abrazan la reforma de los principales abusos que en ella se habían introducido con el transcurso del tiempo . . . . Lima, 1771.

Feyjóo, Benito Gerónymo. *Theatro crítico universal, o discursos varios en todo género de materias, para desengaño de errores comunes.* 8 vols. Madrid, 1753.

Gaceta de Madrid. Madrid, 1776.

Haënke, Tadeo. *Descripción del Perú.* Lima, 1901.

Juan, Jorge, and Antonio de Ulloa. *A Voyage to South America.* The John Adams Translation. Abridged and edited by Irving A. Leonard. New York, 1964.

Kalendario manual, y guía de forasteros en Madrid (Madrid, 1793, 1796).

Memorias de los vireyes que han gobernado el Perú, durante el tiempo del coloniaje español. 6 vols. Lima, 1859.

Mercurio peruano de historia literatura y noticias públicas que da á luz la Sociedad Académica de Amantes de Lima. 12 vols. Lima, 1791–1795; reprinted 1964–66.

Miralla, José Antonio. *Breve descripción de las fiestas celebradas en la capital de los reyes del Perú con motivo de la promoción del excmo. señor D.D. José Baquíjano y Carrillo . . . al supremo consejo de estado. Con una regular colección de algunas poesías relativas al mismo obgeto.* Lima, 1812.

Novísima recopilación de las leyes de España. 6 vols. Madrid, 1805; reprinted, 1976.

Recopilación de leyes de los reynos de las Indias. 4 vols. Madrid, 1681; reprinted 1973.

Relaciones de los vireyes y audiencias que han gobernado el Perú. 3 vols. Vol. I, Lima, 1867; Vols. II and III, Madrid, 1871–72.

Salia, José. *Elogio del excmo. señor don José Baquíjano y Carrillo . . . .* Lima, 1813.

Terralla y Landa, Estevan de. *Lamento métrico general llanto funesto, y gemido triste . . . Carlos III . . . .* Lima, 1790.

SECONDARY SOURCES

Books

Addy, George M. *The Enlightenment in the University of Salamanca.* Durham, 1966.

Amunátegui Solar, Domingo. *Mayorazgos i títulos de Castilla.* 2 vols. Santiago 1901–1904.

Arcila Farías, Eduardo. *El pensamiento económico hispano-americano en Baquíjano y Carrillo.* Caracas, 1976.

Ardao, Arturo. *La filosofía polémica de Feijóo.* Buenos Aires, 1962.

Barreda Laos, Felipe. *Vida intelectual del virreynato del Perú.* Buenos Aires, 1937.

Benson, Nettie Lee, ed. *Mexico and the Spanish Cortes, 1810–1822: Eight Essays.* Austin, 1966.

Borah, Woodrow. *Early Colonial Trade and Navigation Between Mexico and Peru.* Berkeley and Los Angeles, 1954.

Bromley, Juan, and José Barbagelata. *Evolución urbana de la ciudad de Lima.* Lima, 1945.

Burkholder, Mark A. and D. S. Chandler. *From Impotence to Authority: The Spanish Crown and the American Audiencias, 1687–1808.* Columbia and London, 1977.

Campbell, Leon G. *The Military and Society in Colonial Peru 1750–1810.* Philadelphia, 1978.

Céspedes del Castillo, Guillermo. *Lima y Buenos Aires.* Sevilla, 1947.

Deustua Pimentel, Carlos. *José Baquíjano y Carrillo.* Biblioteca Hombres del Perú, Primera edición, Primera serie, VII. Lima, 1964.

Eguiguren, Luis Antonio. *Catálogo histórico del claustro de la Universidad de San Marcos 1576–1800*. Lima. 1912.

———. *Diccionario histórico, cronológico de la Real y Pontificia Universidad de San Marcos y sus colegios. Crónica é investigación*. 3 vols. Lima, 1940–1951.

———. *Guerra separatista (1777–1780)*. Lima, 1942.

Espejo, Juan Luis. *Nobiliario de la Capitanía General de Chile*. Santiago, 1967.

Fisher, J. R. *Government and Society in Colonial Peru: The Intendant System 1784–1814*. London, 1970.

———. *Silver Mines and Silver Miners in Colonial Peru, 1776–1824*. Liverpool, 1977.

Hamerly, Michael T. *Historia social y económica de la antigua provincia de Guayaquil 1763–1842*. Guayaquil, 1973.

Herr, Richard. *The Eighteenth-Century Revolution in Spain*. Princeton, 1958.

Izcue, Luis de. *La nobleza titulada en el Perú colonial*. Second edition. Lima, 1929.

James, Preston E. *Latin America*. Rev. ed. New York, 1950.

Kagan, Richard L. *Students and Society in Early Modern Spain*. Baltimore, 1974.

Kany, Charles E. *Life and Manners in Madrid 1750–1800*. Berkeley, 1932.

Kuethe, Allan J. *Military Reform and Society in New Granada, 1773–1808*. Gainesville, 1978.

Ladd, Doris M. *The Mexican Nobility at Independence 1780–1826*. Austin, 1976.

Lanning, John Tate. *The Eighteenth-Century Enlightenment in the University of San Carlos de Guatemala*. Ithaca, 1956.

———. *The University in the Kingdom of Guatemala*. Ithaca, 1955.

Lockhart, James. *Spanish Peru, 1532–1560*. Madison, 1968.

Lohmann Villena, Guillermo. *Los americanos en las órdenes nobiliarias (1529–1900)*. 2 vols. Madrid, 1947.

———. *Los ministros de la audiencia de Lima en el reinado de los Borbones (1700–1821)*. Seville, 1974.

Lynch, John. *Spain under the Habsburgs*. 2 vols. New York, 1964–69.

Marañón, Gregorio. *Las ideas biológicas del Padre Feijóo*. 3rd ed. Madrid, 1954.

Mendiburu, Manuel de. *Diccionario histórico-biográfico del Perú*. 8 vols. Lima, 1874–1890.

Palacio Atard, Vicente. *Areche y Guirior. Observaciones sobre el fracaso de una visita al Perú*. Seville, 1946.

Palacio Atard, Vicente. *Los españoles de la ilustración*. Madrid, 1964.

Phelan, John Leddy. *The People and the King: The Comunero Revolution in Colombia, 1781*. Madison, 1978.

Pike, Fredrick B. *The Modern History of Peru*. New York, 1967.

Ponte Domínguez, Francisco J. (ed.). *José Antonio Miralla y sus trabajos*. Publicaciones del Archivo Nacional de Cuba, LII. Havana, 1960.

Probst, Juan. *Juan Baltasar Maziel el maestro de la generación de mayo*. Buenos Aires, 1946.

Ramos, Demetrio. *Trigo chileno, navieros del Callao y hacendados limeños entre la crisis agrícola del siglo XVII y la comercial de la primera mitad del XVIII*. Madrid, 1967.

Restrepo Sáenz, José María. *Biografías de los mandatarios y ministros de la real audiencia—(1671 a 1819)*. Bogotá, 1952.

Riva-Agüero, José de la. *Historia del Perú: Selección*. 2 vols. Lima, 1953.

Rubio, David. *La Universidad de San Marcos de Lima durante la colonización española (datos para su historia)*. Madrid, 1933.

Shafer, Robert Jones. *The Economic Societies in the Spanish World 1763–1821*. Syracuse, 1958.

Silva i Molina, Abraham de. *Oidores de la real audiencia de Santiago de Chile durante el siglo XVII*. Santiago, Chile, 1903.

Spell, Jefferson Rea. *Rousseau in the Spanish World Before 1833. A Study in Franco-Spanish Literary Relations.* Austin, 1938.
Tibesar, Antonine. *Franciscan Beginnings in Colonial Peru.* Washington, D.C., 1953.
Valcárcel, Daniel. *Reforma de San Marcos en la época de Amat.* Lima, 1955.
Vargas Ugarte, Rubén. *Historia general del Perú.* 6 vols. Lima, 1966.
Villalobos R., Sergio. *El comercio y la crisis colonial.* Santiago, Chile, 1968.

Articles

Barbier, Jacques A. "The Culmination of the Bourbon Reforms, 1787-1792." *The Hispanic American Historical Review* 57:1 (February 1977):51-68.
Bertrando del Balzo, Conde. "Familias nobles y destacadas del Perú en los informes secretos de un virrey napolitano (1715-1725)." *Revista del instituto peruano de investigaciones genealógicas* (Lima) 14 (1965):107-33.
Brading, D. A., and Harry E. Cross. "Colonial Silver Mining: Mexico and Peru." *The Hispanic American Historical Review* 52:4 (November 1972):545-79.
Bromley y Seminario, Juan. "Alcaldes de la ciudad de Lima en el siglo XVIII." *Revista histórica* 24 (1960-1961):295-378.
Burkholder, Mark A. "From Creole to Peninsular: The Transformation of the Audiencia of Lima." *The Hispanic American Historical Review* 52:3 (August 1972):395-415.
Campbell, Leon G. "A Colonial Establishment: Creole Domination of the Audiencia of Lima During the Late Eighteenth Century." *The Hispanic American Historical Review* 52:1 (February 1972):1-25.
Défourneaux, M. "Pablo de Olavide, L'Homme et le Mythe," *Cahiers du monde hispanique et luso-brésilien.* Toulouse, 1966.
Deustua Pimentel, Carlos. "El Visitador Areche y el "Elogio" de don José Baquíjano y Carrillo." *Boletin del Instituto Riva-Agüero* (Lima) 8 (1969-1971):124-34.
————. "Nuevos datos sobre José Baquíjano y Carrillo," in Pontificia Universidad Católica del Perú, *La causa de la emancipación del Perú: Testimonios de la época precursora 1780-1820.* Lima, 1960, pp. 137-44.
Febres Villarroel, Oscar. "La crisis agrícola del Perú en el último tercio del siglo XVIII." *Revista histórica* (Lima), 27 (1964):102-99.
Konetzke, Richard. "Ideas políticas del Virrey Francisco Gil de Taboada." *Mar del sur* (Lima) 7:20 (March/April 1952):44-55.
López Soria, José Ignacio. "El pensamiento de José Baquíjano y Carrillo." *Historia y cultura* (Lima) 5 (1971):94-185.
Maticorena Estrada, Miguel. "Documentos para la historia de la Universidad Nacional Mayor de San Marcos," *Boletín bibliográfico* (Lima) 19:1-2, año XXII (July, 1949):136-52.
————. "José Baquíjano y Carrillo, reformista peruano del siglo XVIII," *Revista de estudios americanos* (Seville) 15:76-77 (January-February 1958):53-101.
————. "La proscripción del 'Elogio' de Baquíjano y Carrillo," *Mar del sur* (Lima) 6:18 (August 1951):95-101.
————. "Nuevas noticias y documentos de don José Baquíjano y Carrillo, Conde de Vista-Florida," in Pontificia Universidad Católica del Perú, *La causa de la emancipación del Perú: Testimonios de la época precursora 1780-1820.* Lima, 1960, pp. 145-207.
Millares Carlos, Agustín. "Prólogo." *Clasicos Castellanos* 48 (Madrid, 1923):5-86.
Pacheco Vélez, César. "José Baquíjano y Carrillo en Cádiz." *Quinto Congreso Internacional de Historia de América.* 5 vols, II, 531-593.
Palacio Atard, Vicente. "La influencia del P. Feijóo en América," *Simposio sobre el Padre Feijóo y su siglo.* Oviedo, 1966, pp. 21-31.

Riva-Agüero, José de la. "Un capítulo inédito de la nueva biografía de Baquíjano y Carrillo," *Boletín del Museo Bolivariano* (Lima) 1:12 (August 1929):492–502.

————. "Don José Baquíjano de Beascoa y Carrillo de Córdoba, tercer conde de Vistaflorida en el Perú (1751–1818)," *Revista de archivos, bibliotecas, y museos* (Madrid), 3º Epoca, 46 (1925):465–89 and (1926):68–86.

————. "Don José Baquíjano y Carrillo," *El Ateneo de Lima*, 7:38 (1905):1946–79, and 7:39 (1906):5–47.

————. "Don José Baquíjano y Carrillo," *Boletín del Museo Bolivariano* (Lima) 1:12 (August 1929):453–91.

Tiryakian, Josefina Cintrón. "La Disertación de José Baquíjano y Carrillo: plagio o parelelismo." *Latinoamérica* Mexico, 1973, pp. 65–83.

Manuscripts

Burkholder, Mark Alan. "José Baquíjano and the Audiencia of Lima." Ph.D. diss., Duke University, 1970.

Dale, William Pratt. "The Cultural Revolution in Peru, 1750–1820." Ph.D. diss., Duke University, 1941.

Dilg, George Robertson. "The Collapse of the Portobelo Fairs: A Study in Spanish Commercial Reform, 1720–1740." Ph.D. diss., Indiana University, 1975.

Ganster, Paul Bentley. "A Social History of the Secular Clergy of Lima During the Middle Decades of the Eighteenth Century." Ph.D. diss., University of California, Los Angeles 1974.

Tiryakian, Josefina C. "The *Mercurio peruano:* Herald of the Modernization of Peru in the Eighteenth Century." Ph.D. diss., Harvard University, 1969.

Woodham, John E. "Hipólito Unanue and the Enlightenment in Peru." Ph.D. diss., Duke University, 1964.

Index

A Note on the Author

Mark A. Burkholder is a professor of history at the University of Missouri-St. Louis and an associate vice president for academic affairs of the University of Missouri System. He received his doctorate from Duke University. His publications on colonial Latin American history have opened important new vistas on the topic of Spanish colonial administration.